THE
COMPLETE
IDIOT'
GUIDE® TO

D1308800

The Psychology
of Happiness

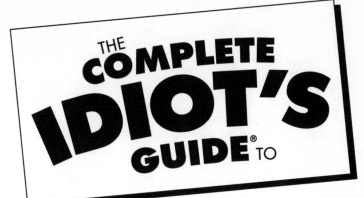

THE COMPLETE IDIOT'S GUIDE® TO

The Psychology of Happiness

by Arlene Matthews Uhl

ALPHA

A member of Penguin Group (USA) Inc.

For Marcello, who got us started.

ALPHA BOOKS

Published by the Penguin Group

Penguin Group (USA) Inc., 375 Hudson Street, New York, New York 10014, USA

Penguin Group (Canada), 90 Eglinton Avenue East, Suite 700, Toronto, Ontario M4P 2Y3, Canada (a division of Pearson Penguin Canada Inc.)

Penguin Books Ltd., 80 Strand, London WC2R 0RL, England

Penguin Ireland, 25 St. Stephen's Green, Dublin 2, Ireland (a division of Penguin Books Ltd.)

Penguin Group (Australia), 250 Camberwell Road, Camberwell, Victoria 3124, Australia (a division of Pearson Australia Group Pty. Ltd.)

Penguin Books India Pvt. Ltd., 11 Community Centre, Panchsheel Park, New Delhi—110 017, India

Penguin Group (NZ), 67 Apollo Drive, Rosedale, North Shore, Auckland 1311, New Zealand (a division of Pearson New Zealand Ltd.)

Penguin Books (South Africa) (Pty.) Ltd., 24 Sturdee Avenue, Rosebank, Johannesburg 2196, South Africa

Penguin Books Ltd., Registered Offices: 80 Strand, London WC2R 0RL, England

Copyright © 2008 by Arlene Matthews Uhl

International Standard Book Number: 978-1-59257-711-8
Library of Congress Catalog Card Number: 2008920997

10 09 08   8 7 6 5 4 3 2 1

Interpretation of the printing code: The rightmost number of the first series of numbers is the year of the book's printing; the rightmost number of the second series of numbers is the number of the book's printing. For example, a printing code of 08-1 shows that the first printing occurred in 2008.

Printed in the United States of America

Note: This publication contains the opinions and ideas of its author. It is intended to provide helpful and informative material on the subject matter covered. It is sold with the understanding that the author and publisher are not engaged in rendering professional services in the book. If the reader requires personal assistance or advice, a competent professional should be consulted.

The author and publisher specifically disclaim any responsibility for any liability, loss, or risk, personal or otherwise, which is incurred as a consequence, directly or indirectly, of the use and application of any of the contents of this book.

Most Alpha books are available at special quantity discounts for bulk purchases for sales promotions, premiums, fund-raising, or educational use. Special books, or book excerpts, can also be created to fit specific needs.

For details, write: Special Markets, Alpha Books, 375 Hudson Street, New York, NY 10014.

Publisher: *Marie Butler-Knight*
Editorial Director: *Mike Sanders*
Senior Managing Editor: *Billy Fields*
Senior Acquisitions Editor: *Paul Dinas*
Senior Development Editor: *Phil Kitchel*
Production Editor: *Kayla Dugger*
Copy Editor: *Tricia Liebig*

Cartoonist: *Shannon Wheeler*
Cover Designer: *Bill Thomas*
Book Designer: *Trina Wurst*
Indexer: *Celia McCoy*
Layout: *Brian Massey*
Proofreader: *Laura Caddell*

Contents at a Glance

Appendixes

Contents

Appendixes

Introduction

What would make us happier than we are? How can we hold onto happiness after we've achieved it? These are the sort of questions most of us think about a lot. Increasingly, psychology is asking the same things. It's also coming up with some eye-opening answers as it turns its attention to people who are successful, satisfied, and resilient enough to flourish in their lives even after setbacks and disappointments. What are their secrets? Can they apply to us all?

Since its inception, psychology—the scientific study of mental states and behavior—has devoted a great deal of time and effort to the understanding and treatment of problems and disorders. And although much progress has been made and much has been learned, there came to be a growing sense that something was missing. The new field of positive psychology, which officially dawned at the turn of our millennium, aims to fill in the gap as it explores the causes and effects of happiness.

The Complete Idiots Guide to the Psychology of Happiness is your guide to the lessons that positive psychology is learning. It's not an instant feel-good fix filled with smiley faces and affirmations. It's a compilation of information and *proven techniques* that will enable you to access your innate strengths, reframe your perceptions, and enhance your repertoire of behaviors in ways that will make you more fulfilled within yourself, within your relationships, and in your work.

Life can be a roller coaster, and circumstances are always shifting. But those who choose to cultivate happiness can remain strong, steady, and ready to make the most of every opportunity. Soon new choices, new habits, and new perspectives may profoundly alter the way you greet each day, relate to others, care for yourself, and anticipate your future.

How This Book Is Organized

This book is divided into six parts:

Part 1, "The Study of Happiness," examines the nature of true happiness and explores humankind's attempt to understand and obtain it—from ancient times through today's burgeoning new field of positive psychology.

Part 2, "The Secrets of Character," tells how our character strengths and values have a profound impact on our level of satisfaction with our lives. It also looks at the phenomenon of altruism and explores why doing good can lead to feeling good.

Part 3, "Positive Thoughts, Attitudes, and Actions," looks at how certain habits of thought, perception, and behavior—such as cultivating humor, optimism, gratitude, and a sense of play—can help us increase our inner propensity for happiness. It also explores why people who consider themselves spiritual seekers tend to feel more content with their lives.

Part 4, "Happy at Work," discusses how and why the principles of positive psychology are being increasingly applied in the workplace in hopes of boosting employee engagement, fostering constructive communication, and engendering more creativity. It also shows how individuals can improve their personal job satisfaction and success by utilizing positive psychology tenets.

Part 5, "Happy Together," explores the impact of strong marriages, supportive friendships, and community involvement on happiness. It also examines the principles of positive parenting—the art of raising children who are optimistic and resilient.

Part 6, "Wellness and Happiness," addresses the roles of both body and mind in generating and sustaining happiness—as well as how happiness itself can play a role in keeping the body healthy and the brain supple. Here you'll learn how practices such as regular aerobic exercise, yoga, meditation, and sound sleep can positively impact the mind-body system, how positive attitudes can help us heal, and how happiness may impact the length of our lives.

Happiness Helpers

Sidebars have been placed throughout this book to make it even more useful and to make it simple to begin understanding the psychology of happiness and its findings. Within them are all sorts of instructive tips and nuggets of knowledge. There are five types of sidebars:

Happy Thought

Here are wise thoughts on living the happy life from experts, including psychologists, philosophers, and spiritual leaders.

Stumbling Blocks

Warning: the behaviors or situations noted here are likely to jeopardize your happiness quotient.

Happiness Trivia

Look here for assorted tales and details—all intriguing attractions along the road to happiness.

def•i•ni•tion

Look here for an elaboration of terms used in the text.

Helping Hand

Here are tips to help you maintain a positive outlook, use your strengths, and seek out happiness-inducing situations.

Trademarks

All terms mentioned in this book that are known to be or are suspected of being trademarks or service marks have been appropriately capitalized. Alpha Books and Penguin Group (USA) Inc. cannot attest to the accuracy of this information. Use of a term in this book should not be regarded as affecting the validity of any trademark or service mark.

Part 1

The Study of Happiness

Much of our behavior is aimed at increasing happiness. Yet many of us find that obtaining things we thought would make us happy only satisfy us for the briefest while. What's at the root of lasting happiness? Is it externally caused or internally determined? This part examines historical perspectives and looks at a new branch of psychology that seeks to learn from people who seem to know the secret.

What Happiness Is ... and Isn't

In This Chapter

♦ When there is confusion of pleasure and happiness

♦ Why money won't buy happiness

♦ Whether falling in love means lasting happiness

♦ Why lasting happiness comes from within

♦ Why there are many obstacles to happiness

You've just heard that it's freezing cold back home, but you don't mind because you're on vacation in the tropics. In fact, right now you're floating in a raft chair in a crystal-clear swimming pool, twirling a cool drink with a festive umbrella stirrer, and taking a long sip. Are you happy?

You've been working outdoors on a hot, humid day. You're parched and perspiring. Suddenly you hear the merry tinkling of a familiar tune. It's the ice-cream man! Someone brings you a double-dip cone. It's got two scoops of your favorite flavor—and sprinkles on top. Are you happy?

Well *of course* you're happy! In both of these scenarios, you're experiencing highly pleasurable sensations. But what if the question went a little deeper?

What if it had been, "Are you deeply satisfied with your life and the way you live it?" or "If you could change anything about your life, would you?" or "Do you believe your future is bright?"

Ah, that's more complicated, isn't it? If you're like most of us, you'd really have to think. What exactly does it take to make you content in the present, at peace with the past, and hopeful about the future? Certainly there's nothing wrong with tropical vacations or double-dip ice-cream cones, but there's got to be more to the story.

And indeed, as social scientists are beginning to show, there is a lot more.

Is Pleasure the Same as Happiness?

Until recently, finding happiness was largely considered a personal matter. But currently the question of whether we're happy has come to be considered a pivotal issue. It has captured the attention of psychologists, economists, educators, business leaders, and health specialists.

One of the main paradoxes that these interested parties want to unravel is why, in a society where so many of us spend so much time and energy seeking pleasure and attempting to avoid pain, are so many of us depressed, anxious, pessimistic, and just plain confused? Why does enduring happiness and joy still feel so far out of reach to so many?

The Problem with Pleasure

To begin with, there is a significant fundamental difference between happiness and pleasure. Pleasure is a fleeting feeling that comes from external circumstances: a sumptuous dinner, a relaxing massage, beautiful surroundings, and so on. Pleasure involves nice things happening to us—things that have to do with sating or exciting the senses. Pleasurable experiences can certainly give us momentary positive feelings, but pleasure-based happiness does not last long—unless you try to organize all your days around pleasure, but that in itself presents other problems. Even if we could afford to chase pleasure all day, every day, the thrill of doing so would soon be gone.

Our brain cells are wired to respond to novel events. After awhile, repeated events or ever-present circumstances become background noise to which we barely react. This process, known as orientation and habituation, begins when we are infants and is part of the way we learn about the world. Introduce, say, a new squeeze toy to a baby and she registers intense interest and excitement (orientation) as she learns that by pressing on the toy she can elicit a fascinating noise. But after awhile, the squeeze toy becomes old hat (habituation). The baby has learned all it can do, has gotten used to it, and will only be aroused by something fresh and unexpected.

All pleasurable events are subject to the same dynamics. No matter what our age, we eventually tire of things we formerly got a big kick out of. Your week's vacation would not be so enthralling if it went on for a year without a change in climate or venue. Your ice-cream cone would not seem so delicious if you were given one every day at the same time.

The result of habituation to pleasure is that the only way to keep it going is to raise the stakes. Sometimes this results in cravings and subsequent addiction. We become enslaved by a behavior or a substance, such as alcohol or a narcotic, and we require more and more of the same to recreate a sensation we hope will be just like our initial rush of pleasurable feeling. (It doesn't, and so we want more yet again.) But even if we do not become addicted to some *thing*, we all too often become addicted to the mental habit of dreaming of a tomorrow where pleasure will prevail over any unpleasant feelings we have in the present.

This phenomenon of continually searching for the next pleasure has been called *destination addiction*. We all probably know people who exemplify this dynamic. They continually promise themselves—and everyone else—that *if only* they can get past this problem or that obstacle and attain this or that pleasurable reward, they will finally be completely happy. But as soon as they have whatever they were wishing for, they repeat the entire *if only* process again. In the end, they appear to be wishing their lives away. There's no happiness in that.

def•i•ni•tion

The term **destination addiction,** meaning a preoccupation with finding satisfaction "tomorrow," was coined by Dr. Robert Holden, founder of the United Kingdom's Happiness Project—a research and training institute. He defines it succinctly as "living in the not now."

A Place for Pleasure

None of this is to say that happiness *excludes* pleasure. It's not as if true happiness seekers are *against* vacations or ice-cream cones. (What humbugs they would be!) So you needn't worry that searching for enduring happiness means living in a secluded cave, eating rice rations, and contemplating your navel—unless, of course, that's what would give you great joy.

But on a hierarchy of happiness, pleasure does not command the top slot. How could it? Anything dependent on circumstance can disappear in an instant, because circumstances are always changing. Your pleasant float in the pool chair can be interrupted when the weather turns threatening or when that cell phone you carefully tucked into your swimsuit starts to ring. Your ice-cream cone might drop to the ground or melt before you've had more than a bite.

Besides, pleasure has no profound, far-reaching consequences for your overall state of mind. In any given day, you might have more pleasant experiences than unpleasant ones, but at the end of the day it's possible that you might still be a dissatisfied, pessimistic grouch.

Pleasure, spaced at reasonable intervals so that we don't become blasé about it or addicted to it, is certainly a wonderful thing. But it would be wrong to confuse it with the kind of abiding happiness that is always accessible through all the ups and downs of life.

> **Happiness Trivia**
>
> Pleasure that comes as a surprise can often produce a more positive feeling than one we've grown used to or planned for. So although planning for pleasure is fine, stay open to spontaneity. Who knows what pleasure waits around the next corner?

Can Money Buy Happiness?

If true happiness cannot be equated with moment-to-moment pleasures, can it be equated with material riches? Certainly many of us behave as if this were the case, devoting much of our lives to spending and getting, getting and spending. But the old adage that "you can't buy happiness" appears to be, for the most part, true.

It is true that if you are poor, a change in wealth status will certainly boost your well-being and improve your state of mind. But research shows that after achieving a certain earnings level (in the United States this is around $40,000, or double the government-defined poverty level for a family of four), increased affluence does not really affect people's overall subjective sense of happiness. What's more, cross-national studies indicate that people in richer countries are not any more apt to report satisfaction with their lives than those in poorer ones. A University of Illinois study found no significant difference between the overall well-being of Fortune 500 billionaires and Maasai herdsmen in eastern Africa.

In fact, too much focus on money can have an emotionally negative effect. A University of Rochester professor who studied how the desire for material wealth impacted mental health concluded that college students who put the most emphasis on affluence were prone to depression and anxiety. And jackpot lottery winners have shown that negative outcomes—including divorce, alcoholism, gambling, and loss of friends—are not uncommon when a windfall occurs.

> **Happiness Trivia**
>
> Some economists argue that we shouldn't use economic growth as a means of measuring the success of a society. Instead, we should measure how happy we are as a nation, or how much unhappiness we've managed to reduce. In 1998, the Himalayan kingdom of Bhutan actually replaced a common measure of national progress—the GNP or Gross National Product—with the GNH, the Gross National Happiness, which measures what its prime minister calls The Four Pillars of Happiness: sustainable economic development, environmental conservation, the promotion of national culture, and good governance.

When More Is Less

Why doesn't being better off in material terms make us any happier? Nobel prize–winning economist Daniel Kahneman says one reason is the *hedonic treadmill*. As our lives improve and we attain more wealth and goods that attest to our wealth—the new car, the designer wardrobe, the state-of-the-art home entertainment center—we want even more. The luxury convertible we bought last year is nice, but not as nice as this year's model. The plasma television is great, but the next generation sets have higher resolution.

def•i•ni•tion

> The **hedonic treadmill** is the phenomenon of continual dissatisfaction with the consumption of material goods. As individuals earn more money, they take their current standard of living for granted while their aspirations ratchet up. They continually aspire to the next level, which will again fail to satisfy.

Like hamsters on an ever-turning wheel, we keep racing and racing toward the next purchase—the one we imagine will finally do the trick of rendering us completely satisfied human beings. Many of us go ahead and make that purchase even if it means overextending ourselves financially, which creates anxiety and means we have to work the treadmill even harder and faster.

Keeping Up with the Joneses

Another reason that material gain doesn't usually coincide with happiness is that we tend to compare ourselves to those who are financially better off than us, rather than

def•i•ni•tion

The **social treadmill** denotes the dissatisfaction that occurs when we compare ourselves negatively to those whom we perceive as financially better off than we are. It is sometimes called *comparison anxiety* or *reference anxiety*.

Helping Hand

To feel more satisfied with your financial standing and happier overall, compare yourself with those who are less well-off than you are. Doing so will remind you to count your blessings, and may also tempt you to spend less and avoid going into anxiety-provoking debt.

to those who are not as well-off. This puts us on the *social treadmill*. We feel we have to keep up with, and then surpass, our neighbors, relatives, co-workers, and friends.

This phenomenon of constant comparison anxiety is backed up by research that shows the following:

◆ Many of us would choose to earn less annual income if our position relative to others improved.

◆ Much of our satisfaction with our income is related to the earnings of our spouse, families, or colleagues.

◆ Our levels of dissatisfaction go up when we perceive those around us are significantly better off than we are.

Social comparison anxiety tends to be even more aggravated in a generally well-off society where many people possess the same outward signs of status. When everyone in our neighborhood has the same SUV in the driveway, it's hard to know where we stand. You might think this would make us calmer, but instead it makes us feel more financial stress. We wonder: what can we do, or buy, that will distinguish us as more affluent and more successful?

Some Happy Uses of Money

The good news: money's not all bad. Although prosperity so often brings with it the paradox of dissatisfaction, money can bring some satisfaction to our lives *if* we use it not to outdo our neighbors or satiate cravings for a surplus of material goods, but to do certain other things.

Among the uses of money most likely to bring emotional fulfillment:

◆ **Creating and holding onto memories.** Spending money on good times— a vacation or a day out at the ballpark—with friends and loved ones is a sounder happiness investment than purchasing expensive material goods. (Although it's not a bad idea to spend a little on memory-boosters, such as photos and souvenirs.)

- ◆ **Celebrating personal accomplishments.** Going out to dinner—even a very casual one—after you finish a triathlon or after your child brings home a good report card can reinforce a sense of pride and personal accomplishment.

- ◆ **Seeing friends.** Making it a priority to spend quality time with people you like is its own reward, even if it means spending a little less time working.

- ◆ **Being more generous.** You can up your happiness quotient by earmarking some of your money for philanthropic causes. Giving to others (about which a lot more will be said in Chapter 6) is as beneficial to us as it is to those to whom we give. So donating money to a worthy cause is a win-win situation.

Can Someone Else Make Us Happy?

It is sometimes tempting to believe that our ultimate happiness will arrive in the form of another person. A fair damsel or brave, charming prince will "rescue" us from any unwanted feelings and suffuse our every moment with bliss. But if that sounds like a fairy tale, it is!

As we'll see in Part 5 of this book, companionship is, in fact, a crucial element in achieving lasting happiness. However, to confuse the euphoric feelings of "falling in love"—which actually releases feel-good brain chemicals and gives us a temporary mood lift—with the lifelong satisfaction of *acting lovingly* is to buy into an illusion (albeit a popular, Hollywood-style illusion).

Long-term happiness does not result so much from "falling" in love as from "rising" in love. When we act in a loving way toward someone, we are ultimately more ful-filled than we are when we dwell on the fact that we are desired and admired (though that, certainly, is not a bad thing).

Acting in a loving way is not always easy. It can be quite a challenge when the people whom we love (who are, after all, only human) disagree with us, behave in ways that frustrate us, or simply have a bad day. Nevertheless, when we manage to remain kind and compassionate under trying circumstances, and when we do things that bring joy to those we love, we are more apt to achieve long-lasting personal satisfaction.

The Pursuit of Inner Happiness

The bottom line is that being dependent on anything that emanates from outside of ourselves—pleasurable experiences, material goods, money, or the approval of some-one else—can bring us, at most, transient positive feelings. But when we adapt to these externals, or if they are suddenly withdrawn, we then typically endure negative feelings: cravings, anxiety, perhaps even despondency.

As virtually all who study happiness agree, and as this book will show at length, genuine, lasting happiness is an internal quality, at least partially determined by developing a particular skill set. Those who report a high level of subjective well-being have cultivated traits, attitudes, and behaviors that bolster them not only in good times, but also when circumstances are far less than ideal.

> ### Happy Thought _____
>
> "Happiness cannot come from without. It must come from within. It is not what we see and touch or that which others do for us that makes us happy; it is that which we think and feel and do, first for the other fellow and then for ourselves."
> —Helen Keller

Why Happiness Can Be Hard

As with all things worth achieving, however, achieving happiness is, for most of us, not necessarily a simple matter. Apart from the setbacks we often encounter in the quest to cultivate positive traits, attitudes, and behaviors, there are some genuine biological and cultural reasons why happiness can be difficult to attain and even more difficult to maintain.

The Fear of Happiness

Is a kind of happy-phobia possible? In some ways, it is not only possible, but also probable. At a certain level, many of us resist happiness for a number of fear-induced reasons:

♦ We worry that if we feel happy now we will experience a sense of letdown later—we don't let ourselves feel happy so we won't risk disappointment.

♦ We are afraid that if we appear happy we will draw the envy and wrath of others—and that possibly these others will go so far as to wish us or cause us harm.

♦ We fear looking frivolous or selfish if we are overly concerned with being happy.

♦ We associate happiness with a lack of intellectual acuity ("Ignorance is bliss").

- We feel guilty that pursuing happiness is not right or fair in a world where some people lack basic necessities.

- We don't believe we deserve to feel happy.

The fear of happiness is not to be confused with *anhedonia*, which is the actual inability to experience pleasure. Most people who feel phobic about happiness are able to enjoy pleasurable circumstances. They imagine, however, that if they are too happy, negative consequences will ensue.

def•i•ni•tion

> **Anhedonia** is the inability to experience pleasure from normally pleasurable life events such as eating, exercising, and social or sexual interactions. It is recognized as one of the key symptoms of depression according to the Diagnostic and Statistical Manual of Mental Disorders (DSM). Sometimes also seen in schizophrenia and other mental disorders, it may be caused by a breakdown in the brain's reward system that affects dopamine distribution pathways.

The Prediction Problem

We are notoriously bad at predicting what will make us happy. Ask people in the Midwest if they think those in warm, sunny California are happier and they'll say yes. But in fact, people who live in warm climates are no happier than those who live in cold ones. (Think how many of those people have picked up and moved across the country only to find their mental state is pretty much the same!)

Our predictions are off for a number of reasons. First, they're based on the way we feel at the moment. (If you just walked in from a blizzard, a walk on the Santa Monica pier sounds pretty good.) Second, we tend to have a short memory about times when certain remedies didn't work as well as we had hoped.

Some theorize that we are actually programmed by evolution to be deficient predictors of what will bring us satisfaction.

> **Stumbling Blocks**
>
> If you are trying to forecast what will make you happy in the future, you need a reality check. If you're thinking of switching careers, for example, don't ask people in that career if they are happy—instead, observe them and draw your own conclusions.

From the standpoint of pure survival, they say, our "mean genes" need to be selfish. The illusory promise of happiness is the carrot-and-stick that motivates us to keep on keeping on.

Stuck at the Happiness Set Point?

Whatever you believe the role of evolution is in happiness, one thing is certain. Like our blood pressure and our cholesterol count, our capacity for happiness is partially determined by our genetic makeup. Researchers David Lykken and Auke Tellegen, who studied 254 sets of identical and fraternal twins, estimated that 50 percent of the traits that contribute to people's satisfaction levels are inherited. In each of us, happiness tends to fluctuate more or less around a predetermined *happiness set point*.

def•i•ni•tion

The **happiness set point**, similar to a set point for body weight, is a kind of default setting to which we tend to return over and over again. Its baseline is genetically predetermined, handed down from generation to generation.

When something exhilarating happens (we got into a great school; we said yes to a marriage proposal) we tend to exceed the set point, but after a couple of weeks we revert to our usual state of mind. Likewise, when we experience a setback (we got fired; we had a romantic break up) we sink below the set point, but ultimately rise to it again as we adjust to our new circumstances.

This set point dynamic might lead one to believe that how happy we'll be is a foregone conclusion. If we're stuck, we're stuck. But keep in mind that, although we do seem to come into the world with a happiness threshold, the other 50 percent of our happiness is self-determined. It is altogether possible that we can, in effect, raise our set point by the ways in which we think, act, and react.

Things that might help us reset our happiness thermostat include the following:

◆ Thinking as an optimist.

◆ Finding opportunities to laugh.

◆ Helping others.

◆ Having close friendships and a satisfying marriage.

◆ Choosing work and leisure activities that engage our skills.

◆ Having a meaningful religious faith or spiritual practice.

- Getting enough exercise and rest.

- Meditating regularly.

Researchers continue to make great strides in determining other variables that can boost the happiness set point. Meanwhile, don't rule out the possibility that you might find something on your own that does the trick for you. Each of us can be our own experimental subject in the quest for happiness.

The Least You Need to Know

- Although lasting happiness does not exclude pleasurable states, these states alone (even lots of them) won't lead to deep, enduring life satisfaction.

- More money generally does not mean more happiness because we adapt to our current level of creature comforts and want more, and because we tend to compare ourselves to those who have more than we do.

- Although strong interpersonal relationships can profoundly contribute to happiness, "falling in love" brings only a transient lift—it's the loving, not the falling, that raises our happiness quotient.

- Our inner state will generate more genuine happiness than any external circumstance—be it a highly pleasant experience, a coveted material object, or the admiration and approval of another.

- Cultivating a happy state of mind can be a challenge due to fear of happiness and to genetic limitations; nevertheless, much of our potential happiness is within our control.

Chapter 2

A Brief History of Happiness

In This Chapter

- ◆ The Greek philosophers on happiness
- ◆ Eastern perspectives on fulfillment
- ◆ Christianity and eternal happiness
- ◆ Happiness as a democratic right
- ◆ The credo of positive thinking

Novelist Edith Wharton once quipped, "If only we'd stop trying to be happy, we'd have a pretty good time." Nearly a century later, singer Bobby McFerrin echoed such sentiments in his signature tune, "Don't Worry, Be Happy." Yet part of our nature is not only to seek happiness but also to give doing so a great deal of thought. Since the beginnings of recorded history, and long before happiness became a topic of scientific interest, philosophers and spiritual leaders had much to say on the subject.

The Ancient Greeks on Happiness

Is happiness just a matter of luck? The notion of happiness and luck being linked are reflected in the very origins of the word *happy*. The root *hap* means "chance" or "fortune." *Hap* is also found in the word *happenstance*, meaning a random event.

If you read the classic Greek dramas, most of which were written in the fifth century B.C.E., you would have to conclude that happiness is, in fact, random. In most of the plays, the protagonist would somehow collide with the gods, who themselves were portrayed as fickle and reckless. Just when the hero thought things were going well, a proverbial thunderbolt would skewer his hopes and dreams. Or, conversely, things would suddenly work out as the gods intervened to resolve a hopeless situation.

def•i•ni•tion

Eudaimonia is a Greek term that literally translates as "good spirit," and connotes "human flourishing" and "life well-lived." Noted Greek philosophers—including Socrates, Plato, and Aristotle—used the term to distinguish virtues-based happiness from pleasure-based happiness.

Yet the most famous of the Greek philosophers of the same era were beginning to think differently about happiness. Socrates (469–399 B.C.E.) concluded that happiness was inseparable from goodness, and that a happy life was one in which an individual was in touch with his nobler, higher feelings. Both Socrates and Plato used the term *eudaimonia* (good spirit) to distinguish a kind of happiness that was separate from the mere pleasures of the flesh.

Aristotle (384–322 B.C.E.) expanded on the concept of eudaimonia. He said it was constituted not by wealth or power but by practicing virtue over the course of one's life. He said that achieving eudaimonia topped the hierarchy of human purposes, and he enumerated some of the virtues of character that contributed to eudaimonia. These included:

- Courage
- Honesty
- Friendliness
- Wittiness
- Rationality

The philosopher Epicurus (341–270 B.C.E.), from whose name we get the word *epicurean* (meaning one devoted to sensual pleasure), actually agreed with Aristotle that eudaimonia, not pleasure, was the highest good. He said, "Happiness is man's greatest aim in life. Tranquility and rationality are the cornerstones of happiness."

Although Epicurus believed it was in our nature to chase pleasure, he emphasized that one should calculate what would bring the most pleasure in the long term and aim for that, even if it meant foregoing short-term pleasures. Ironically enough, Epicurus turned out to be one of the earliest recorded advocates of delayed gratification as a path to happiness.

Taoism and Confucianism

Two ancient spiritual traditions overlapped in China. Taoism and Confucianism both trace their roots to around the fifth century B.C.E. (at about the same time the great Greek philosophers lived and Buddha taught in India). Both traditions have much to say on the subject of happiness.

Taoism, as outlined in its signature text, the *Tao Te Ching*, reveres the natural order of the universe and teaches that man cannot reach fulfillment through restless striving, but rather by "inaction." By "inaction," Taoists do not mean loafing around. This easily misunderstood concept actually means acting in concert with the ways of the universe, understanding and accepting the cyclical nature of existence, and acting with spontaneity and creativity.

The sayings of Lao-Tzu, the presumed author of the *Tao Te Ching*, reinforce the idea that struggling for worldly goods is *not* the way to happiness. According to Lao-Tzu, "He who is contented is rich," and, "He who knows that enough is enough will always have enough."

Stumbling Blocks

Confucianism was greatly concerned with manners and with the dynamics of everyday social life. Confucius offered this wise aphorism, which addresses a common obstacle to happiness then *and* now: "We take greater pains to persuade others that we are happy than in endeavoring to think so ourselves." In other words, don't try to impress others; focus on being happy rather than pretending to be.

Unlike mystical and esoteric Taoism, Confucianism is a complex system of moral, social, and political teachings as well as spiritual teachings. The scholar Confucius (551–479 B.C.E.) built the system on a foundation of ancient Chinese tradition. Confucianism focused on the obligation to live a virtuous life, which consisted of the following:

- Sincerity
- Benevolence
- Propriety (politeness and conventional morality)
- Filial piety (profound respect for one's parents)

Confucianism taught that virtue was its own reward; without it no fulfillment was possible. But it also taught that children owed the performance of virtuous actions to their dead parents. In acting honorably, they would contribute to their mothers' and fathers' happiness in the spirit world.

The Christian View

Christianity, like the great spiritual traditions that predated it, preserved the link between virtue and happiness. For 2,000 years, Christian faiths have promulgated the idea that happiness can be won via good works.

According to the gospel of St. Matthew, there are particular types of good works and pure, humble attitudes that will be rewarded:

- Blessed are the poor in spirit: for theirs is the kingdom of Heaven.

- Blessed are the meek: for they shall inherit the earth.

- Blessed are they who mourn: for they shall be comforted.

- Blessed are they that hunger and thirst after justice: for they shall have their fill.

- Blessed are the merciful: for they shall obtain mercy.

- Blessed are the clean of heart: for they shall see God.

- Blessed are the peacemakers: for they shall be called the children of God.

- Blessed are they that suffer persecution for justice's sake: for theirs is the kingdom of Heaven.

It was, however, Christianity's recurrent idea of reward in the kingdom of Heaven that added a new dimension to the quest for happiness. Earthly woes themselves, according to Christian thought, do not constitute obstacles to happiness. Indeed, suffering earthly trials while still taking refuge in Jesus, who Christians revere as the son of God, ensures the attainment of eternal bliss in Heaven.

Also significant in Christianity is the idea that its followers are not excluded from the possibility of eternal happiness even if they sinned. Christians acknowledge that achieving an earthly life of perfect virtue is difficult, if not impossible. However, through acknowledging and confessing imperfections, it is believed that one can still attain heavenly reward.

Many Christian theologians have written on the subject of happiness, but perhaps the most well-known is St. Thomas Aquinas (1225–1274 C.E.). Considered by many to be the greatest theologian of the Catholic church, Aquinas wrote in his best-known work, *Summa Theologica*, that complete happiness can consist only in contemplating the Divine Essence. But he is clear that that possibility eludes us until we are in the heavenly kingdom to come.

Aquinas also appears to agree with the Buddhist precept that craving pleasure is, in fact, the greatest source of *un*happiness. "As long as man desires and seeks something, he remains unhappy."

Happiness as a Democratic "Right"

In the seventeenth and eighteenth centuries, the respective periods of the Age of Reason and the Age of Enlightenment, new ideas began to take shape with regard to many concepts—including that of happiness. Throughout Europe, in the centuries leading up to this time, happiness was seen as a matter of virtue, and the path toward it was a religious one. Moreover, happiness might not ever manifest itself in this life, but only in an afterlife. Some prominent thinkers began to take a more pragmatic and worldly view of happiness—a secular view that put religion to one side.

Today we may take it for granted that people have their own opinions about what constitutes personal happiness, and find nothing odd in the idea that it is an individual's prerogative to seek happiness in their own way. But at a certain time these were bold, even radical constructs. Enlightenment thinkers were the first in modern times to dare to proclaim such things. Among their pivotal new philosophical constructs were the following:

◆ Scottish philosophers Francis Hutcheson (1694–1746) and David Hume (1711–1776) argued that we do virtuous things less for their own sake than to experience pleasurable feelings.

◆ Hume also posited that humankind's thirst for happiness kept all of humankind gainfully occupied.

◆ English philosophers known as Utilitarians argued that "the happiness of the greatest number" should be the guiding principle behind action. (Jeremy Bentham [1748–1832] argued that "The greatest happiness of the greatest number is the foundation of morals and legislation.")

> **Happy Thought**
>
> "The great end of all human industry is the attainment of happiness. For this were arts invented, sciences cultivated, laws ordained, and societies modeled, by the most profound wisdom of patriots and legislators."
>
> —David Hume

- The French writer Voltaire (1694–1779) contended that happiness depended on the creation of a just, tolerant society in which men and women lived freely and in peace.

By the time America achieved its independence, Thomas Jefferson (1743–1826) believed individual happiness to be so important and so integral to democracy that he included it in the Declaration of Independence. That 1776 document included the words: "We hold these truths to be self-evident, that all men are created equal, that they are endowed by their Creator with certain unalienable Rights, that among these are Life, Liberty and the pursuit of Happiness."

Happiness Trivia

The phrase "life, liberty, and the pursuit of happiness" is often said to be based on the writings of philosopher John Locke and economist Adam Smith. But neither of these men actually included happiness in their enumerations of rights (Smith actually coined the phrase, "Life, liberty and the pursuit of property.") The expression "pursuit of happiness" was coined by Dr. Samuel Johnson in his 1759 novel *Rasselas*.

The Rise of Positive Thinking

Thanks to Thomas Jefferson, Americans were left endowed with a remarkable legacy: it is our right—maybe even our obligation—to pursue happiness. The question was, how? In the late nineteenth and early twentieth century, some prominent Americans embraced an individualistic, "can-do" approach to happiness that caught on with millions. That approach was one of positive thinking.

Dale Carnegie

Dale Carnegie (1888–1955) was one of America's original personal growth gurus. Born a poor farmer's son in Missouri, he managed to get a college education and became a salesman of legendary success. What distinguished Carnegie was his firm belief that anyone could be successful and happy if they truly desired positive outcomes.

Carnegie developed famous courses on self-improvement and authored numerous best-selling books, including *How To Stop Worrying and Start Living* and *How to Win Friends and Influence People*. Among his core ideas were the credos that life is what we make it, and that we each can substantially shape our own experiences by altering the kinds of thoughts we think.

Carnegie was a proponent of what has come to be known as *responsibility assumption—* the concept that we each bear significant, if not total, responsibility for the events that unfold in our lives. According to Carnegie's way of thinking, whether or not we are happy is a result of whether or not we really *want* to be happy.

def•i•ni•tion

> **Responsibility assumption** is the belief that individuals' mental mechanisms contribute substantially to the events that occur in their lives. Whether an outcome is good or bad, someone who subscribes to responsibility assumption would concede that this is what they must have wanted.

Norman Vincent Peale

Norman Vincent Peale (1898–1993) was one of America's most famous Christian preachers, who for more than 50 years was pastor of the Marble Collegiate Church Manhattan. He is one of the key progenitors of positive thinking. His seminal book, *The Power of Positive Thinking*, stayed on *The New York Times* best-seller list for 186 consecutive weeks, has been translated into 15 languages, and has sold some 7 million copies worldwide.

According to Peale, our biggest obstacle to happiness and success in all endeavors is self-doubt. He offered specific techniques—including a type of autohypnosis and intercessory prayer—for visualizing the achievement of goals and for eliminating negative thoughts.

Peale was a spiritual man, yet he did not see his faith as being at odds with the idea that we exert control over our lives through thinking, and that a happy life is available to anyone who is willing to truly change their thoughts. Peale did not invoke God as a punitive power, nor as an arbiter of who attained heavenly rewards, but rather as a benevolent source of support. He often repeated the question, "If God is for us, who can be against us?"

Happiness Trivia

In our own century, the so-called Law of Attraction has gained great popularity as a potential self-help path to happiness. The Law of Attraction is a concept similar to that of positive thinking. It states that we can get what we want by asking the universe for it, acting as if we already have it, and being open to receiving it. Both positive thinking and the Law of Attraction actually have roots traceable at least as far back as various Buddhist and Hindu texts that speak of the mind's influence on the nature of worldly events.

The Ongoing Search

Throughout the ages, the nature and causes of happiness have been pondered, debated, and dissected by some of our greatest writers, philosophers, theologians, and statesmen. Yet happiness, as it happens, has been an elusive concept to pin down. Is it a matter of luck? Is it inextricably connected with virtue or with spirituality? Is it our right or obligation to pursue individual happiness, or to contribute to the happiness of others? Is achieving happiness simply a matter of desiring happiness and thinking happy thoughts?

In the next chapter, we'll see why—and how—science decided to weigh in on this fascinating field of inquiry.

The Least You Need to Know

- Greek dramatists seem to attribute happiness to luck and fate, but the great Greek philosophers, including Socrates, Plato, and Aristotle, equated happiness with the deliberate cultivation of goodness and virtue.

- Eastern philosophies offer a long, venerable tradition of inquiry into the nature and attainment of happiness: Buddhism, Hinduism, and Taoism stress stilling the mind and rising above worldly concerns as the path to the sublime.

- Christianity teaches that earthly trials need not deflect from happiness for people of faith, but that ultimate happiness and reward will occur only in Heaven.

- Thinkers in the seventeenth and eighteenth century Age of Enlightenment took a secular view of happiness—their ideas culminated in America's Declaration of Independence naming the "pursuit of happiness" as a right.

- The twentieth century saw the rise of positive thinking as a route to happiness—writers such as Dale Carnegie and Norman Vincent Peale promoted the belief that we contribute substantially to creating happy outcomes by the ways in which we think.

Chapter 3

The New Science of Happiness

In This Chapter

- ◆ The beginnings of positive psychology
- ◆ The three types of happiness positive psychologists study
- ◆ The learning boom in happiness
- ◆ The pioneers in the science of happiness
- ◆ The importance of understanding happiness now

As our new millennium dawned, so did a new branch of psychology—one that gave a name to humankind's long-standing quest to understand the nature of happiness. The so-called "psychology of happiness," or positive psychology, garnered a great deal of attention. In the media, stories about how psychology was now looking at the good things in life—and good ways of experiencing life and developing oneself—abounded. The idea was intriguing, both to the general public and to psychology students who promptly packed the hundreds of courses that came to be offered at universities around the country.

Yet despite the field's burgeoning popularity, many people have a rather limited view of positive psychology. This chapter looks at the precepts of positive psychology and at its founders. It also looks at why understanding happiness is perhaps more critical now than at any other time in human history.

The Dawn of Positive Psychology

In January 2000, two founders of the positive psychology movement, Martin Seligman and Mihaly Csikszentmihalyi, edited a special issue of the journal *American Psychologist*. It was devoted to the new field of positive psychology. In this seminal issue, the two men stated that psychology, for all its accomplishments, was not producing enough "knowledge of what makes life worth living."

Previously, the discipline of psychology had focused much of its efforts on problems and pathology. That was about to change. Using an empirical approach, positive psychology aimed to learn about happiness by studying people who actually *were* happy and positive. Observation and experiment would be favored over theory.

Happiness Trivia

Some psychologists estimate that more than 90 percent of research into emotion has concentrated on various forms of mental illness such as depression and anxiety. However, during the last few years more than 3,000 scientific papers have explored the benefits and impacts of happiness. Many of these are chronicled on the World Database of Happiness (http://worlddatabaseofhappiness.eur.nl).

Three Rooms in the House of Happiness

But what exactly did positive psychologists mean by happiness? Did the word signify positive subjective experiences, virtue and values, positive goals and intentions? The answer, according to Seligman, was all three. He said the psychology of happiness would address the pleasant life, the good life, and the meaningful life.

Positive Experience

The pleasant life is what most of us probably think of when we first hear the word happiness. If what we're experiencing in the moment makes us feel good (this can be anything that we deem pleasant, from listening to a symphony to making love to watching NASCAR), we say we're happy. And if we are in a phase of life where pleasant experiences outweigh unpleasant ones, we might even say we're very happy—on a roll.

But the pleasant life has its limitations. For one thing, our subjective sense of how much pleasure we're having and how cheerful we are about it relates to our happiness set point. As explained in Chapter 1, at least half of this is hereditary. There are things we can do to raise our set point within limits, and positive psychologists are certainly interested in studying those practices. But if pleasantness is our full measure of happiness, we may be short-changed.

A second challenge to the pleasant life is that it is very much about the moment. Yet many of us have difficulty staying in the moment. Even in the midst of a pleasurable experience, we tend to dwell on anxiety about the future—and sometimes even regrets about the past. Before we know it, we have lost our focus, and the pleasure has slipped through our fingers.

Stumbling Blocks

We undermine our own pleasant experiences when we interject "spoiler" thoughts such as "Sure, I'm happy now, but later I have to get a bunch of work done and do the laundry," or "This is nice, but something is bound to go wrong sooner or later." Catching yourself thinking this way is the first step to changing this habit. Try to bring your thoughts back to the present when the present is pleasant.

It's easy to take shortcuts, sometimes dangerous shortcuts, to a pleasant experience. If we think "happiness is chocolate cake" we might mindlessly eat, or overeat, chocolate cake. If we think "happiness is driving fast," we might drive fast—maybe too fast. But in the end, especially if we do not stop to mindfully notice and appreciate our pleasures, there's an inevitable "so what" factor.

All in all, living the pleasant life is, well, pleasant—as far as it goes. But it only goes so far. No matter what we do, there will be times of unpleasantness and times of sadness in life. That's why positive psychology is also paying a lot if attention to two additional dimensions of happiness—dimensions that can see us through the not-so-good times.

Life Well-Lived

What positive psychologists mean by "the good life" is essentially living life well by drawing on our strengths. Researchers are intensely interested in the underlying character traits, values, talents, and attitudes that allow people to thrive *in spite* of setbacks and to achieve resilience in the aftermath of negative events.

The well-lived life based on character harkens back to the ideals of the ancient Greeks and their theory of eudaimonia (as described in Chapter 2). But positive psychology goes well beyond theory. Social scientists' very pragmatic goal in methodically identifying positive traits is to help all of us learn to recognize our own strengths, build on them, and consciously make the most of them. For example, if you get fired from your job, but recognize that you have a great deal of persistence and creativity, you can deliberately use those traits to help yourself find an even better job. You won't give up when other people might (persistence) and you will find ways to be noticed above the crowd (creativity). If you break your leg but are aware that you are basically a hopeful person who keeps things in perspective with a great sense of humor, you can not only tolerate your recovery period with equanimity, but also appreciate its potential for generating some amusing "let me tell you about my time on crutches" stories.

When we become familiar with our key strengths, we can even contemplate restructuring our lives so that we use those characteristics more and more. We may find ourselves creating new opportunities in our careers, expanding our social lives, and enhancing our family lives. In addition, we may use the strengths to help others. The more we use our positive traits, the more they develop. Like a set of well-flexed muscles, they grow ever more powerful.

Helping Hand

Using your strengths for personal growth or to help others might well give you more satisfaction than pursuing a sensual pleasure. Researcher Veronika Huta of McGill University devised an experiment where she paged people at random intervals throughout the day and asked them what they were doing and how they were feeling. Pursuits that involved developing one's potential, achieving excellence, and contributing to the well-being of others significantly correlated with reports of life satisfaction; hedonic pursuits did not.

A Purposeful Path

The meaningful life involves following a personal path lighted by purpose. It may involve devotion to a particular institution (a charity, a religious organization, a political party, an environmental group). But it can involve any commitment to and belief in any cause greater than ourselves. We can find meaning in something as close to home as nurturing our family and supporting our friends.

When we pursue a purpose, we are motivated. The meaning we ascribe to our path provides us with energy, drive, and intellectual and emotional engagement. We know the all-important *why* of our existence: why we are getting up in the morning, why we are expending so much effort, why we persist even in the face of obstacles, why we may even be sacrificing things that might be considered pleasurable.

Leading a purposeful life also gives us the satisfying feeling that we matter, that we are making a difference, and that the world will change for the better because of us having been here. And although it's certainly true that pursuing a larger purpose generally involves more hard work than moment-to-moment "fun" (picture washing cars at a Boy Scout fundraiser or helping your middle schooler with algebra versus soaking in a hot tub), studies show it provides more long-lasting feelings of happiness to be of use to others than to simply indulge ourselves.

As positive psychologists have pointed out, finding a particular meaning and purpose is up to each of us. And unlike embracing momentary pleasure, seeking meaning can be a lengthy journey—with no shortcuts and no feel-good substances to help us along the way. But after we come to a realization about why we are here and how to be useful, our satisfaction can soar.

Happy Thought

"There will likely be a pharmacology of pleasure, and there may be a pharmacology of positive emotion generally, but ... it's impossible that there'll be a pharmacology of meaning."

—Martin Seligman

Who's Curious About Happiness?

Since positive psychology took shape at the turn of the twenty-first century, the number of people who decided they wanted to learn more about it has steadily grown. Who is creating this learning boom? And how is this learning taking place?

Students from All Walks of Life

In the past several years, classes on positive psychology have sprung up on more than 200 college campuses across America. These include such institutions as the University of North Carolina at Chapel Hill, the University of Wisconsin, and Virginia's George Mason University. As of the spring semester 2006, positive psychology was officially the most popular course at Harvard. With an enrollment of 855 students who craved knowledge of living "a fulfilling and flourishing life"—as the course description said—positive psychology surpassed the enrollment of even introductory economics. The psychology of happiness is also becoming popular abroad, especially in England. In 2006, the Well-being Institute, devoted to positive psychology studies, was founded at Cambridge University.

The formal study of positive psychology is not limited to undergraduates. At the University of Pennsylvania, it's now possible to obtain a Master's degree in Applied

Positive Psychology (MAPP). The program attracts psychologists, educators, life coaches, and health and business professionals. Some of these graduate students want to build a specialization within a clinical practice; others want to access the means of positively influencing businesses, schools, or other social institutions. Still other students want to focus intensely on research.

> **Happiness Trivia**
>
> Currently, research in the field of positive psychology is thriving, thanks to millions of dollars contributed to this end by nonprofit organizations—and to the more than 125,000 people who have signed up so far to participate in web-based positive psychology studies conducted at various institutions.

But perhaps most significant of all, countless people who are not students per se are beginning to take an interest in studying happiness. They are taking adult education courses, workshops, and seminars in positive psychology. The members of this ever-widening community are simply interested in learning what they can about getting the most out of life.

Homework Required

Although positive psychology is a serious, evidence-based scientific discipline, learning about it, whether in a classroom or workshop, is likely to require more than reading textbooks and articles and examining research studies. In addition to such things, anyone who takes a course should be prepared to use *themselves* as research subjects—at least in an informal sense.

Students would be gaining a very limited understanding of the field and its discoveries if they did not merge theory with some practice. So courses in the psychology of happiness typically incorporate practical assignments on an ongoing basis. A student might be asked to do the following:

- Record journal entries
- Take life-satisfaction surveys
- Identify their personal character strengths
- Seek out and thank people to whom they feel grateful
- Contrast how they feel after indulging in fun versus how they feel after helping someone else

All students of positive psychology should be prepared to undertake personal happiness homework. The assignments might seem unorthodox at first, and perhaps provoke a little anxiety. But there is no "wrong way" to do them, and in undertaking them the abstract will become concrete.

Founders of Positive Psychology

It's said that good ideas have many parents, while bad ideas are orphans. The psychology of happiness has multiple parents. We'll look here at some of the key people who founded the contemporary movement, as well as a few who nudged psychology in a positive direction in the recent past.

Martin Seligman

For all intents and purposes the "father" of positive psychology, Martin Seligman officially gave the field its name in 1998. Doing so was one of the initiatives undertaken by Seligman in his role then as president of the American Psychological Association.

Seligman is the Fox Leadership Professor of Psychology at the University of Pennsylvania. He also heads that school's Positive Psychology Center, a hub of ongoing research, learning, and discussion in the field. He has authored a number of very accessible books on happiness and optimism (see Appendix B), and currently devotes much of his time to training those pursuing higher academic degrees in positive psychology.

Seligman has talked openly about a transformative event that ignited his personal drive to understanding positivity. When his then 5-year-old daughter accused him of being a grouch, he apparently took it to heart. Acknowledging that she might have a point, he decided to turn his attention and talents to exploring what made life worthwhile and what made people happy.

In the early part of his career, much of Seligman's renowned research had been in the field of depression, in which he explored the concept of *learned helplessness*. Later he became known as well for the concept of *learned optimism*.

def•i•ni•tion

> **Learned helplessness** is essentially a giving-up or quitting response. It grows out of the belief that whatever actions we take are futile and will have no impact on how events turn out. **Learned optimism** is the process of altering our outlook by changing the way in which we evaluate and explain our circumstances.

Mihaly Csikszentmihalyi

Mihaly (a.k.a. Mike) Csikszentmihalyi (pronounced *chik-SENT-me-hi-ee*), a professor of psychology at the University of Chicago, coedited the pivotal January 2000 issue of *American Psychologist* that heralded widespread interest in a psychology of happiness. But by then Csikszentmihalyi's seminal contribution to the understanding of the positive aspects of human experience had been well-known for a decade. That contribution was the concept of *flow*.

Flow, about which more will be said in Chapter 11, is essentially a process of total involvement with life that is achieved when one is pursuing a creative and challenging activity—making music, writing poetry, scaling a mountain, planting a garden, running a marathon—with single-minded concentration. Allowing oneself to be engaged and immersed in this way, Csikszentmihalyi showed, boosts feelings of self-worth, well-being, calm, and joy.

Csikszentmihalyi's unique personal history no doubt played a role in helping him discover his own joy-inducing passion. The son of an aristocrat who served as Budapest's ambassador to Rome, his world was shattered when Hungary was taken over by Stalin in 1948. Csikszentmihalyi noticed that while some of his compatriots fell into hopelessness and despair, others who faced the same obstacles rose to the challenge and brilliantly created their lives anew. His desire for an explanation of the difference prompted him to embark on his psychological quest, which involved interviewing thousands of people from all around the globe and from all walks of life about what gave them joy and satisfaction. Along the way, he also engaged his wide-ranging creative impulses by sculpting and painting and by writing for *The New Yorker*. In a sense, Csikszentmihalyi was one of his own case studies.

> **Happy Thought**
>
> "People who learn to control inner experience will be able to determine the quality of their lives, which is as close as any of us can come to being happy."
> —Mihaly Csikszentmihalyi

Christopher Peterson

Christopher Peterson is often cited for his work in the areas of optimism, health, character, and well-being. He is, along with Martin Seligman, the author of *Character Strengths and Virtues: A Handbook and Classification*.

Peterson's ambitious research, undertaken from a positive psychology perspective, helped to identify the signature strengths most likely to contribute to life satisfaction.

Petersen is a professor of psychology at the University of Michigan. He is a consulting editor of the *Journal of Positive Psychology* and a member of the Positive Psychology Steering Committee.

Ed Diener

Ed Diener is a psychology professor at the University of Illinois in Urbana-Champaign, where his social science laboratory is devoted to studying subjective well-being (how happy we perceive ourselves to be). Diener is well-known for his research relating to material wealth and happiness. Along with fellow researcher David Myers, Ph.D., he has documented the fact that after individuals have enough money to cover basic needs, personal income does not have much impact on personal happiness—or, as some have put it, "the goods life" does not affect "the good life."

Abraham Maslow

It would be a mistake to conclude there was no interest in human fulfillment and happiness within the general psychological community before the turn of the millennium. On the contrary, a movement that laid down roots as long ago as the 1960s and 1970s set the stage for today's positive psychology. That movement was humanistic psychology, which looked at what experiences gave meaning to life and at how human beings could fulfill their highest potential.

Within the context of the humanism, Abraham Maslow was well-known for developing the *hierarchy of human needs*. This theory contended that as we humans meet our basic needs (food, shelter, safety) we are driven to pursue higher needs, such as the quest for knowledge, the search for truth and beauty, and—at the top of the hierarchy—the need to achieve *self-actualization*.

def•i•ni•tion

Maslow's **hierarchy of human needs** is a theory of motivation. It posits that after basic biological and social needs are met, humans will innately move toward satisfying higher needs—pursuing wisdom, aesthetics, spirituality, and personal fulfillment. Maslow's hierarchy is often pictured as a pyramid comprised of numerous levels.

Self-actualization, according to Maslow, is the process of working to become one's best possible self and fulfilling one's highest potential.

Carl Rogers

Humanist psychotherapist Carl Rogers became known for applying the human potential perspective to the practice of psychotherapy. Rogers developed a positive approach to treatment that he called "client centered." This approach …

- ◆ Focused on the present and future rather than on the past.

- ◆ Focused on the conscious mind rather than the unconscious.

- ◆ Encouraged clients to take responsibility for their actions.

- ◆ Took promoting growth—rather than "curing illness"—as its goal.

Rogers's goal for therapeutic treatment differed markedly from the goal that Sigmund Freud laid out for psychoanalytic treatment. Psychoanalysis, Freud said, was equipped to transform "neurotic misery" into "ordinary unhappiness."

For Rogers and the other humanists, happiness did not seem an unreasonable goal to set our sights on. We might never fully realize our highest potential, but we would be better off for trying.

Why a Happiness Movement Now?

Why is the psychology of happiness engendering so much interest at this juncture in history? As with most things that seem to catch on quickly, enthusiasm has actually been building up for quite a while. Nevertheless, it seems clear that we have reached a tipping point. Positive psychology will likely continue to gain momentum, and the reasons why are many.

A Globalized Perspective

More than ever in history, individuals are aware of the challenges experienced by people all over the world. Mass media and modern technology may have made the world "smaller," but in doing so they have also made us aware of global inequities.

Positive psychologists believe that by examining the dimensions of the well-lived life and the meaningful life that have to do with compassion and altruism, the discipline can be instrumental in helping to address such inequities. It can increase the chances that those who are suffering are helped by those who are doing well. Rather than being a luxury, positive psychology can be looked at as a necessity for helping people cultivate attitudes and strengths that will benefit not just one, but all.

An Emphasis on Prevention

Traditional psychology has made great strides in treating emotional problems and psychological disorders when they manifest themselves. Positive psychology can play a role in fortifying us so that some of these psychological problems and disorders—and the negative physical consequences sometimes associated with them—may not arise or may be less severe.

Highly persuasive evidence, for example, tells us that factors such as optimistic attitudes play a role in maintaining psychological and physical health. Optimists (about whom more will be said in Chapter 7) are better at deflecting stress-related ailments and even appear to live longer overall.

It is much less costly, in terms of dollars and in terms of quality of life, to protect ourselves against illness rather than to treat illness after it has set in. That's why positive psychologists say it makes sense to invest more funds, time, and research in a discipline that can help people develop attitudes and behaviors that can promote and preserve long-term wellness.

Although positive psychology is by no means seen as a replacement for traditional psychology, it is, as Martin Seligman has put it, "another bow in its quiver." We overcome damage not just by repairing it but by trying to identify and eradicate its causes.

More Life to Live

Finally, there is this: as a populace we are living longer than ever before. Naturally we are concerned with maintaining a high quality of life for as long as possible. The potential for a psychology of happiness to assist us in this quest is alluring. We are eager to learn its lessons and apply them throughout our increasing life span. Why live longer, after all, if we cannot live happier?

The Least You Need to Know

- ◆ The field of positive psychology was given its name by Dr. Martin Seligman in 1998, and has been garnering a great deal of interest since the turn of the millennium.

- ◆ Positive psychology examines three dimensions of happiness: pleasurable experiences; the good life driven by character strengths; and meaningful, purposeful existence. Of the three, the latter two create the most life satisfaction.

- Learning about positive psychology in any setting involves putting theory into practice and doing "homework assignments" that involve discovering what makes us happy and why.

- Contemporary founders of positive psychology, including Martin Seligman and Mihaly Csikszentmihalyi, were preceded by theorists and practitioners in the human potential movement.

- The psychology of happiness continues to gain momentum for social reasons, such as its emphasis on compassion, and for medical reasons, such as its promise for developing effective preventive measures to help us maintain wellness.

Part 2

The Secrets of Character

Are you curious, creative, determined? Do you appreciate beauty? Do you keep things in perspective? If so, you possess character traits that can predispose you to happiness. In this part of the book, you'll learn why such traits are critical and how you can enhance your own personal strengths. You'll also learn about practicing altruism and discover why people whose character leads them to do good tend to feel good as a result.

Chapter 4

Why Character Is Crucial

In This Chapter

- How character can transform life
- How to distinguish temperament, personality, and character
- What comprises character
- How character develops

"Character is destiny," asserted Heraclitus, the ancient Greek philosopher. Positive psychologists would agree. Our character—our innermost convictions, values, and virtues—plays an essential part in determining how happy we will be throughout our lifetime.

For a long time psychology steered clear of studying character. The subject had a moral connotation that many felt was an inappropriate focus for science. But such is no longer the case. As this chapter shows, it is virtually impossible to understand happiness without considering what character is, how it is formed, and why it has the potential to drive our most positive actions.

The Happiness-Character Link

According to Christopher Peterson, one of positive psychology's founders, good character is regarded by positive psychology as "a family of positive dispositions." The components of character are known as character strengths. Positive psychologists believe that each of us has various strengths in varying degrees. The more strengths we have, and the greater their potency, the better able we will be not only to appreciate happiness but to actively choose and create it—even in difficult circumstances.

But even people who may never have consciously considered exactly what good character consists of tend to recognize it when they see it. As the following example shows, you don't need to be a psychologist to appreciate the powerful way in which character can shape an individual's response to life events.

Quite a Character: One Man's Example

In the fall of 2007, Randy Pausch, a Carnegie Mellon University computer-science professor, gave what was billed as his "last lecture" to 400 students and colleagues. The "last lecture" is a popular title for talks on college campuses in which top professors give hypothetical "final" talks about the things that matter most to them. The difference in this situation was that Pausch, a 46-year-old father of three, had been diagnosed with terminal pancreatic cancer. He was literally, not figuratively, imparting his final words of wisdom to his audience.

The professor began his talk by showing CT scans of the tumors that would prematurely end his life within a few months. He then announced that if anyone expected him be "morose," he was sorry to disappoint them. On the heels of that statement he gleefully segued into a series of one-handed push-ups.

During the lecture that followed his display of physical prowess, Pausch talked about his very specific childhood dreams—to walk in zero gravity, to write a World Book Encyclopedia entry, to design Disney rides, and to win enormous stuffed animals whenever carnivals came to town. He noted that he had achieved each and every goal—and then distributed his stuffed animal cache among audience members, saying he would not need them anymore.

In another section of his talk, Pausch flashed across a screen a series of rejection letters he'd been sent in the course of his career. Obviously relishing his setbacks, he told his listeners that "Brick walls are there for a reason. They let us prove how badly we want things."

Pausch advised his listeners to be patient: "Wait long enough, and people will surprise and impress you." He encouraged creativity: after showing photos of his childhood bedroom, decorated with math notations he'd scrawled on the walls, he said, "If your kids want to paint their bedrooms, as a favor to me, let 'em do it." He espoused the joys of altruism: "Helping others fulfill their dreams is even more fun than achieving your own."

Pausch talked about his legacy, saying he would "live on in Alice," a Carnegie Mellon software project he helped create that allows users to create 3-D animations. He paid homage to his parents, who'd let him write on his walls; brought out a birthday cake for his wife, whose birthday had been the day before; and noted that he was having the talk videotaped so that his children, ages 5, 2, and 1, could watch it when they were older.

After the professor's speech, the audience rose for an ovation. They were applauding more than the talk, however. They were applauding a life well-lived—a life filled with pleasure, meaning, and purpose. In a sense they were applauding the unfolding of one man's exemplary character.

Happy Thought

"Be such a person and live such a life that if everyone lived a life like yours, this would be God's paradise."

—Anonymous

How Character Carries Us Through

Randy Pausch might be defined as a paragon of good character. His final message strikingly summed up a lifetime of attitudes and actions that enabled him not only to achieve his dreams but to manifest resilience in the face of defeat and even death. What are the elements that made Pausch a man of strong, virtuous character, and, by extension, a happy man?

Among the qualities he displayed were:

- ♦ The imagination and creativity to envision unique and complex goals
- ♦ The perseverance and determination to pursue these goals
- ♦ Zest and enthusiasm for life's pleasures
- ♦ A love of learning
- ♦ Self-motivation
- ♦ Gratitude for the entirety of his life experience
- ♦ Love for his family
- ♦ Respect for his students and colleagues

- ◆ A spirit of giving

- ◆ A sense of humor and whimsy

- ◆ Courage

- ◆ A sense of optimism and perspective

Helping Hand _____

The final lecture of professor Randy Pausch is available for viewing on www.youtube.com. Full versions and shorter highlight versions are both available.

From Pausch's stories it appears that many of these traits were constant influences in both his personal and professional life. Some, like his creativity, love of learning, and self-motivation, were evident even in boyhood. But how might Pausch's character have developed? For that matter, how does character develop in any of us? Are we simply born with character?

Temperament, Personality, and Character

Social scientists studying character contend that any character strength may have its prodigies—precocious children or adolescents who display the trait early and naturally. But positive psychologists do not assume that character traits are fixed or grounded in an immutable genetic code.

In other words, we're not born with character. We are born with a bundle of predispositions known as temperament. As babies we are more than blank slates.

The Foundation of Infant Temperament

Temperament refers to an infant's individual way of interacting with and adapting to the world. Temperament does have a biological component. To some extent, it is based on genetic traits that determine factors such as the nature of chemical receptors in the brain, and to some extent, it can be impacted by the baby's in-utero environment and the hormones to which the developing infant is exposed.

Manifestations of temperament are present very early in life. Some are observable from birth, and others are clearly measurable within the first few weeks and months of life. Developmental psychologists have identified many characteristics of behavior that comprise temperament. These include the following:

- ◆ Activity level

- ◆ Smiling and laughing

- ◆ Regularity in eating and sleeping

- ◆ Approaching or avoiding new situations and people

- ◆ Adaptability to change

- ◆ Sensitivity to stimulation

- ◆ Intensity of responsiveness

- ◆ Attention span and distractibility

- ◆ Distress when experiencing limitations

- ◆ Soothability

- ◆ General mood (cheerful or grumpy)

Parents—especially mothers or any primary caregiver—are acutely aware of the aspects that comprise infant temperament, but they usually describe them in a different way. They tend to describe their babies as "happy" or "fussy," "difficult" or "easy."

So-called easy babies are amenable to change. They tend to approach new situations and people in a positive way. Their eating and sleeping behavior is predictable. And their mood, overall, is positive. On the other hand, so-called difficult babies withdraw from new people and situations. They adapt to change slowly, if at all. Their schedules are erratic. Their mood is generally negative, and they complain loudly when upset.

Labels notwithstanding—and as any parent knows—it does *not* turn out that easy babies end up with "good character" or that difficult babies end up with "bad character." What will evolve into characterological dispositions and strengths are still a long way from solidifying, with many factors intervening over many years.

Is Personality the Same as Character?

In the months after birth, early manifestations of temperament are already subject to change. The changes occur as babies interact with their caregivers. Parents' reactions to their child's style of behavior can strengthen it or weaken it. For example, parents can react to a "difficult" child by becoming more rigid about scheduling and less responsive to outbursts. But this in turn can make the infant even *more* difficult to handle. On the other hand, parents can respond in ways that nudge temperament in a more positive direction—perhaps by becoming more adaptable themselves, or by reframing a child's boisterous cry as a sign of hardiness rather than an accusatory commentary on their parenting skills. (*That kid's got some pair of lungs. What a ball of energy!*)

Parents' response to their infant's temperament is only the first of countless environmental factors that will contribute to an individual's overall personality. Soon the child will be influenced by peers, teachers, neighbors, the media, and the sum total of cultural messages. The adult personality that develops over ensuing years is a complex overlay of behavioral patterns and attitudes, emotional reactions, and social roles.

> **Happy Thought**
>
> "Character is what you do in the dark, it is what you do when no one is watching."
> —Anonymous

As personality develops, character is also formed and also influenced by these multiple and overlapping factors. But personality and character are not the same things. The first is overt, the latter internal. Put another way: when we interact with anyone, personality is what we see; character is what we get.

Characteristics of Character Strength

It's possible to spend 10 minutes in a casual exchange with someone and come away with a fairly strong sense of their personality traits. We might describe that person as shy or outgoing, serious or merry, forceful or laid back. However, it usually takes far longer to assess someone's character. We don't know if they are brave or loyal or compassionate until we see them put to some sort of test and have to choose between courses of action. As Aristotle pointed out, when we speak of an excellence of character, the emphasis is not on mere distinctiveness or individuality, but on the combination of qualities that people find admirable.

Character is complex. It involves the interplay of many traits and many influences. But there are some constants.

Good Character Takes Work

Everyone develops a personality, and everyone develops character. But to develop the sort of character that can generate happiness is not a passive act. It requires conscious choice and volition. In other words, we have to work at it.

As positive psychology movement founder Martin Seligman has pointed out, there are many shortcuts to pleasure, from drugs to casual sex to TV to shopping, but there are no shortcuts to the good life that is derived from character strengths. Indeed, to make life decisions based on character-linked convictions can often seem like anything *but* the easy way out. Traits such as self-control, loyalty, and humility can sometimes get in the way of, say, turning a quick (albeit unethical) profit or indulging in an illicit love affair.

But in the end, an individual can derive more satisfaction from habits that derive from good character than from giving in to impulses to quench an immediate desire.

Character Is Values-Based

What makes character strengths a matter of conscious choice is that they are based on values. Life's important decisions involve choosing from among a variety of options. When we select goals we consider worthy, we are acting out of a sense of personal values. For example, if we value knowledge, we may decide to spend our time reading books, attending seminars, or pursuing an advanced degree. If we value the love of family, we may decide to arrange our life to encompass more family time. If we value kindness, we will be aware of how we speak to people, even when we are angry.

Everyone has beliefs about what is valuable to them, so everyone has values. And most people are aware of the sorts of virtuous values that their culture, society, and spiritual traditions hold dear. The values prescribed by spiritual traditions throughout the world and throughout time are strikingly similar. So presumably everyone has an idea of what options they *should* pursue to embody good character and reap the rewards of doing so. But whether they do so—and to what degree—is another matter.

Ideal values are not always easy to achieve; even if you value honesty highly, try being totally honest with everyone you meet for 24 hours and you will understand the challenge. Understandably, many people find it easier to *articulate* admirable values than to actually *practice* them. And virtually everyone at sometime or other will need to make some compromises between, say, self-interest and self-sacrifice, or between calculation and compassion.

Still, some people's words match their deeds more often than other people's. In the end, exhibiting the kind of character that generates happiness involves not simply talking the talk but actually walking the walk. Character strengths can be considered values on which action is taken with some degree of consistency, even—or especially—in times when circumstances are trying and the proverbial chips are down. As Napoleon said, "To have the right estimate of a man's character, we must see him in adversity."

> **Helping Hand** _____
>
> Research shows that our beliefs are most apt to be reflected in our actions when we define our self-image by a particular value. For example, the more we authentically think of ourselves as generous people, the more likely we are to be generous in a variety of situations. Periodically examining and enumerating our values may actually help us employ our character strengths more often and in new and diverse ways.

Emotions Pass, Character Lasts

Even people who are arguably of sterling character and who frequently put their strengths into practice are perfectly capable of experiencing emotions that run counter to the behavioral choices they see as more valuable and productive. However, one thing such individuals appear to understand is that emotions pass, while character lasts. Often, they can *feel* like behaving badly and still do what will, in the end, produce a more positive outcome. They may feel angry, but still behave kindly—most of the time. They may feel lazy, but still behave industriously—most of the time.

As for those situations when their behavior does not follow their beliefs, these individuals do not forsake their values and strengths afterward but use them as a home base they can return to. Their character strengths anchor them even after a rush of powerful emotion may succeed in temporarily derailing them.

Some social scientists say character is a mere matter of *situationalism*, and that any of us will sacrifice our character strengths under certain combinations of circumstances, such as when fear of authority causes us to follow questionable orders. But positive psychologists contend this is a simplistic way of looking at character. Even if they do stray, fundamentally happy people do not consider a character transgression an excuse to surrender their usual virtues any more than successful dieters consider an occasional ice-cream cone a reason to give up their weight-loss plan.

Character Can Be Improved

Is character malleable or fixed? With neurobiologists searching for brain-linked causes or contributors to virtually every human behavior, it's not surprising that they are also currently looking for neurochemical forces that drive our impulses to do good or do wrong. At the University of Zurich, for example, researchers relate a person's level of trust to a measure of their neuropeptide levels. They also relate an individual's level of fairness to the electromagnetic pattern in their right prefrontal cortex—and have noted that if you disrupt that pattern with a strong magnet, a person's sense of fair play will be snuffed out like a match flame in a brisk wind.

However, additional research has yielded far fuzzier results on how the brain makes values-based decisions. Ask an individual a series of increasing knotty ethical questions, and with each escalating layer of complication, more and more regions of the brain become active—presumably doing battle while the individual ponders a course of action. It appears that values-based actions are a holistic affair, with many cognitive and emotional "moving parts" factoring in.

Happiness Trivia

In a scenario known as the "trolley dilemma," researchers pose a series of ethical questions that grow more and more complex. The premise is that you are standing near a track as an out-of-control trolley careens toward five unwitting people:

Would you pull a switch that diverted the train onto an empty siding?

Would you do the same if pulling that switch meant one person would be killed instead of five?

Would you sacrifice that one person for five if you had to push him in front of the trolley yourself?

With each successive level, multiple areas of the brain fire up, displaying the complex nature of values-based decisions.

Positive psychologists certainly believe some aspects of character strengths may be linked to brain chemistry and heritability. But they wouldn't be spending so much time studying character strengths if they didn't believe we could take proactive steps to develop the character traits that lead to a more positive life.

But just what would such steps involve?

Where Does Character Come From?

Humans are social creatures, and our character dispositions have a significant social learning component. Whether we are aware of it or not, the values that inform our character are, in part, shaped and molded by influential people around us and by institutions in whose circle of influence we fall.

Moms, Dads, Models, and Morals

Our species is skilled at imitation. Humans are born mimics, naturally imitating the people around us as we develop. Developmental psychologists have long observed that as we grow we absorb and recreate not only the actions of those around us but also their attitudes and values. We "read" what those close to us are thinking and notice how they are deliberating when faced with a challenge or dilemma. We hear what they say, and—more importantly—we observe what they do. This is known as *modeling*. We use these people as role models—templates on which to pattern our own values-based behaviors.

def•i•ni•tion

Modeling refers to emulating what influential people say and do. It is a cornerstone concept of social learning theory as put forth by psychologist Albert Bandura.

Not surprisingly, the people in our immediate families—most notably our parents—are our first role models of character and instructors of values. They may or may not sit us down and say, "Let me tell you about courage," or "Here's what I know about the rewards of persistence," but we observe the decisions they make and the values those decisions embody, and we learn what their hopes and expectations are for our own behavior.

In addition to modeling, parents can also influence our values by behavioral means, by doling out rewards and punishments. Through this type of reinforcement, we learn that acting on the values our parents consider positive will get us something positive. Acting in opposition to those values, on the other hand, will yield unpleasant consequences.

Finally, parents are early gatekeepers of our worldly information. The books and films and television shows they expose us to when we are small are also filled with ideas, behaviors, role models, and values-based lessons. Thus *The Little Engine That Could* teaches us about perseverance, Aslan of *The Chronicles of Narnia* teach us about bravery, and *The Simpsons* teaches us that a sense of humor is important, too.

Influential Institutions

As we move out into the wider world, we encounter institutions and organizations that impart values-based lessons in a cognitive way. Many children attend some form of religious instruction classes that fulfill this role. Many belong to groups such as Boy Scouts, whose values lessons can be summed up in the Boy Scout law, which stipulates that a Scout is "loyal, helpful, friendly, courteous, kind, obedient, cheerful, thrifty, brave, clean, and reverent."

Helping Hand

In the United States, many families who subscribe to no formal religion are participating in a growing trend to enroll their children in Humanist Sunday schools and summer camps that reinforce their parents' morals and values. The children learn secular lessons linked to, among other things, collaboration, self-reflection, and intellectual curiosity.

Schools, those ubiquitous institutions in which young people spend so much of their time, have always been influential in shaping values, whether they acknowledge this or not. Today, however, many schools formalize this role by implementing character education programs. (More about this in Chapter 16.) These programs systematize values-driven lessons, attempt to create an environment where the school itself functions in accordance with those values, and often recognize students for displaying character traits that are consistent with those values, such as responsibility, self-control, fairness, tolerance, and consideration of others.

Organizations and institutions can certainly play a part in forming our values and in creating character strengths. However, they are most effective when the lessons they impart and the virtues they endorse resonate with those taught at home.

The Self-Examination Factor

Modeling, reward and punishment, and cognitive instruction all work together to form our values and, in turn, our character strengths. But positive psychology does not believe they tell the whole story.

At any juncture in our life from childhood on, positive psychologists say we may face a challenging situation that compels us to look within and ask ourselves, "What is the right thing to do?" As we make such choices over and over—with "no one watching," as it were—we can actually map the landscape of our own virtues.

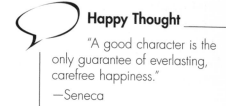

Happy Thought

"A good character is the only guarantee of everlasting, carefree happiness."

—Seneca

As far as the psychology of happiness is concerned, character strengths are always capable of evolving. We are always capable of discovering a new strength, of resurrecting a dormant strength, or of enhancing a strength we use routinely. Life will be our instructor if we let it be. And the more we let life instruct us, the happier that life will turn out to be.

The Least You Need to Know

◆ Good character is regarded by positive psychology as "a family of positive dispositions." The components of character are known as character strengths.

◆ Personality and character are not the same thing—personality is what we see when we interact with someone, but character is what we get.

◆ Good character requires effort and involves identifying and acting on one's values; although character issues are complex, positive psychologists believe character strengths are malleable and can be improved upon.

◆ Our character is formed under the influence of individual role models and social institutions, but according to positive psychology we can always discover or enhance strengths whenever we are faced with a challenge.

Chapter 5

Sustaining Strengths

In This Chapter

- ◆ Seeking areas of character strength
- ◆ Evaluating your strengths
- ◆ Identifying your skills and talents
- ◆ Making the most of strengths and skills

If someone were to ask you about your character strengths, you might not know how to answer. It's possible you never thought about yourself in those terms. If you did answer, you might say something general, such as "I'm a nice person" or "I have integrity."

But positive psychologists believe that each and every one of us has specific strengths and virtues we can draw upon to promote happiness. Identifying them is the first step to making the most of them. This chapter looks at what constitutes happiness-enhancing strengths, as well as how we can recognize and build upon our own.

Areas of Character Strength

Positive psychologists have considered, and are still considering at great length, exactly which aspects of character can help us live a life that is not

Helping Hand _____

You can evaluate your strengths according to the Values in Action index at the website of Dr. Martin Seligman, www.authentichappiness.com. You can also access other happiness questionnaires at this site.

only enjoyable but also filled with meaning and purpose. Dr. Martin Seligman and Dr. Chris Peterson, along with other top scholars in the country, spearheaded the research to create the extensive Values in Action (VIA) classification, which defines six general categories of overriding virtues—wisdom, courage, justice, humanity, temperance, and spirituality. They then defined the paths by which each of these virtues is expressed, resulting in 24 character strengths.

Other positive psychologists have grouped strengths somewhat differently. For example, Dr. Stephen Post, professor of bioethics at Case Western University and president of the institute for Research on Unlimited Love, conceives of character strengths in 10 major rubrics: celebration, generativity, forgiveness, courage, humor, respect, compassion, loyalty, listening, and creativity.

Yet the essence of the strengths and virtues remains the same, regardless of which listing or categorization one consults. All the strengths link to values and to virtue, and all require expending positive effort via our minds, hearts, and spirits. They relate to how we treat ourselves, how we treat others, and how we relate to the human condition at large.

The summary of strengths that follows is an encapsulation of those most frequently cited, grouped into categories of cognitive strengths, goal-oriented strengths, self-mastery strengths, interpersonal strengths, and transcendent strengths.

Cognitive Strengths

Cognitive strengths are strengths of mental focus. They spring from valuing knowledge. Individuals who display these strengths are interested in accumulating knowledge not just for their own sakes but also because of what that knowledge may enable them to do. Among the focus-oriented strengths positive psychologists most often cite are creativity, curiosity, reason, and social and emotional intelligence:

- Creativity involves inventiveness and imagination—the ability to generate ideas, artifacts, and solutions to problems that are both novel and useful.

- Curiosity involves the love of learning and an eagerness to discover more about a wide range of things, including people, places, ideas, and natural phenomena.

♦ Reason involves the ability to think critically and logically, to make sound decisions with regard to oneself and others without being unduly swayed by fleeting emotions.

♦ Social and emotional intelligence involves knowledge of one's own intrapsychic workings and knowledge of the most effective means of relating positively to other people.

Creativity can contribute to happiness in myriad ways. To actively be in a creative state is to be highly energized and attentive to the process at hand—so engaged that time flies, and everyday worries and mundane concerns seem to vanish for the duration. (For more about this state of mind, known as "flow," see Chapter 10.) But creativity does more than temporarily distract people from their problems. Creative people think in flexible and divergent ways that can actually help them resolve their problems and meet life's challenges.

Curiosity connotes an openness to new experiences. Curious people continually want to know more about various aspects of the world around them, about others, or about themselves. They are never bored or apathetic, because there is always something more to understand and appreciate. Not surprisingly, curiosity correlates highly with physical health and longevity (more about this in Chapter 21), probably because curious people always want to know what tomorrow will bring and are curious about matters pertaining to their own well-being.

Reason can contribute to life satisfaction by orienting us toward reality and positive ways to cope with and adapt to it. Emotional and social intelligence helps us negotiate the complex landscape of emotions and interpersonal relationships in thoughtful, constructive ways.

Goal-Oriented Strengths

Goal-oriented strengths are related to accomplishment. They spring from the values of achievement and determination. People with goal-oriented strengths are self-motivators. They are proactive rather than reactive. Perseverance, courage, and conscientiousness are among the key strengths in this category:

♦ Courage comes in many forms; it can involve taking great risks and changing the world, but it can also involve the everyday heroism needed to face a new day in spite of hardships and difficulties.

♦ Perseverance involves making a commitment—to an ideal, to a course of action, to a relationship—and holding fast to that commitment in spite of challenges.

♦ Conscientiousness encompasses thoroughness and diligence in performing tasks.

> ### Happy Thought _____
>
> "Great works are performed not by strength, but perseverance."
>
> —Samuel Johnson
>
> "Where fear is, happiness is not."
>
> —Seneca

Courage, persistence, and conscientiousness can help individuals become successful in whatever they pursue. But even when worldly success per se is elusive, these strengths can uplift the spirits and increase pride and self-respect. The brave are also often very influential people. Their courage inspires others, which in turn makes the courageous feel gratified.

People rich in goal-oriented strengths are adept at finding meaning and articulating their purpose in life. They know what they want to do and are brave and dedicated enough to do whatever it takes.

Self-Mastery Strengths

Strengths of self-mastery are, in essence, traits of self-discipline and balance. They relate to the value of self-control. They require the ability to refrain from impulsivity and overindulgence. Typical self-mastery strengths include *moderation* and *modesty:*

♦ Moderation involves resisting the temptation to give in to recklessness, destructive excess, or deprivation in any and all activities, even in one's attitudes.

♦ Modesty means being humble enough to know that one cannot know all, do all, or have all.

Moderation is the art of controlling cravings, addictions, and unreasonable desires that can prove excessive or harmful. And almost *anything* can prove harmful in extremes. Having a goal and working toward it, for example, can lead to happiness. But obsessively working toward that goal to the exclusion of fulfilling relationships and personal health will lead to a lack of balance and perspective.

Modesty is itself a kind of moderation—a moderation of grandiosity and boastfulness. It is true that happy people have high self-regard, but those with inflated egos and arrogant attitudes are not displaying healthy self-esteem but actually indicating a deficit in their self-image. Those who possess modesty and humility are more open-minded, more flexible, and more accessible to other people.

Interpersonal Strengths

Other-oriented strengths relate to the values of compassion, cooperation, and basic regard for others with whom we share our lives and the planet. The strengths include kindness, fairness, empathy, generosity, trust, loyalty, forgiveness, and genuineness:

- ◆ Kindness involves treating people with universal goodwill, as we ourselves would wish to be treated.

- ◆ Fairness involves open-mindedness and a respect for equity and justice for all.

- ◆ Empathy is the ability to understand other people's points of view, to listen to them nonjudgmentally, and to experience the world through their eyes.

- ◆ Altruism involves a spirit of generosity, a willingness to share one's resources—not only wealth but time, effort, and spirit—with others.

- ◆ Trust means displaying an optimistic view of human nature that gives people the benefit of the doubt.

- ◆ Loyalty involves the ability to make enduring commitments to those we love and respect.

- ◆ Forgiveness involves the ability to stop dwelling on hurts, to put the past behind and move forward.

- ◆ Genuineness encompasses openness, authenticity, honesty, and receptivity to others.

Many interpersonal strengths contribute to forging strong, close, supportive relationships. Research overwhelmingly shows that strong relationships on the individual and community level are direct instigators of happiness. The same is true of altruistic behavior (more on this in Chapter 6).

Stumbling Blocks

Some people are reluctant to forgive because they confuse forgiveness with weakness and condoning hurtful behavior. But forgiveness does not connote approval. Moreover, the benefits of forgiveness accrue primarily to the person who does the forgiving. Forgiveness boosts mood, alleviates depression, and reduces anger. A study at the University of Michigan showed that forgiving others unconditionally linked to well-being even more strongly than did forgiving others who offered apology and expressed contrition.

Transcendent Strengths

Transcendent strengths allow us to rise above negative circumstances. They enable us to weather the ups and downs of daily life with greater peace and equanimity, and—on occasion—to surpass what we may have thought of as our limits. Transcendent strengths include hope, reverence, gratitude, enthusiasm, and humor:

◆ Hope involves an optimistic spirit, a belief that the best can come to pass, and a faith that whatever happens may be for the best even if we don't understand why at the time.

◆ Reverence means allowing oneself to enter a state of awe, amazement, wonder, and deep appreciation—it has a spiritual component even if not tied to a formal religious faith.

◆ Gratitude involves the active expression of thankfulness for the positive things in one's life.

◆ Enthusiasm means embracing life, going forth into the world each day with a joyous anticipation and a tendency to say "yes."

◆ Humor was aptly defined by comedian Mel Brooks as "a defense against the universe"—it allows us to dispel frustration, counter stress, and reframe experience in a more positive way.

Transcendent strengths are tied to what psychologists in the human potential movement called self-actualization. People strong in transcendent qualities tend to value the ideal of reaching their highest potential. That noble quest itself can be a source of immense contentment.

Evaluating Your Strengths

Look down any list of character strengths and some will probably resonate or ring a bell. You might have shocks of recognition and think, "that describes me exactly," or "I'm like that—at least sometimes." That's a good start toward identifying your strengths.

But which strengths would you say are your trademark strengths? Which ones do you tend to use repeatedly and effectively to enhance your life? Which ones have you drawn on when the going got tough?

Identifying these can be invaluable. When you know what strengths define you, you can consciously build on them to boost your overall happiness.

Recall When Strengths Saved You

Did you ever use your social intelligence and sense of humor to deflect the menace of a schoolyard bully? Did you ever use your creativity to improvise your way through a presentation at work when your projector failed and your PowerPoint slides proved useless? Have you ever been told you could not possibly achieve something and still found it within yourself to persevere and prevail? Have you ever faced a dire personal situation—perhaps a serious illness or loss—where your courage and hope sustained you?

Try recalling and then writing down stories in your life that involve such situations. It doesn't matter how old you were, and the outcome needn't have changed the world—it need only have made your personal experience richer and more gratifying.

Write Yourself a Letter of Recommendation

Another way to identify your strengths is to take a third-party perspective. Step back and try to view yourself through the eyes of those whom you've most impressed in your life: teachers, coaches, co-workers, bosses, parents, spouses, or even your own children. Now write a letter as if it were coming from one of the people that hold you in high regard. How would they recommend you for a job, a promotion, a college acceptance, or even a blind date? If your imagination needs a jolt, fill in the blanks in the following example:

To Whom It May Concern:

It is our pleasure to recommend _____ to you. We know you will find her to possess a fine mind that is extremely capable of _____. For example, we remember the time she _____.

When it comes to achieving her goals, I know you will find her to be _____. She was extremely determined to accomplish _____ and succeeded in doing it.

She is also very self-disciplined when it comes to _____.

When it comes to interacting with other people, we are certain that you will be impressed with her _____ and _____. She is remarkable when it comes to making other people feel _____. I recall the time that her skill in dealing with others made a particular difference. Here's what happened: _____

_____

_____.

Finally, when the chips are down, you will find that she always has her _____ and _____ to fall back on. These qualities will help her be resilient in the face of any challenge.

Sincerely,

_____

Seeing your strengths in writing can be a satisfying experience in itself. But when you have your list you'll want to review it periodically. Doing so will give you a chance to add to it, amend it, and note which skills you employ most often. Remember especially to consult your list in times of difficulty or when you need ideas and inspiration. The list will remind you of all the tools you have in your tool belt.

Stumbling Blocks

Modesty is a virtue, but don't confuse humility with self-effacement. Enumerating and evaluating your character strengths is anything but an act of inappropriate boastfulness. This process is between *you* and *you*. Approach it with honesty and a realistic perspective, and it will make you not only a happier person, but also more capable of making others happy.

Skills and Talents

In addition to character strengths, each of us possesses specific talents and abilities that can also contribute to our happiness. We tend to experience pleasure and a sense of meaning and purpose when we are actively using our talents.

def•i•ni•tion

Multiple intelligences is a concept introduced by Harvard education professor Howard Gardner. The idea posits that intelligence can best be understood not as an all-inclusive IQ number but as a distinct group of abilities that individuals may possess in varying degrees.

Our skills and talents often tie in to something termed *multiple intelligences*. For example, an individual may have talents in one or a number of realms.

Athletic skills involve grace, dexterity, stamina, and "muscle memory," or recalling things through one's body rather than verbally or visually. Athletic and body movement abilities can translate into being good at anything from basketball to boxing to ballet.

Linguistic skills involve anything related to language, including a facility with reading, writing, and persuasive speaking. People with language abilities may excel in anything (or everything) from doing crossword puzzles to writing poetry to debating to teaching. They are also likely to have excellent memories for information they hear and read.

Math and logic skills have to do with numbers, patterns and sequence recognition, abstractions, and inductive and deductive reasoning. Those who have talent in this area are often good at complex calculations and scientific investigation.

People with spatial and visual skills are good at envisioning how things will look and how they will fit together. They are good at manipulating objects. Their visual memory is strong and they have a good sense of location and direction. They may be artistically inclined or have a strong aptitude for engineering.

Musical skills relate to sound, rhythm, pitch, and all aspects of music. People with such abilities may be good at singing, at playing instruments, and at composing. They also have excellent audio memory.

Naturalistic skills involve relating well to one's natural surroundings. People with these skills have an exceptional sensitivity to nature. They may be good at growing and gardening, at analyzing climates and environments, and even at relating to animals.

Unlike character strengths, which take effort and will to enact, our talents may seem to come naturally to us. We might feel we have a "knack" or even a "gift" for certain activities. But we are usually most happy when we are not only using our skills but also honing them and stretching them.

Building and Renewing Strengths and Skills

Not everyone possesses every talent or character strength. Skills and strengths can certainly be acquired, but one surefire path to *un*happiness is to sit around pining about what you don't have. If you want to cultivate a skill or strength, by all means do so! But, according to the psychology of happiness, one of the best paths to happiness is to build on the skills and strengths you already possess.

Dust off dormant skills and strengths and take them to new heights. Think of ways you can merge and use them together. And whenever you can, use a strength or skill in a new way. This combines the pleasure of novelty with the satisfaction of purpose.

Suppose, for example, you have a talent for language and a strong sense of fairness and justice. Find a compelling issue and start a "letter to the editor" campaign to speak out for the underprivileged. Suppose you are creative and funny. Think about taking the stage for "open mike" night at your local comedy club. (This ought to brush up your courage as well!) Suppose you have athletic agility and a tremendous amount of perseverance. Are you up for running a marathon?

> **Happy Thought**
>
> "Most folks are as happy as they make up their minds to be."
> —Abraham Lincoln

These are just a few of myriad possibilities. The idea is to maximize your existing potential to make yourself happier. Life will never feel stale to those who take this approach.

The Least You Need to Know

- ◆ Positive psychologists believe each of us has numerous character strengths we can draw on to promote happiness—the wide range of strengths can emanate from our heads, our hearts, and our spirits.

- ◆ Identifying your most potent strengths is the first step to consciously employing them to boost your happiness to a higher level.

- ◆ In addition to mining your character strengths, you can increase your happiness by identifying your skills and talents.

- ◆ To enhance happiness, dust off dormant strengths and skills, combine the ones you currently use, and employ them in new and exciting ways.

Chapter 6

Altruism: The Golden Rule

In This Chapter

- ◆ Why altruism comes naturally
- ◆ How altruism makes us feel good
- ◆ How to increase altruism
- ◆ How helping "too much" can harm
- ◆ Why healthy altruism creates more of the same

Imagine you wanted to take a crash-course in character instruction. If you asked your instructor for one guiding rule or principle by which to live with pleasure, meaning, and purpose, he would probably cite some version of what we know as the Golden Rule:

"Do unto others as you would have others do unto you."

As it turns out, this principle is not only the Golden Rule of morality and spirituality, but also a path to cultivating a high level of personal happiness. By living altruistically, we can make the most of all our best character traits by using them to benefit others.

That such "selfless" actions also benefit us is a key discovery of positive psychology.

The Altruism Urge

Acts of compassion, generosity, and everyday kindness all fall under the collective heading of altruism. The word *altruism* comes from the Latin word *alter*, meaning "other," and refers to helping others. But altruism generates a high rate of return for those who bestow it as well as those who receive it.

Altruism is a phenomenon as ancient as humankind itself. Some researchers believe that altruism played a role in the development of the human race, because our ancestors gained evolutionary advantages by helping one another to hunt, gather food, and defend against predators. Altruism probably contributed to the development of many other kinds of positive social behavior, such as sharing, communication, and laughter.

If we hear someone contend that altruism is a universal part of human nature, however, we might be prone to skepticism. It's sometimes all too easy to think of individuals whose blatantly selfish actions seem to embody the opposite of altruism: ruthless dictators, hardened criminals, con artists, and terrorists. But consider two things: first, those people who are decidedly nonaltruistic don't seem very happy, do they? Second, as with any so-called universal trait, there is always variation among individuals. Our species thrives on altruism, but some of us are more prone to altruism than others.

Still, all humans have within us the capacity to be altruistic. Moreover, we can expand our altruistic actions if we consciously choose to do so. Why would we choose to do this? The answer is something of a paradox. Although altruism is defined as a form of selflessness, it is actually a form of enlightened self-interest. When we help someone, they get something and we get something. With altruism, everyone's a winner.

Happy Thought _____

"Every man must decide whether he will walk in the light of creative altruism or in the darkness of destructive selfishness."
—Martin Luther King Jr.

"I do not know what your destiny is, but I know this. Those who seek and find ways to help others will find true happiness."
—Dr. Albert Schweitzer

Do Good, Feel Good

A common assignment to students who take courses in positive psychology is to indulge in an activity that provides pure sensory pleasure and then engage in an activity that involves helping someone else. On completing the assignment, many students are amazed to find that they felt appreciably happier after helping someone else (for example, tutoring a fellow student, volunteering at a soup kitchen or animal shelter, or shoveling snow for a neighbor) than they did after engaging in pure pleasure (for example, eating a sumptuous meal, attending a concert, or making love on the beach).

Research backs up what those students have discovered on a personal level. It consistently shows that when we act with kindness and compassion on behalf of other people, we experience a sense of emotional well-being and comfort as well as a diminished sense of stress.

How does this work? Altruism stimulates the brain's positive emotion centers. Using MRI scans, scientists have noted that regions of the brain associated with generating positive emotion are highly active when we experience empathetic and compassionate emotions.

Helpful behavior also triggers feel-good hormones. The brain's pleasure-linked chemicals, such as dopamine and various endorphins are released into the bloodstream when we engage in helpful behavior. These hormones can create a burst of euphoric energy, a so-called *helper's high*.

A recent study has identified high levels of the hormone oxytocin in people who are being generous toward others. Oxytocin is

def•i•ni•tion _____

The term **helper's high** was coined in 1988 by researcher Allen Luks, on noting that 50 percent of those who helped others reported feeling "high" when doing so. Forty-three percent felt stronger and more energetic.

connected to an adaptive positive response to stress known as "tend and befriend." An alternative to the "fight or flight" response, which can create edginess and aggression, "tend and befriend" prompts us to manage stress by affiliating with others and working cooperatively. Oxytocin is best known for its role in preparing mothers for motherhood, but the hormone is present in both men and women, and spikes when a member of either gender lends a helping hand.

Helping behavior alleviates depression across the life cycle. Various studies have shown that giving and generosity reduce teen depression and that teens who are giving are happier than their less-altruistic peers. Additional research has shown that the same holds true at the other end of the life cycle. A study conducted by sociologists at the University of Texas at Austin found that volunteering substantially reduces symptoms of depression for adults older than age 65.

Helping others raises our self-esteem and enables us to forgive our own mistakes. A study of older Americans revealed that those who lent emotional support to others demonstrated an increased willingness to forgive themselves for their own failings and shortcomings. This self-forgiveness is key to a sense of well-being.

Altruism not only puts us in a happier state, but also enables us to remain in that state for a longer stretch of time. Researchers conducting longitudinal studies—the sort that follows subjects for decades, interviewing them extensively at various intervals—have concluded that people who are givers suffer fewer stress-created illnesses and add years to their life span.

Active Altruism

Not surprisingly, those who demonstrate altruistic behavior early in life tend to keep on doing so. No doubt their behavior brings them a great deal of gratification, and this positive reinforcement keeps them behaving in a helpful, generous way.

Happiness Trivia
In 2006, according to *Time* magazine, 61.2 million Americans dedicated 8.1 million hours to volunteerism. States where the most volunteerism occurs are Utah, Nebraska, Minnesota, Alaska, and Kansas—in that order.

But not everyone practices helping their neighbors—or anyone else—at an early age. Those who have positive role models in their families or are involved in community-based or faith-based organizations that stress service are usually more likely to make helping a habit than those who lack such affiliations. The good news, of course, is that it is never too late to catch up. There are many ways to make contributions, both large and small, to the well-being of others.

Looking Within Your Community

Who would benefit from your help? Who would appreciate some generosity and kindness? The first place it might seem natural to look is in your immediate surroundings. You can get some ideas by simply walking down your street.

There are your elderly neighbors. Could they use help with their errands—or could they just use some friendly company? There's the local elementary school. Perhaps you can do something for the students—or the teachers. There's the local park—could it do with a cleanup?

If you are hesitant to jump in on your own, don't worry. An abundance of volunteer organizations can help you figure out how to give some of your time on a regular basis. And joining a group will also add to your happiness (more on this in Chapter 17) because you will have the added satisfaction of meeting like-minded people, sharing ideas, and pitching in to achieve a goal you might not have been able to achieve on your own.

To find an opportunity that is right for you, first consider your talents and strengths. People are happy when they are doing what they're good at—and volunteering is no exception. If you have a way with animals, that SPCA dog-walking position might be right up your alley. If you're a natural mentor type, Big Brothers or Big Sisters can be your perfect match. If carpentry is your thing, consider Habitat for Humanity—an organization that builds houses for the underprivileged and for disaster victims.

> **Stumbling Blocks**
>
> Not enough time to volunteer? Many of the busiest and most successful people do so. In the end it will buy you more time. Two large studies found that volunteers live longer than nonvolunteers. And one of those found a 44 percent reduction in early death rates among adults who volunteered on a regular basis. That effect on longevity is greater than that of exercising four times a week.

Consider your values, too. What is important to you in terms of what is happening in your community? Are you concerned about the environment? Look for an organization that works to preserve, protect, or restore natural habitats. Are you concerned about education? Consider tutoring or homework help opportunities, or consider Literacy Volunteers. Are you interested in furthering public health? Look for service opportunities at local hospitals or at organizations that conduct blood drives, free clinics, and the like.

Consider the level of personal contact you're comfortable with. It can be somewhat gratifying to do the kind of volunteering that is "once-removed," such as collecting clothes for the Salvation Army or books for library drives. But many people find that volunteering is ultimately more satisfying if they meet and spend time with the people they are helping. The same holds true if you enjoy working with animals. Selling raffles so the local shelter can care for more cats is great, but it will most likely be even more happiness-inducing if you are at least occasionally able to stroke and snuggle some real-live kittens.

What level of commitment are you looking for? Many organizations need volunteers solely in response to a particular problem or situation (such as in the aftermath of a hurricane or earthquake). Other organizations have seasonal needs for helpers (perhaps to distribute food or gifts to needy families at holiday time). These are worthy causes and no one should hesitate to pitch in. But beyond this, it is a good idea for happiness-seekers to integrate volunteering into their schedule on a regular weekly basis. This way the benefits of giving will remain a steady factor in your emotional well-being.

If no perfect-fit volunteer groups immediately come to mind, you can easily find a local nonprofit group that needs your help by simply looking in your local telephone book. You can also conduct a very specific Internet search. If you belong to a church, mosque, or temple, that is a wonderful place to inquire about helping opportunities in the general community.

Helping Hand

You might wish to consider devoting some of your vacation time to a "volunteer vacation," which is an increasingly popular way of spending one's leisure time both pleasurably and purposefully. Many faith-based groups organize trips for such purposes. You can also contact an organization such as the aforementioned Habitat for Humanity, (which has numerous international affiliates) or Earthwatch (which has volunteers join scientific expeditions with the purpose of saving endangered species), or visit websites such as www.globalvolunteers.org, www.unitedplanet.org, or www.crossculturalsolutions.org.

Spontaneous Altruism

Some people are reluctant to help others because they are preoccupied with their own problems. Yet after you start to help others, you will find that your preoccupation with your own problems recedes, and with it the anxiety that can block your happiness. This can be especially true when you stay open to the possibility of helping others in the moment as opportunity presents itself. If you cultivate an attitude of alertness to what others need, you will be less prone to self-absorbed worry and rumination. You will be broadening your perspective and opening up your inner world.

Naturally you may find lots of opportunities to offer in-the-moment assistance to members of your immediate family and circle of friends. Providing such help is part of the implicit bargain we make in family life and friendships: you help me and I'll help you. Your helpfulness, in such instances, will contribute to your loved ones' well-being and to yours, because your needs mutually impact one another. *Quid pro quo.*

But let's take it one step further. What if you make it a point to remain alert to opportunities to perform some sort of altruistic act for casual acquaintances or even for complete strangers whom you most likely will never see again: the driver who needs a break getting into your lane in traffic, the shopper laden down with too many grocery bags, the novice exerciser at the gym who needs a word of encouragement?

How would that make you happy? Here's what's in it for you:

Helping Hand

We are most likely to help others when we are feeling happy and secure. This well-documented phenomenon is known as the "feel good, do good" effect. But don't rule out helping out when your mood is less than great. It's good medicine for the blues, because helping can be an instant mood booster.

- An expanded sense of community. Isolation and loneliness can result from our feeling that we are "separate" from everyone else. Keeping an eye out for one another reinforces the idea that, although we are all unique individuals, we are all connected. To help one is to help all, including yourself.

- A "helper's high." Pitching in where you can and making yourself universally useful increases your chances of achieving a helper's high on a routine basis. A random act of kindness can release your endorphins and stimulate the positive emotion centers in your brain.

- A contagious smile. When you help a stranger, your immediate "payment" is often a smile of acknowledgement and gratitude. A smile is something we can easily "catch" from someone else. It's infectious. Someone smiles at us and we smile back without even thinking about it. The mere physical act of smiling enhances our mood.

- A diminished stress level. The physiological sensations that occur within us when we help can counter our level of negative stress. Being ready, willing, and able to help acquaintances and strangers throughout the day can be an ongoing strategy for keeping stress in check.

- Moral or spiritual satisfaction. The obligation to help others is a basic tenet of virtually every faith and of any service organization. Acts of spontaneous kindness can help us feel more in tune with such uplifting positive teachings.

Helping at random requires an attitude of empathy and compassion, and a willingness to keep at least part of your focus on something other than yourself. The Boy Scouts exhort their members to "do a good deed daily." Judaism reminds its followers to perform a daily *mitzvah*, or good turn. Buddhism reminds its followers of the principle of *karma*, a law of cause and effect that implies our positive intent resonates universally and, eventually, returns to us in some form. And Christianity teaches that we reap what we sow.

But fear not: there is no need to give up your worldly possessions, quit your job, and wander the earth helping needy souls. It is perfectly possible to change nothing about your life except to open your eyes to opportunities to be kind and still raise your happiness quotient substantially. Moreover, most spontaneous helping does not necessitate devoting your entire day, or even a substantial fraction of it. It takes only moments to pay a compliment, laugh at someone's joke, hold a door open, or wave someone ahead of you in the supermarket express line. Research shows that even the brief simple act of praying for others has a positive impact on the well-being of the person who prays.

Overhelping: A Happiness Hazard

Though the happiness engendered in helping others is clear, anything can be taken to drastic extremes and thus become unhealthy. Helping others will not help you, or them, if you martyr yourself and neglect your own needs—or if you do things that diminish the other person's ability to help himself and pursue his own path toward happiness.

Beware of helping people so much that they become overly dependent on you. It is more effective to engage in activities that help others help themselves to discover and use their own strengths. (This is one reason why teaching a skill to others is often an especially gratifying volunteer experience.)

Beware of confusing compassion with control and of trying to get others to do what you want in the name of "helping" them. When you try to control people, your ego becomes tied up in the outcome of events. That is the antithesis of no-strings-attached altruism and will most certainly not lead to happiness but to added stress and worry.

Also beware of enabling people to pursue self-destructive habits. You won't help a gambling addict by buying them a lottery ticket. You won't help a child you are tutoring by doing the homework they neglected to do.

Beware of volunteering for activities or in settings that are poor matches for you. The situation may not be right for you if ...

  ◆ You are not utilizing any of your skills and strengths.

  ◆ You are experiencing a lot of anxiety (the usual beginner's adaptation aside).

  ◆ You are being assigned tasks that are over your head.

- ◆ You find the setting depersonalizing.

- ◆ You are continually asked to do more, even if it means sapping time from your work or family.

- ◆ You are made to feel guilty when you cannot do more.

Beware of feeling bad if you cannot "fix" or "solve" everything. The idea that any one person can do so is irrational and will prevent you from achieving anything because you will be so completely overwhelmed by what you *cannot* do. Don't be too hard on yourself; remember, you didn't create the problem you are trying to alleviate. Keep things in perspective. Being altruistic does not mean you can save the world, or even "save" one person. You can support and assist people in their journey, but in the end everyone must take responsibility for their lives or they will not find their own pleasure and meaning. To begin helping, think small. In the words of William Blake, it is best to be helpful in "minute particulars."

Stumbling Blocks

Try to keep your ego out of the helping process. Examine your motivation. If you are performing altruistic acts so that others will notice and praise your sacrifice and "selflessness," you are setting yourself up for disappointment and unhappiness. There is nothing wrong with recognition, but you will gain more contentment if you neither expect it nor think of it as your ultimate goal.

Finally, remember that kindness begins with being kind to yourself. Beware of overdoing your altruism to the point of burning out. Compassion starts with self-compassion. In the Buddhist tradition, even meditation on compassion (known as the practice of *metta*, or "loving kindness," begins with affirming one's compassion for oneself). The practitioner begins by silently repeating the phrase, "May I be happy; may I be at peace." Only then do they begin to direct the phrase toward loved ones and then ultimately to all: "May all beings be happy; may all beings be at peace." The progression of this meditation demonstrates the importance of carefully caring for ourselves. If we don't, we will be too stressed, tired, and overwhelmed to effectively care for anyone else.

The Feedback Loop of Happiness

When we help in healthy ways we do not feel pressured or burned out. We feel satisfied and gratified. And the more satisfied and gratified we feel, the more we will continue to help.

This is a highly positive feedback loop. If we give it a chance to initiate, we are likely to make helping a regular part of our life as opposed to an occasional dabbling. That consistency will, in turn, help to insulate us from the effects of stress and from a buildup of negative emotions. Certainly it won't take away stress or sadness (these things are a part of life), but engaging in altruism will, over time, make us more optimistic and resilient.

We often think of life as a zero-sum game, the kind of endeavor where someone must win (and be happy) and someone must lose (and be unhappy). But this does not appear to be the case. In fact, just the opposite appears to be true: the more we make others happy, the happier we are likely to be.

Happy Thought

> "It is one of the most beautiful compensations of this life that no man can sincerely try to help another without helping himself."
> —Ralph Waldo Emerson

Today, science has confirmed what spiritual teachers have long expounded. The Golden Rule of happiness works precisely because there is more than enough happiness to go around. And one true "secret of happiness" is that we are happy when we make others happy.

The Least You Need to Know

◆ The scientific evidence is in: doing good makes us feel good by lowering our stress level, enhancing our health and well-being, and generating pleasurable emotions (the "helper's high").

◆ Those who practice helping early in life are motivated to continue, but it is never too late to cultivate altruism and to reap the emotional rewards of doing so.

◆ To find the right volunteer opportunity for yourself, consider your strengths, talents, and values, and find a situation where you can contribute on an ongoing basis with a personal touch.

◆ To maintain happiness and decrease the self-preoccupation that leads to anxiety and worry, remain alert to the needs of others and practice small, spontaneous kindnesses even with strangers.

◆ Altruism begins with self-compassion. Refrain from flirting with burnout or from becoming a martyr who lives *only* for others, or you will help no one to be happier, including yourself.

Part 3

Positive Thoughts, Attitudes, and Actions

Some people have a more innate inclination to happiness than others. Yet, happily, that's not the whole story. To some extent, it appears that happiness can increase by consciously acquiring certain habits of thought and action. In this part, you'll see how cultivating humor, optimism, and gratitude, along with a sense of play and a willingness to seek life's deeper meaning, might just turn up your happiness thermostat.

Chapter 7

Laughing Your Way to Happiness

In This Chapter

- Discovering the power of humor to transform emotions
- Finding humor and social bonding
- Opting for humor in frustrating situations
- Assessing your humor capability
- Creating more laughter opportunities

The ability to appreciate and generate humor is a character trait that has attracted special interest from those who study happiness—no doubt because humor has so many beneficial effects. There is nothing like a good, hearty laugh to make us feel both instant emotional cheer and immediate physical release.

But humor is also a way to bond with others and enhance our social connections. Perhaps most significant of all, humor can help us rise above our troubles, maintain perspective and flexibility, and even reevaluate our circumstances in a new, more positive light.

The Transformative Power of Laughter

In many cultures and communities, it is a tradition to bring food to the homes of grieving families. The gesture is one of love and respect, and an acknowledgement that although death comes to us all, life goes on. I once had a neighbor who ritually baked a coffee cake for anyone in the neighborhood who'd had a death in the family. Her coffee cake was delicious, but this was the only sort of occasion for which she baked it. One day a mutual friend lost her elderly father quickly and unexpectedly. The next morning the bereaved family had gathered and my friend arrived bearing her coffee cake. The bereaved daughter saw my friend coming up the walk clutching a baking pan, rushed out to greet her, and threw her arms around her. Through her tears she smiled and asked, "Is that the famous 'heavenly coffee cake?'" Everyone in earshot burst out laughing. For a few moments, sorrow had been banished—replaced by a feeling of warmth, gratitude, and camaraderie.

> **Happy Thought**
>
> "Humor is the fastest, fleetest form of giving. It can change pain to joy in a mere millisecond."
> —Stephen Post, Ph.D.

When we laugh, we feel good. In fact, it is impossible to feel bad when we laugh. Even if we are in the midst of a highly stressful or sad time, laughter offers us an oasis. Research shows it can even help us recover from the extreme distress that accompanies life-changing losses.

When a University of Tel Aviv researcher interviewed Holocaust survivors, humor was repeatedly mentioned as a mechanism for helping people to survive trauma. When a researcher at the University of California at Berkeley studied widows and widowers whose spouses had died six months before, he noted that those who had re-established the ability to laugh within weeks of their loved one's passing displayed less stress and many more positive emotions two to four years later.

Humor, it turns out, is not only a unique human tool to facilitate survival, but also a mechanism to facilitate thriving and resilience. The more laughs we have in our life, the better able we are to handle whatever comes our way and the more we are able to take pleasure from each day.

The Physiology of Laughter

Part of the curative power of humor is purely physiological. It has to do with the impact of laughter on our bodies and our brains.

Laughter is a form of *eustress*—that is, of positive stress (that's "eu" as in euphoria). It's a stimulus that brings body and brain to an alert state. But unlike *dis*tress or negative stress, which generates anxiety, it's helpful rather than harmful. It makes us feel alive, vibrant, and "up."

In a nutshell—and in the most basic layman's terms—laughing is an enjoyable sensation: it's fun. But looked at more scientifically, laughter is doing a lot more "behind the scenes."

def•i•ni•tion

The term **eustress** was coined by renowned stress researcher Hans Selye in 1980. It refers to a modest but necessary level of stress of limited duration—a commodity we all require to feel satisfied, engaged, and capable in all areas of life.

Laugh Chemistry

Laughter elevates natural mood-enhancing endorphins and releases the feel-good brain chemical dopamine. At the same time, laughter turns *down* our stress hormone spigot. Studies show it also significantly lowers the chemical cortisol, which is associated with negative stress and can dangerously raise blood sugar, as well as other stress-related hormones that constrict blood vessels.

Experiments have been specifically designed to test the connection between laughter and the decrease of potentially harmful stress hormones. In one, blood samples were drawn from volunteers before, during, and after watching a one-hour comedy video. Sure enough, stress hormones decreased as participants were exposed to humor.

In another experiment, two groups of cardiac patents were treated for a year following heart attacks. The group that watched 10 minutes of comedy a day as a complement to medical therapy had lower stress hormone levels (not to mention lower blood pressure, fewer heartbeat irregularities, and fewer repeat heart attacks) than did the group that received medical treatment alone.

Happiness Trivia

Laughter is, literally, a rush. The breath released during a hearty laugh has been clocked at speeds of up to 170 miles per hour. As it erupts, laughter stimulates the brain, the nervous system, the respiratory system, the hormonal system, and the muscular system.

Humor and Health

There's more good news about laughter as well. According to Dr. William F. Fry, a Stanford University psychiatrist, a hundred laughs provides the aerobic equivalent of 10 minutes spent rowing. So, on those days when you can't exercise, it might be a good alternative to hang around with some of your funny friends or pop in a video of your favorite funny film.

Finally, it is hard to be happy when you're sick, and there appears to be substantial truth to the adage that laughter is the best medicine. After exposure to humor, there is a general increase in our immune system activity, specifically in the production of the disease-fighting antibodies known as IgA and IgB (immunoglobulins A and B) and in natural killer cells that attack virally infected cells and some types of cancer cells; an increase in a substance known as Complement 3, which helps antibodies pierce dysfunctional or infected cells; and an increase in gamma interferon, which signals various components of the immune system to "turn on."

Perhaps best of all: laughter's effects on happiness and health are residual. The brain and body chemicals released by laughter remain at higher levels even after your funny bone has stopped being tickled. Laughter might be fleeting, but its effects are lasting.

Humor and Social Connection

Humor's benefits also extend into the social realm. Humor helps us build and maintain bonds with others—bonds that are themselves essential to happiness (more about such bonds in Part 5 of this book).

To see how this works, consider it from an evolutionary perspective. Why do we humans appreciate humor and why do we laugh in the first place? What on Earth did Mother Nature have in mind?

Social Survival

Some primates other than humans (such as chimpanzees and bonobos, our close genetic relations) exhibit grins and sounds that signal availability for friendly social interaction. But humans appear to be the only species that exhibits full-fledged laughter (aptly termed *social playization* by anthropologists) as a routine part of communication and not simply as a response to physical stimulation (such as tickling).

Communicative laughter probably evolved as our ancestors climbed down from the treetops in search of new habitats. At this important turning point, laughter served a number of critical social purposes:

- It signaled to other group members when an environment was safe and free of predators.

- It let everyone know it was an appropriate time to relax.

- It enhanced the trust and cooperation needed to take risks as a group.

- It eased individuals' sense of isolation or loneliness—especially because the sound of laughter carries across relatively long distances.

We may have left the treetop canopy behind long ago, but we *still* use laughter as a mechanism to fulfill all these very necessary functions. We use it to decrease social stress. We use it to reassure. We use it to motivate. We use it to bond.

Social Success

We are much more likely to laugh in social situations than alone. If you don't believe this, try watching your favorite *Seinfeld* rerun alone and then with friends. On which occasion did you laugh louder, longer, and more frequently? Most people would probably agree they laughed a good deal more with companions. That's because they're not only taking pleasure from the antics of the characters, but also communicating to others—saying, in effect, "Hey, I can relate to that, can't you?"

Laughter is wordless conversation. This powerful dialogue begins when we are babies, bonding with parents who simply cannot resist eliciting our endearing giggles. It continues throughout childhood, facilitating friendships. And it pays a powerful role in the mating game, where humor can be a potent flirtation strategy. (Check out personal ads to see how many romance seekers cite "a sense of humor" as essential in a potential boyfriend or girlfriend.) Throughout life, in virtually any setting, humor and laughter can make pleasant situations more pleasant and unpleasant ones more tolerable. It can grease the wheels of negotiation in a tough business setting. It can help sway a jury. It can win voters over to a politician.

Humor can do all these things because we are far less likely to feel separate from people when we are laughing with them. There is nothing like a shared laugh to instantly communicate, "You and I are on the same wavelength." It is also, in the moment that we are laughing with someone, virtually impossible to feel hatred or fear toward them. Even when the moment passes, residual good feeling lingers. How bad can someone be, after all, if we both "get it"?

Stumbling Blocks _____

Not *all* kinds of humor lead to bonding. While self-deprecating humor says you are self-aware, humble, and empathic, humor that denigrates others marks you as cruel and insensitive. If bonding is your social goal, go for healthy laughs, avoid sarcasm, and avoid eliciting sneers and jeers. Remember, there's a difference between laughing *with* someone versus *at* them.

Laughter as Reward

Experiencing a social laugh is good. Even better, perhaps, is the happy feeling of reward we get from instigating one. When we make someone laugh, we have a feeling of instant success. And if the situation was a potentially thorny one, we feel a sense of relief as well.

When we intentionally and successfully make others laugh, we feel confident, brimming with self-esteem. Their laughter is, in effect, an invitation to go on—to continue communicating. When we make a crowd laugh we can feel like "king of the world," as though we have everyone in the palm of our hand. And indeed, for a moment, we actually do.

Choosing to See the Light Side

Sometimes laughter erupts spontaneously, but sometimes we can make a conscious choice to see the humor in a situation. When we do so, we are consciously reframing our experience and, in a very real sense, choosing a positive interpretation over a negative one.

We have all experienced times in our lives when we "don't know whether to laugh or cry." Exasperated and frustrated by circumstances, uncooperative people, maddening machinery—or all those things together—we throw up our hands. We might not actually cry, but we might grit our teeth, hunch our shoulders, and clench our fists in classic stress-saturated poses.

But what if we actively reframed our experience so that we could stop stressing and laugh instead? This may seem unlikely, but chances are you have already done this—albeit with a bit of a time lag. Surely there were events in your life that seemed hopeless and when you felt helpless: pubescent crushes that weren't reciprocated, job interviews that went painfully awry, plans that didn't work out no matter how hard you tried. But as time passes, you have probably learned to see some of the humor in those situations—especially if, in the end, they all worked out for the best. (Who would have wanted to marry their first crush anyway?) Moreover, you have probably transformed these events, once perceived as negative, into some of your funniest stories—those tales you tell about yourself that are always bound to incite warm laughter and nods of understanding.

Now the challenge is to try and appreciate some of life's frustrations and even its absurdities as they are unfolding. If we interpret them with a humorous bent, we can transcend the negative feelings that we might typically attach to them.

Happy Thought

"Some of us suffer from a debilitating mental disorder called irony deficiency. Seeing a doctor won't help, but seeing a paradox will."

—Swami Beyondananda

So, the next time you "don't know whether to laugh or cry," or perhaps when you simply feel like screaming, try one of these strategies:

- **Create a late-night monologue.** If you're stranded at an airport while your luggage has moved on without you, or if you're trying to get off "hold" in an automated telephone system and speak to a human being, imagine retelling the story later that night to an appreciative audience. What would Jay Leno or David Letterman say to get everyone to recognize their "pain" and laugh it away?

- **Jot down your jokes.** Office air-conditioning gone out on the hottest day of the year? *How hot was it?* Go on, take a stab at it. You can amuse yourself, and may even come up with something so good you'll want to share it.

- **Find an immediate audience.** Stuck in an interminable line at the Department of Motor Vehicles? Find someone ahead of you or behind you who looks like they need cheering up, and then say something to make them smile.

- **Grin while you bear it.** Even if you're all alone in your plight, try to find something humorous about it and smile. The mere act of smiling will brighten your mood and make you feel happier.

Finding the humor in a situation that could "go either way" is empowering. It gives you a greater sense of control over whatever situation you are in. That sense of control can, in turn, help you maintain an upbeat frame of mind.

Do You Get It?

As with most traits and behaviors, the ability to appreciate humor, and to generate humor, comes to each of us in varying degrees. Underlying genetic factors may influence how often and how enthusiastically we tend to laugh. Animal researchers can actually determine which individuals in a population of lab rats are most playful and most receptive to tickling, and then breed for these traits. In humans, it's been noted that babies born with extroverted temperaments tend to do more laughing than those with introverted temperaments.

> **Happiness Trivia**
>
> In the Western world, the country where people laugh the most is Italy. Supposedly the average Italian devotes 21 minutes a day to laughter.

Experts say the average American adult laughs 15 times a day. Some stress researchers say we need at least 20 daily laughs to ease our angst. That would make many of us laugh-deprived.

Of course, it has never occurred to most of us to count our outbursts of laughter. But what if you tried? Try keeping a laugh diary (as in the following example), or devising a simple system such as making a check mark in your day planner or putting a coin in a jar each time you laugh out loud? This would give you a rough idea of your "humor benchmark."

While you're at it, give yourself a point for each time you make someone else laugh, be they family member, friend, co-worker, or total stranger. That not only makes you happy, but gives to others.

The Laughter Tracker

	Laughed Out Loud	Made Someone Laugh
Monday	_____	_____
Tuesday	_____	_____
Wednesday	_____	_____
Thursday	_____	_____
Friday	_____	_____
Saturday	_____	_____
Sunday	_____	_____

Enter a plus sign or check mark each time you laugh and/or inspire laughter. Track your totals. Then you can make a concerted effort to up your laugh score.

Enhancing Humor Appreciation

No matter how much you laugh in adulthood, chances are you laughed more as a child. Those same experts who peg the average number of daily adult laughs at 15 for grown-ups say that many small children laugh hundreds of times a day. Based on this, each of us has the potential to laugh—and to generate and share laughter—more.

Here are some ways to do so:

- **Create a video humor library.** Collect DVDs of movies and television shows that you find hilarious, no matter how many times you watch them. Fill some shelves with these comic gems, and remind yourself to insert one when you need a lift in spirits.

- **Leave funny books and magazines around the house.** Leave these in strategic spots that will make them easy to access—on coffee tables, the bedside stand, or in the bathroom.

- **Share a "funniest ever" list.** Now that you have identified the materials that make you laugh most, make a list and share it with friends. Ask them to do the same. You all might discover a few new films and books that crack you up.

- **Write a humor bio.** Give yourself an assignment to write down the funniest (in retrospect!) things that have ever happened to you. You'll make yourself laugh while reminding yourself that things often work out for the best. Now you'll also have plenty of material to amuse your friends with.

- **Keep a "You Said It" jar.** Keep your ear out for "funny and true" aphorisms that strike a chord with you. (For example, Steve Jobs offered a piece of advice in a commencement speech that advised everyone to "live every day as it was your last—because someday you'll be right.") Write them on slips of paper and store them in a jar for when you need some quick, philosophical, and funny advice.

- **Hang out with the lighthearted.** Seek out companions who like fun, who are funny, and who are ready, willing, and able to laugh. Limit your exposure to grouches, whiners, and fussers.

- **Socialize in big groups.** Research shows that the larger the group, the more likely laughter is to occur. Just as you're more likely to catch a cold in a big group, you're more likely to "catch" a laugh. (Don't worry about the cold part. Remember that laughter boosts your immunity.)

Helping Hand

If you're not in the mood to laugh, you can seek a structured class that will help you "fake it 'til you make it." During the past decade, workshops in a practice known as *laughter yoga* have been catching on in settings as diverse as corporations, hospitals, schools, and even military installations. The practice, said to benefit emotional and physical well-being, combines yogic breathing exercises and heavy doses of group mirth. Though practitioners at first generate laughter "without a reason," the contrived laughter invariably leads to genuine laughter.

Increasing your capacity for humor and laughter will help you feel more relaxed and more optimistic. It will help you develop empathy and be more sensitive to others—and thus improve your relationships. All in all, humor is a potent tonic for maintaining a happiness-enhancing perspective.

The Least You Need to Know

- Humor can serve as a powerful transformer of emotions, helping us to recover from loss and other negative events.

- Laughter ignites the bodily chemistry of happiness by stimulating feel-good brain chemicals and inhibiting levels of hormones associated with stress.

- The use of humor can enhance social bonding (which in itself increases happiness) by creating a relaxed atmosphere of trust and cooperation.

- Choosing to see the lighter side of a frustrating situation can help us reframe our experience in a more positive light.

- Each of us can increase our propensity for laughter by keeping humorous materials handy, spending time with humorous people, and generally increasing the amount of time we spend socializing in large groups.

Chapter 8

The Power of Optimism

In This Chapter

- ◆ Finding the benefits of an optimistic outlook
- ◆ Having optimists explain events
- ◆ Assessing and expanding optimism
- ◆ Realizing the power of positive memories
- ◆ Merging optimism and realism

Is happiness a self-fulfilling prophecy? To a large degree, the answer seems to be *yes*. Research shows that people who are optimists—that is, those who are inclined to *expect* good outcomes—are more content, more resilient, and have fewer physical and emotional disorders than pessimists who anticipate negative outcomes.

But there's good news for pessimists (at least for those willing to hear it). A bleak outlook can be transformed. Research also shows that it is possible to become more optimistic.

The Happy Rewards of Optimism

For a long time optimists were not much studied by psychology. As with most people who were doing pretty well, they were not considered squeaky wheels that needed grease. For many decades we knew a lot more about pessimists and how their penchant for feeling helpless created anxiety, depression, and—in the end—increased helplessness itself. Today, however, positive psychologists acknowledge there is a lot to learn from optimists. To illustrate what some of those things are, consider the following scenario.

A Matter of Attitude

Jill, a pessimist, and Jane, an optimist, each go to their physician for an annual check-up and take a number of routine tests. They are both called the following day and told that the results of one of the tests was irregular and they need to retake it the following week it to see if there is a problem. "Don't worry," they are told. "We sometimes get false positives, and that is why we want you to retake the test."

Jill interprets the situation as negative from the moment she gets the call. She assumes that the test will show she has a dire medical condition, which she begins researching on the Internet immediately. Preoccupied with what she is sure is a grave illness, she begins sleeping poorly and losing focus at work. She snaps at her co-workers and at her spouse. (*If only they knew my terrible fate*, she thinks!) All week long her mood plummets and she becomes more and more nervous.

Jane also feels an initial pang of anxiety as she puts down the phone. But she counsels herself to take to heart the advice not to worry, that such tests can give a false result. She goes on about her business, and if a stressful thought intrudes she reminds herself that everything will turn out fine. Even if the test turns out to reveal a problem, she is confident that she will be successfully treated and that those around her will help her with their love and support. *Things tend to work out*, she remembers, *but if there's an issue, I can deal with whatever comes my way.*

If the results of the second test indicate that Jill and Jane are both perfectly fine, Jane, the optimist, would think, *I knew that was nothing to be concerned about.* But Jill, the pessimist, would have already suffered a significant amount of stress, grown fatigued and irritable, alienated those close to her, and generally made herself miserable. By force of habit, she would simply start to worry about something else, such as, *What if the second test was wrong?*

But what if the tests indicated there was an illness after all? You might think that Jill would fare better, because she had prepared herself for the worst. But in fact, her spirits would likely sink further as she affirmed her belief that *nothing ever goes right*. Jane, on the other hand, would, after experiencing some initial letdown, mobilize her considerable internal resources and her external support system and determine that she would vanquish her illness. Even if she had setbacks, she would count her blessings. All other things being equal between her treatment and Jill's, her positive attitude could be a significant factor in her recovery.

The Optimist's Advantage

Things can go well or badly for optimists or pessimists alike—the difference is in the reaction. Optimists tend to fare better and feel happier in any circumstance:

- They avoid anticipating the worst, limiting their stress and the toxic biochemical reactions that stress can trigger.

- They exhibit a variety of active coping strategies.

- They have more positive relationships (and thus more social support) because they are more trusting and cooperative.

- Although they may certainly experience emotional distress, they are not immobilized by it, do not let it impair their judgment, and tend to rebound quickly.

- They not only bounce back from crises faster than pessimists, but bounce back to a more positive and energetic level than where they started out.

Optimists even outlive pessimists: studies show that they have higher immunity and that optimism appears to reduce the risk and lessen the severity of cardiovascular disease, pulmonary disease, hypertension, diabetes, and colds and upper respiratory infections.

There is even a strong case to be made that optimists play a part in creating some of the positive outcomes they anticipate. To prove that positive expectations can help shape reality, consider the placebo effect. In every study of a potentially helping drug, a certain number of subjects are given an inert sugar pill—a placebo—instead of actual medication. Typically, about a third of these subjects improve even though their cure was a "fake." Likewise, many subjects who are told they are being given pain relief medication—when in fact they are being given a placebo—immediately report a decrease in pain. Their brains have actually kicked in and produced more endorphins, which are natural pain relievers.

> **Happiness Trivia**
>
> Researchers say that optimism and pessimism are two ends of a continuum. About 80 percent of the U.S. population ranges from mildly to unremittingly optimistic.

Putting a Happy Spin on the World

So what exactly makes one an optimist? Once again, heredity can get the ball rolling. A study that measured the optimism of identical and fraternal twins showed a higher correlation of attitudes between identicals, which suggests that genetics may play a substantial role in predisposing us toward embracing a glass-half-full outlook. But even those who conducted the study acknowledge that optimism is a complex trait that can be transmitted by indirect means. We can learn to be more optimistic, for example, from optimistic role models—especially those who are close to us, such as our parents.

def•i•ni•tion

Explanatory style is the way we explain the causes and effects of our circumstances to ourselves. It is the "spin" we put on events that occur in our lives.

But what behaviors would these role models be modeling? What would we emulate to become more optimistic? Martin Seligman, Christopher Peterson, and other leading positive psychologists contend that we can start moving toward a more optimistic outlook by noticing and addressing our *explanatory style*.

Now versus Always

One of the key factors that make an optimist an optimist, according to Seligman, is their ability to view negative events as temporary. Pessimists, on the other hand, view them as permanent.

Feeling tired?

If you're a pessimist you'd say, "I'll never have the same energy I used to."

If you're an optimist you'd be more likely to say, "I feel tired *today;* I'm sure it will pass with a good night's sleep."

Sick of a long, rainy spell?

If you're a pessimist you'd say, "Climate change has ruined the weather patterns around here for good."

If you're an optimist you'd probably say, "I'll really appreciate the sunshine when it comes."

Disappointed with yourself because you cheated on your weight-loss diet?

If you're a pessimist you'd say, "I knew it. I might as well throw those skinny jeans away."

If you're an optimist you'd slap yourself on the wrist and say, "I'm getting right back on the wagon—and not the chow wagon!"

When negative events occur, pessimists insist that they're *always* wrong, that they'll *never* succeed, that they're *constantly* failing, that their slump will last *forever*, and that they are unlucky *all the time*. Optimists, on the other hand, will tell you they made a mistake *this time*, that they're in a slump *at the moment*, or that things didn't work out so well *today*—but their luck is *bound to change*.

However, it's important to note that optimists have a wonderful way of altering their perspective so that it stays cheerful. That means that when things go *right*, they are more than willing to switch scripts. On a roll, an optimist will foresee that fortuitous circumstances will endure. They'll remark that their luck is holding, *as usual*, and that they were *right again*.

Although this is a flip-flop, it is an effective perspective. Optimists limit the distress caused by negative events by minimizing the perception of their duration, and they maximize pleasant and positive events by refusing to dwell on their impermanence.

Situational versus Universal

Optimists also differ from pessimists in that they view negative events as being limited in scope. When one thing goes wrong, they see it as an anomaly. They don't leap to the conclusion that this occurrence is indicative of *everything* going wrong. They compartmentalize their troubles, putting borders around them rather than letting them bleed into other areas.

Someone tells you they don't like your new haircut?

If you're an optimist you'll shrug it off: "Bob doesn't like my new haircut (that jerk!)."

If you're a pessimist you're apt to conclude, "Nobody likes my haircut; I look awful."

Romantic interest cooling things off?

If you're an optimist you'll think, "I'll find someone better."

If you're a pessimist you'll practically convince yourself to join a monastery.

But when things go right, get ready for a style switch again. An optimist in a good relationship says, "I deserve great relationships. I'm a desirable person." The pessimist says, "This person seems to like me—I wonder what's wrong with them?"

> **Stumbling Blocks** _____
>
> The tendency to assess isolated negative events as indicators of ongoing and pervasive problems predisposes pessimists to give up before they give themselves a chance to succeed. Numerous studies confirm that optimists are more likely to stick with tasks, stay with their jobs, and perform better at their work than pessimists do.

Internal Causes versus External Causes

The third side of the optimism versus pessimism explanatory style triangle has to do with exhibiting a kind of *self-serving bias*. Optimists take credit for their successes, but attribute failure to external factors. Pessimists conclude that successes are due to external factors and that failures are "all their fault."

def•i•ni•tion _____

> A **self-serving bias** occurs when people claim responsibility for successes but not for failures. It may also manifest itself as a tendency for people to evaluate ambiguous information in a way beneficial to their interests. People thinking that they perform better than average in areas important to their self-esteem are also an example of self-serving bias.

Got a good grade on an exam?

If you're an optimist you'll attribute it to your innate intelligence: "Of course I got an A; I'm smart."

If you're a pessimist you'll attribute your grade to the fact that "the test was not hard" or that "the teacher is an easy grader."

Scored a goal in the big game?

If you're an optimist you'll cite your strength and skill.

If you're a pessimist you'll cite your opponent's momentary lapse in judgment or attention.

Now for the flip side: optimists who fail a test or miss a goal wouldn't be likely to attribute this to a personal internal flaw. They might say the test was unfair or the referee made a bad call (both external causes). They might say they had a bad day (thus relegating the event to one-time status). They might even say they need to study more or practice harder (thus putting the matter within their sphere of personal control). What they do *not* do is associate poor outcomes with internal shortcomings. Optimists might sometimes lose, but they never see themselves as "losers."

Now, if you're starting to wonder whether an optimistic perspective can go too far or be blind to reality, ultimately creating problems and *un*happiness, you're asking a valid question—one we'll address later in this chapter.

In Search of Optimism

Is there a way to tell if you're more of an optimist than a pessimist? And can you become more optimistic? The answer to both questions is yes.

Psychologists who wish to determine someone's explanatory style can do so by administering an Attributional Style Questionnaire (ASQ), which measures one's level of optimistic versus pessimistic responses and identifies prevalent attitudes. But happiness researchers also became interested in the styles of people who weren't going to take any such test. They wondered: Which sports heroes are optimists? Which politicians? Which business leaders? And how does that optimism affect their performance?

This curiosity led to Dr. Christopher Peterson's pioneering work in what has become known as the CAVE technique: Content Analysis of Verbatim Explanations. The idea is actually very simple—so simple that Peterson began CAVEing by reading the sports pages. If a player or coach lost a game, Petersen noted whether or not they blamed external factors (for example, inclement weather) or put the onus on themselves. He noted whether they viewed the defeat as part of a trend or as an exception. He used the participants' direct quotations to create explanatory style profiles. Later researchers began CAVEing a broad range of material, both spoken and written—speeches, interviews, press conferences, diaries, letters, and even wills. Using the technique they could determine the pessimistic or optimistic tendencies of virtually anyone, living or deceased.

An excellent beginning strategy for anyone who would like to move toward the more optimistic end spectrum should begin observing their own communications by using a similar technique.

Developing Self-Awareness

What kinds of things do you typically say when things go wrong? Some of us are not even aware when we default to a pessimistic stance. Yet out of habit we might say things such as, "I just can't win," "I can never get a break," or "That's just my luck" when things go wrong. We might greet a setback by responding, "Isn't that always the way it is?" We might greet bad news by waiting for the other shoe to drop, by asking "What next?" or by citing Murphy's Law: "Whatever can go wrong will go wrong." (Murphy was no optimist!)

On the other hand we might have our optimistic moments—ones we can notice and expand on. As with those times when we react to negative events by noting that this too shall pass, or, as Scarlet O'Hara put it, "Tomorrow's another day." (Scarlet never gave in to pessimism. Where some take lemons and make lemonade, she took a pair of drapes and made a velvet ball gown.)

Now, what do you typically say when things go right? Do you react with an optimistic "Now we're cooking!" or a pessimistic "This will never last," or "Well, at least *one* thing went right"? Do you say, "I made it happen," or do you chalk it up to dumb luck?

Self-awareness is the first step on the road to change. Charting your responses to events during a brief period of time—even as little as a week or two—can yield some remarkable insights. To keep track of your habitual responses to events, put a check mark next to your verbal reactions as you respond to events in your daily life. (This table is based on interpretation of Dr. Martin Seligman's criteria for optimistic and pessimistic explanatory styles.)

Negative Event Reaction

❏ Now	❏ Always
❏ Situational	❏ Universal
❏ Outside cause	❏ Caused by me

Positive Event Reaction

❏ Now	❏ Always
❏ Situational	❏ Universal
❏ Outside cause	❏ Caused by me

If your attitudes are predominantly pessimistic, you will have more check marks in the right column of the first box and in the left column of the second. If your attitudes are predominantly pessimistic, you will have more check marks in the left column of the first box and in the right column of the second.

Retrospective Optimism

A recent research trend points to yet another potential strategy for increasing one's level of optimism. This research centers on *personal narrative,* the stories that each of us tell about our own lives and how we got to where we are today.

To conduct this research, psychologists at Northwestern University conducted two-hour, life-story interviews. Typically, subjects describe phases of their lives as if they were outlining chapters from childhood through adolescence to middle age. They also describe a number of pivotal scenes in detail, including high points (winning that scholarship); low points (being left at the altar); and turning points (deciding to go to law school rather than medical school).

When the transcripts were analyzed, researchers noted some interesting trends. Those with mood-related problems reported negative details even in predominantly positive memories (*I spoke at my graduation, although the day would have been better without the rain*) and tend to close "chapters" on notes of disappointment. On the other hand, those whom researchers called *generative adults* (energetic, involved, and civic-minded) tended to focus on themes of redemption (*I got left at the altar but on a trip to recover met the man of my dreams*).

These life stories shape not only how we think about ourselves, but also how we behave, those behind the studies say. But these narratives are not set in stone. As it turns out, each of us is gradually but continually revising our story treatments—and therein lies their potential to benefit us.

Those who have studied the power of these personal narratives contend that interpretations of past behavior shape how we envision the future. If we go back and revise our tales with a more positive bent—noting how challenges led to growth and failures led to new opportunity—we are likely to look forward with a more positive attitude.

Helping Hand

Many successful people display retrospective optimism when they recount their life stories. Steve Jobs, for example, gave a widely quoted commencement address at Stanford in which he described three potentially devastating events—dropping out of college, being fired from his own company, and receiving a cancer diagnosis—as integral to his growth and vision. Reading autobiographies and speeches by those who recount their stories in this sort of light can help us tap the influence of positive role models.

Tapping the power of positive memory is not dissimilar to changing one's explanatory style in the present. Indeed, accomplishing the first task can help us accomplish the second. As we recall times when we emerged victorious from life's challenges, we can build a reservoir of confidence with which to ground ourselves as new challenges present themselves—and we can use those challenges as chances to achieve resilience and, ultimately, happiness.

Optimistic Realism: A Contradiction in Terms?

Having a firm grasp on reality has long been considered the gold standard of mental health, but we can acknowledge that optimists are biased in a self-serving way. They are not completely objective when it comes to evaluating risks, which in extreme cases could lead to, say, an optimistic cigarette smoker continuing to smoke despite evidence that doing so is detrimental to her health, or an investor sinking his life savings into a new and unproven investment scheme.

This is a conundrum that has led to many further studies of optimistic perspectives and their limitations. Researchers now suggest that there may be an *optimal margin of illusion* that, while allowing people to slightly overestimate their abilities and chances of success, does not typically lead to irresponsible behaviors based on false assumptions.

In other words, balance is the key. Optimism and realism need not be mutually exclusive terms. Optimists may be more inclined to take a calculated risk, but those who plunge headlong into situations of immeasurable uncertainty based on an inflated understanding of their skills or their luck are not optimists. They could more accurately be described as narcissists with grandiose delusions.

Most situations in life allow room for some ambiguity. Given the same set of facts, we can still legitimately speculate about outcomes. For example, a group of scientists who agree that climate change is occurring may be divided into one group that sees the problem as insoluble and one that sees it as reversible. Both groups can offer objective evidence that backs up what they see as their logical assessment. Yet the group that sees the problem as reversible is, of course, the group likely to seek solutions. In this situation, as in so many others, "truth" is an imprecise commodity, yet this latter group is willing to act on its interpretation of the truth in an optimistic, proactive way. (Note that their attitude is *We can do it*, rather than *It will happen*. They are not betting on a magical outcome, but planning to address genuine obstacles and challenges.)

Optimistic thinking will not lead to long-term happiness if it isn't based in reality. But being a realistic optimist is possible. Realistic optimism requires not ignoring facts, but collecting and evaluating available information as thoroughly as possible before acting constructively to potentially maximize positive outcomes.

When there is still some level of uncertainty (as is the case in most situations), realistic optimists ...

- Give the benefit of the doubt when considering others' motivations.

- Remain alert to positive elements in the current situation—even while acknowledging the existence of negative elements.

- Accept the challenges that lie ahead while holding on to hope.

Happy Thought

"No pessimist ever discovered the secrets of the stars, or sailed to an uncharted land, or opened a new Heaven to the human spirit."

—Helen Keller

Finally, it's important to note that maintaining realistic optimism requires regular reality checks. The successful optimist will not just set a plan in motion and hope for the best. They will set interim goals, solicit feedback from knowledgeable sources, and alter their strategy when doing so is called for.

Nevertheless, the attitudes that realistic optimists hold about past, present, and future eschew cynicism, complaint, and stagnation in favor of trust, gratitude, and goal-setting. The latter are the habits of the happy.

The Least You Need to Know

- To a significant extent, happiness is a self-fulfilling prophecy—those who expect positive outcomes tend to get them; those who expect to be more content, are.

- Optimists see problems as temporary anomalies that are externally caused; pessimists view problems as long-lasting, pervasive, and "their fault."

- Optimism can be cultivated by becoming aware of one's explanatory style and gradually altering it.

- Focusing on personal triumphs over adversity when telling one's life story can also generate optimism about the future.

- For optimism to lead to lasting happiness, it must be tempered with realism—realistic optimists don't ignore facts but evaluate available information and act in ways that potentially maximize positive outcomes.

Chapter 9

An Attitude of Gratitude

In This Chapter

- Discovering how gratitude increases happiness
- Assessing your thankfulness
- Expressing gratitude
- Finding the forgiveness-gratitude link
- Learning the artful acceptance of gratitude

In America, we traditionally set aside one day a year to officially give thanks. On this Thanksgiving holiday we typically prepare a feast of turkey with all the trimmings. Before we eat we might stop for a few moments to acknowledge how thankful we are for the blessings in our lives. After we eat, we watch football. A year later we remember to give thanks again.

But if gratitude and thanksgiving are significant enough to build beloved rituals around once a year, what if we found ways to acknowledge and express gratitude on a regular—even a daily—basis? According to positive psychology, we would be happier for doing so.

Why the Grateful Are Happy

A number of research groups have studied the effects of asking people to stop and ponder, as a matter of routine, what they are grateful for in their lives. The experiments often involve instructing people to take a few minutes at the end of each day to enumerate what happened during the day that was good and to write or recite a phrase expressing gratitude for those things. The things that inspire gratitude can be major events (*I'm grateful I found out I'm getting a promotion; I'm thankful that my kid got into a great college*), but more often than not they are relatively minor (*I'm thankful that I got to take my dog for a long, enjoyable walk; I'm so glad we got the kitchen faucet fixed*). Even if someone's day was disappointing or frustrating or even downright unpleasant, the assignment holds: give thanks for the good. (*Today it rained buckets—I'm thankful because my lawn needed watering.*)

The results of these experiments show that people who make such a practice a part of their lives report increased happiness and diminished symptoms of depression. The follow-up findings of one such experiment, the "three good things" study (Seligman, Steen, Park, and Peterson, 2005), which asked participants to list each evening three things that went well and why, were especially interesting. Sixty percent of the subjects in the experiment said they were still ending each day this way six months after the experiment ended. To them, the ongoing benefits were obvious.

Stumbling Blocks

Don't assume that only those you might consider "lucky" are adept at expressing gratitude. Individuals who have been through the most trying experiences and weathered the most adverse circumstances are often the most grateful. Hurricane and other natural disaster survivors, for example, tend to express gratitude for what they have *not* lost.

A 1998 Gallup survey of American adults and teenagers found that 95 percent of respondents felt at least somewhat happy when expressing gratitude, and more than 50 percent felt extremely happy while doing so. But science shows that the joy that comes from being grateful lasts longer than it takes to utter or to jot down one's sentiments. An attitude of gratitude is cumulative—it tends to accrue long-term benefits. Those who display such an attitude have been shown to be energetic, optimistic, and empathetic, and even to enjoy significant physical well-being.

Anchoring in the Present

Where does the power of gratitude lie? The very act of giving thanks requires us to stop, look around, and notice where we are and what we have right now. It brings us into the present moment and makes us more conscious of what surrounds us. It frees us from ruminating about past problems or focusing on future-oriented anxieties.

During much of our existence, we may take things for granted, but in these moments of taking stock we allow ourselves to be pleasantly surprised: *Look at all of this!* When we choose to focus on positive aspects of our immediate situation, we acknowledge small but significant good things that might otherwise have passed unnoticed.

It's been said that if happy people painted pictures of their lives, positive elements would be in the foreground, while negative

> **Happy Thought**
>
> "Let us rise up and be thankful, for if we didn't learn a lot today, at least we learned a little, and if we didn't learn a little, at least we didn't get sick, and if we got sick, at least we didn't die; so, let us all be thankful."
> —Buddha

ones would constitute a vague and fuzzy backdrop. Gratitude helps us achieve just this sort of perspective. If we make it a habit to find things to be grateful for, almost anything can be considered a blessing compared to the worst-case scenario. You may dislike your boss, for example, but that can be reframed as *I am grateful to have a job.* You may have broken your arm in an accident, but that translates to, *I'm glad I walked away alive!*

Gaining Security

We can always chase more riches and comforts in the name of attaining security. But this continually grasping state of mind (the hedonic treadmill detailed in Chapter 1) has been shown to detract from happiness. Genuine security entails feeling satisfied with where we are. And although being happy certainly doesn't preclude setting goals, it does mean not being a slave to social pressure or being obsessed by financial status.

Reminding ourselves what we have to be grateful for in the moment can help quell the urge to jump on that hedonic treadmill. It can also remind us to honor ourselves for having gotten as far as we have—and that reminder, in turn, makes us more secure in our own strengths and abilities.

Enhancing Altruism

In keeping with the "feel good, do good" effect (see Chapter 6), people who feel grateful tend to be highly helpful and nurturing to others. It is as if by counting our own blessings we remember the value of being a blessing to someone else.

In addition, gratitude can help sustain those whose acts of caregiving might lead to physical and emotional strain. A study of caregivers who were under the stress of caring for severely ill loved ones showed that those who took the time to write about their gratitude remained in a better state of health themselves.

Lowering Stress, Upping Immunity

Feelings of thankfulness and appreciation have been shown to contribute to overall well-being in a number of ways. Studies show ...

- They stimulate our *parasympathetic* nervous system—the part of our autonomic nervous system that initiates relaxation—and "puts on the brakes" in the aftermath of frustration or anxiety—by lowering heart rate, respiration rate, and blood pressure.

- They increase levels of an immune antibody called IgA (immunoglobulin A), which is part of the body's first line of defense against invading microbes—especially those that cause upper respiratory infections.

- They stimulate the release of a beneficial hormone called DHEA (dehydro-epiandosterone), a hormone said to play a role in weight maintenance and in prolonging youthful energy.

- They correspond to a decrease in the stress-related hormone cortisol, which can raise blood sugar to dangerous levels and cause other adverse health effects when released during sustained periods.

Feelings of gratitude not only help prevent illness, but play a role in helping us heal from illness and recover from surgery. In other words, those who feel thankful in spite of infirmities are most likely to rebound from them sooner.

> **Happiness Trivia**
>
> A study conducted by Case Western University's Institute for Research on Unlimited Love investigated the impact of gratitude on 74 recipients of organ donations. Researchers questioned recipients of hearts, livers, lungs, kidneys, and the pancreas. Those recipients who expressed gratitude either directly to donors or indirectly (by writing their feelings in journals) felt physically better and actually functioned at a higher level than those who did not.

Are You Grateful?

You might never have stopped to think about whether or not you are given to expressing gratitude. You might do it sporadically or as a matter of course. You might have reasons—perhaps as yet unexamined ones—that cause you to resist doing it altogether. The following quiz will help you focus on your gratitude habits and see if there is room to expand them to increase your happiness potential.

Simply note the level to which you agree or disagree with each statement. Then check your results at the end of the quiz:

1. **Looking at the world as a whole, I think we all have much to be grateful for.**
   A. Strongly agree
   B. Somewhat agree
   C. Neutral
   D. Somewhat disagree
   E. Strongly disagree

2. **I personally have a great deal to be thankful for.**
   A. Strongly agree
   B. Somewhat agree
   C. Neutral
   D. Somewhat disagree
   E. Strongly disagree

3. **If I made a list of all I'm thankful for, it would be long and varied.**
   A. Strongly agree
   B. Somewhat agree
   C. Neutral
   D. Somewhat disagree
   E. Strongly disagree

4. **I have personally thanked people to whom I feel grateful.**
   A. Strongly agree
   B. Somewhat agree
   C. Neutral
   D. Somewhat disagree
   E. Strongly disagree

5. **I express general indirect thanks on a regular basis (for example through a journal or through some form of prayer or "acknowledging the universe").**
   A. Strongly agree
   B. Somewhat agree
   C. Neutral
   D. Somewhat disagree
   E. Strongly disagree

6. **I tend to notice good things even during a hard day.**
   A. Strongly agree
   B. Somewhat agree
   C. Neutral
   D. Somewhat disagree
   E. Strongly disagree

7. **Looking back, I see some experiences that were tough but yielded results I am now thankful for.**
   A. Strongly agree
   B. Somewhat agree
   C. Neutral
   D. Somewhat disagree
   E. Strongly disagree

8. **I am afraid of looking weak, sappy, or "uncool" if I openly express gratitude.**
   A. Strongly agree
   B. Somewhat agree
   C. Neutral
   D. Somewhat disagree
   E. Strongly disagree

9. **I am reluctant to express gratitude for fear I'll "tempt fate" to send me some troubles.**
   A. Strongly agree
   B. Somewhat agree
   C. Neutral
   D. Somewhat disagree
   E. Strongly disagree

10. **If I start to count my blessings, I get distracted by thinking about desirable things I do not have.**
    A. Strongly agree
    B. Somewhat agree
    C. Neutral
    D. Somewhat disagree
    E. Strongly disagree

For questions 1 through 7, give yourself 5 points for each "A" response, 4 for each "B," 3 for each "C," 2 for each "D," and 1 for each "E."

For questions 8 through 10, reverse the scoring. Give yourself 1 point for each "A" response, 2 for each "B," 3 for each "C," 4 for each "D," and 5 for each "E."

45–50 points: You go through life being grateful. No doubt you are reaping the emotional rewards of doing so. Keep up your happiness-inducing habits.

35–44 points: Although you have room for improvement, you are not averse to expressing gratitude. The rest of this chapter will show you ways to enhance your habits.

Less than 35 points: Gratitude is not a primary focus of yours. But if you've read this far, there's every reason to be optimistic that you can make it more so.

Expressing Gratitude

When you were a child, your parents probably taught you that it was good and proper to say "thank you." Most of us still honor this social protocol. If someone holds a door open or helps us carry an unwieldy package or pays us a compliment, we say "thanks" in passing. There's nothing wrong with that, of course. However, you're likely to up your happiness quotient significantly if you also make it a point to express gratitude in deliberate, regular—perhaps even daily—ways.

Gratitude Journals

One way to ritualize the expression of thankfulness in your life is to keep what's become known as a gratitude journal. Doing so is a popular assignment in positive psychology courses, but many people are doing it at the behest of their church or synagogue, or simply trying the practice because they've read about it or heard about it through word of mouth.

The process is simple. Devote a notebook to the daily recordings of things for which you are thankful. Set aside some time at the end of each day to record a list of blessings in your life. These can be ongoing blessings, events from the past that have led to good things in the present, or specific events that occurred in the course of the day. In short, they can be about anything that makes you feel grateful.

You can direct your items toward an individual (*I am grateful to my sister Sarah for driving our Mom to the doctor*) or to a spiritual figure (making your list a prayerful experience) or to no one in particular (a blanket acknowledgement to the universe at large).

If you have trouble getting started, try using these prompts:

I am grateful and happy that _____ did _____ for me.

I am so thankful that _____ worked out well.

I am so grateful that I have _____.

I am thankful that my loved ones have _____.

I am so grateful that _____ taught me a lesson about _____.

I am thankful to have the opportunity to _____.

I am grateful for my ability to _____.

No subject is off-limits in a gratitude journal. No topic is too small or inconsequential. You may be grateful that you have a hot cup of tea while you write, grateful that your beloved cat is curled on your lap, even grateful for the air you breathe or for the opportunity to enjoy some sweet dreams when you finish your writing.

From time to time you should read over your gratitude journal. Chances are you will be heartened by how many positive things you have in your life that you have begun to notice, appreciate, and savor. You may also wish to share some of the writings in your gratitude journal with your spouse or significant other. Couples who do so report that this can have a profoundly positive effect on their relationship and bring them closer together.

Helping Hand _____

Writing in a gratitude journal or offering up prayers or similar expressions of gratitude is best done at night. When the day is done we can review it with the aim of discovering the good that it contained. We will be more apt to go to sleep in a positive frame of mind and to wake up in a positive frame of mind.

Gratitude Letters and Visits

Another popular "homework assignment" in positive psychology courses—also a practice that is catching on in other circles—is to write a gratitude letter to a specific person who has positively impacted your life. This could be someone you currently see on a regular basis, or someone you haven't seen in quite some time.

In the letter you would ...

- Say as *specifically* as possible what that person did to help you, teach you, enlighten you, set an example for you, or inspire you.

- Say what qualities you appreciate about them (for example their generosity, their humor, their wisdom, their courage).

- Directly express your feelings of thankfulness toward them.

A gratitude letter might look similar to this:

Dear Bill:

As my big brother you have helped me throughout my life. Whenever I lost confidence in myself, you helped me find that confidence again. You did this when I was a freshman in high school and scared to try out for the football team. I did not think I had the size or the muscle. You not only practiced with me even though you had many other commitments, but you also spent many Sunday afternoons watching pro games with me and pointing out how it wasn't always the biggest guys that played the smartest and the best. You helped me find my talents and believe in them.

Recently you did this again. You encouraged me to start my own business when I was reluctant to give up the security of working for an established company. Once again you reminded me of my own strengths and gave me confidence. You even offered to invest in the company—and that made me realize the tremendous faith you had in me. My business is starting to take off now, and I think every day about the fact that it probably would not exist if not for you.

Bill, you are a loyal, unselfish brother. You are always upbeat and your enthusiasm is contagious. Your "can do" attitude continues to be an inspiration to me.

I know how busy I have been lately. But I wanted to make sure you know that not a day goes by when I don't think of you with affection and gratitude. I hope you will always remember that.

Your brother,

Sam

Or it might look like this:

Dear Mrs. O'Shea:

I have always wanted you to know that, as my eighth grade history teacher, you so positively impacted my life that I never forgot you. As a 13-year-old kid, I was not originally too enthused about studying ancient civilizations. Who cared about what happened so long ago and so far away—I had my own problems!

But you made history come alive for me. The way you told stories had me on the edge of my seat. I felt like Alexander the Great was as present in my life as the kid sitting next to me. You also made me understand the connection between history and what happens in our own time.

Not long after I moved on to high school you retired. I felt bad that the kids who came after me at Lincoln Middle School never got a chance to be your students. But more than that, I felt bad that I never was able to tell you how I decided to major in history and political science in college. Now I have my first job, working for an international nonprofit organization. I will be traveling to some of the places you taught us about, and I will think of you when I am there.

I will always remember you with gratitude. I was lucky to be your pupil. And I am sure there are many other students you influenced in your career who feel the same way.

Sincerely,

Josh Miller

If at all possible, try to combine your gratitude letter with a gratitude visit. Deliver your letter in person and have the object of your thankfulness read it in your presence. The results are generally extremely moving and rewarding for both parties.

If delivering your letter involves tracking down someone you haven't seen in a while, so much the better. Think how surprised and delighted someone's eighth grade teacher would be to see that a former student made that kind of effort.

Stumbling Blocks

Positive psychology professor and researcher Christopher Peterson notes that some of his students have been hesitant to thank one of their parents, fearing that the other will feel slighted. Petersen writes, however, that this has never happened: "Dad is always happy when Mom is thanked."

Grudges or Gratitude

Writing expressions of gratitude to a specific person can also have the beneficial effect of helping you to forgive any past *im*perfect behavior on their part. Sure, your older sibling might have teased and tormented you sometimes, but by focusing on the times when they encouraged you, cheered you up, made you laugh, or set a high standard for you to emulate, you will minimize the negative by accentuating the positive.

Now, think about some of the people to whom you might owe a debt of gratitude who perhaps only indirectly or inadvertently helped you. For example:

◆ The boss who told you that you weren't right for a certain promotion and turned out to be correct in saying you were better suited to another profession—one you are now successful in.

◆ The athletic coach who was rough on you, insisting you could be in much better shape (which you now are).

◆ The college roommate who was incredibly competitive with you and got you so reciprocally competitive that you graduated with honors.

Think how surprised they would be to get a letter of thanks from you!

What will you gain by looking back over your life and considering how certain people whose actions seemed unfair, irritating, or even unreasonable at the time turned out to be just what the doctor ordered? Only a whole new perspective! You are likely to be more tolerant, patient, and forgiving—all traits that serve your personal happiness far more than the negative thoughts that occur when we carry grudges.

In fact, we don't call it *carrying* a grudge for nothing. Those destructive emotions can weigh us down.

Graciously Accepting Gratitude

Finally, what if you are the recipient of someone else's gratitude? It will probably make you very happy, but somehow we have gotten the idea that the polite thing to do when thanked is to minimize what you did. One of the ways we typically respond when someone thanks us is to say, "Hey, it's nothing!" (The Spanish say "*de nada*" and the French say "*de rien*," which literally translate as "it's nothing" as well.)

But there are many other ways we can respond when someone says, "Thank you very much":

"*It means a lot to me to hear you say that.*"

"*It was my pleasure.*"

"*I appreciate your acknowledgement.*"

"*You made my day!*"

and of course,

"*You are very welcome.*"

> **Happy Thought** _____
>
> "The deepest craving of human nature is the need to be appreciated."
>
> —William James

You may value humility, which is all well and good, but it is false humility to deny that you helped someone if you did. Moreover it serves to diminish the effort that person took to express their gratitude in the first place. It is human nature to enjoy being appreciated. Whether you are on the giving or receiving end of gratitude, enjoy the happiness it brings.

The Least You Need to Know

♦ Gratitude ups our happiness level by helping us appreciate the present moment, by increasing our sense of security and self-confidence, by inspiring us to be more altruistic, and by tempering our stress.

♦ We can ritualize our expression of gratitude by keeping a gratitude journal, by writing letters of gratitude, and by paying gratitude visits—we accrue benefits whether we thank individuals directly or indirectly acknowledge the universe.

♦ Focusing on gratitude can help us overlook people's imperfections and let go of old grudges that keep us mired in negative emotions.

♦ When someone thanks you, accept it graciously—don't belittle their efforts by minimizing your own actions.

Chapter 10

Positively Playful

In This Chapter

- Having leisure activities and pleasure
- Finding the meaningful process of play
- Learning how "flow" makes us happy
- Finding time to flow
- Discovering your flow activity

Imagine you are watching children at play. If someone asked you to describe their predominant feeling, chances are you would describe them as happy. And so they are. It's fun to play; to be truly playful is to be light-hearted and entranced.

Adults, too, have fun when they play. Play relaxes us and lifts our spirits. It relieves stress and takes our mind off our troubles. But, as this chapter shows, play can do even more to engender happiness. Play can help us lead not just a pleasant life, but also a life rich in engagement and meaning.

The Pleasure of Leisure

One of the most significant predictors of an individual's life satisfaction, research shows, is how much time that person spends engaged in leisure activities. The correlation is strong for many reasons.

The first and most obvious reason that leisure makes us happy is that many leisure activities directly produce pleasant sensations. If you like to run, bike, or swim, for example, you'll get all the mood-enhancing benefits that aerobic exercise provides—not to mention a boost to your health, vitality, and self-image. If you like to garden or fish or hike in the wilderness, you'll derive the aesthetic pleasures of being outdoors in restorative natural surroundings. If you like to listen to music, you'll also achieve mood enhancement: listening to quiet music raises feelings of contentment; listening to more stimulating music increases pleasurable arousal and excitement levels.

Recreational activities are also often done in the company of friends and family. Sometimes new friendships are formed or old ones strengthened by sharing leisure activities, from deep-sea diving to playing bridge. Because time spent with loved ones and friends is itself a potential source of happiness, leisure time can be doubly rewarding.

What we do with our leisure time can also help us build a sense of personal and community identity—both of which contribute to elevated feelings of self-worth and satisfaction. We enjoy describing ourselves in terms of what sport we prefer, identifying ourselves as golfers or sailors or surfers, and we often respond positively to those who pursue the same pastimes. There is an instant feeling of fraternity and a great deal to talk about. (*Hey, you run marathons? I run marathons!*) Sometimes we join formal organizations or clubs associated with our favorite activities, but even if we simply stand around and shoot the breeze in the most informal way, we appreciate and value the camaraderie.

Helping Hand

Our leisure activities sometimes provide us with a chance to compete. If you thrive on competition, a rousing tennis match, an intense game of chess, or a video game tournament can afford you a special dose of hyper-alertness that's known as *eustress*—positive stress of brief, limited duration that our brains respond to with pleasure.

Of course, there is a seemingly endless variety of experiences that people enjoy in their nonworking hours. Some are interactive, others are solitary. Some take energy, some—such as watching television—are passive. What they all have in common is that they are activities *we choose*. No one insists we do them. And when our choice of how we spend our time is left to our own discretion, that alone is enough to make us happy—at least to some degree.

But pleasurable leisure and recreation do not tell the whole story of the potential of play. Fun is fun—no one will argue with that. But play is a process that has even more to offer. Play can allow us to both lose ourselves—in the best sense—and, ultimately, to find ourselves.

The Higher Purposes of Play

Throughout much of the animal kingdom, play is a widespread phenomenon. If you've ever raised cats or dogs, their propensity for play is no doubt obvious to you. Dolphins also play, and so do chimps, bonobos, and other primates. When no immediate danger threatens and food is plentiful, many creatures spend the better part of their day at play.

Ethologists—researchers who study animal behavior, including the behavior of the human animal—note that play is anything but random. Indeed, it serves many evolutionary and developmental purposes. Play can be useful in developing survival skills, such as the ability to outfox or outrun a predator. It sharpens the mind by promoting mental strategizing. Play builds our ability to anticipate, weigh possible outcomes, and generate multiple solutions to problems. And play builds imagination, allowing the mind to wander and fantasize.

Not all of our enjoyable leisure activities allow us to reach a highly engaged level that sharpens our saw, so to speak. And it's fine that not all of them do. There's nothing wrong with the simple, pleasant relaxation we derive from whiling away a Sunday afternoon browsing through catalogs or watching football. However, those who also integrate more demanding and creative endeavors into their repertoire of pastimes will reap additional benefits. When we engage in play that taps our drive and resourcefulness, we are apt to find ourselves entering the happy state known as "flow."

> **Happiness Trivia**
>
> Couch potatoes take note: if you are spending all your leisure time in passive relaxation, you probably won't be as happy as you could be. When people are interrupted at random intervals to report how much they are enjoying themselves, those who are vegetating report far less satisfaction than those who are participating in an activity requiring physical or mental energy.

Going with the Flow

"Flow" is a concept formulated by Mihaly Csikszentmihalyi, a University of Chicago professor and one of the pioneers of positive psychology (for more about Csikszentmihalyi, see Chapter 3). He defines *flow*, essentially, as an "optimal experience" that results from a maximally engaged state. Csikszentmihalyi observed this state in people engaged in activities as diverse as painting, sculpting, writing, dancing, playing or composing music, playing chess, and climbing mountains.

Flow is said to generate joy in those who achieve it. But this level of happiness far surpasses that experienced during transient diversions. It is deeper and extends far beyond the period that is actually devoted to the activity that brought it on in the first place. After being completely consumed by a flow-inducing experience, one emerges with a heightened sense of well-being and self-confidence.

Finding and pursuing an activity that brings on a state of flow is a means of expanding our potential for happiness. So, just how do you know when you're in flow?

Relishing a Challenge

Overwhelmingly, Csikszentmihalyi says, optimal experiences are reported during activities that require the investment of energy (mental, physical, or both) and present challenges that could not be met without the appropriate skills.

If one has the skills to pursue an activity, that activity or even the prospect of that activity becomes exciting. When involved in the pursuit, an adequately skilled person becomes engrossed in choosing from among myriad opportunities for action. For example, a rock climber must decide where to place his crampons so as not to take a tumble, and a writer must decide how to structure sentences and paragraphs so as to best convey mood and meaning.

Stumbling Blocks

If you're looking for flow, match the *level* of your skill to your chosen pursuit. If you are very good at something, make sure the specific activity is not too easy for you. And if you're competing, seek out worthy opponents. If what you're doing is a piece of cake, you won't be happy, you'll be bored.

If one does not have the skills to undertake a particular activity, then that activity lacks meaning. It becomes not challenging, but frustrating. For example, imagine attempting to complete a crossword puzzle in a foreign language. It would be pointless at best, infuriating at worst. The clues would be a "word salad." Imagine sitting down to a game of bridge if you have no idea what the rules are. It would be confounding to you and infuriating to your bridge partner. The cards would all seem equally valuable or valueless to you. Such an obviously doomed endeavor would hardly make you happy.

Valuing Process Over Product

Flow-inducing experiences tend to be goal-directed, and are bound by a certain set of rules or principles. People who engage in flow activities do so with some sort of plan: they want to accomplish something.

Goals, however, can be short term or long term. And gratification can come sooner, or later. A tennis player who wants to win a tennis match has a short-term goal, as does a mountain climber who wants to reach a summit. But a musician practicing piano may have the long-term goal of improving over time, even if each practice session advances this goal only imperceptibly (at least to an outside observer).

Yet, although flow pursuits tend to ultimately produce results, it's important to note that the end result or product itself is not the *cause* of the flow. Flow experiences are primarily *autotelic experiences.* Exhilaration comes from the doing, not from being done.

def•i•ni•tion

> *Autotelic* combines two Greek words—*auto* (self) and *telos* (goal). An **autotelic experience** is a self-contained activity that is done not for the sake of future reward or benefit but simply for the joy of doing it. On the other hand, an *exotelic experience* is one in which the results are of primary importance. If you are singing because you love to sing, you are having an autotelic experience. If you are singing strictly to get on *American Idol,* you are having an exotelic experience.

People engaged in optimal experience enjoy the process of doing whatever it is they are doing. The gardener in flow loves to turn the soil, to plant, to prune, and to care for his flowers and plants. If his goal is to grow a prize-winning rose, his success will likely make him happy—but not *as* happy as he was when he was working *toward* that success. Before you know it, he'll be out in the garden planting again. It is the same for the composer, the painter, the sculptor. After they complete their work, they long to begin the creation process anew. Like children at play, they don't want the game to end, and when it does they want to start another game.

Intensely Focusing Attention

One of the most common attributes cited about the state of flow is that it involves a complete, intense focus of one's attention. Awareness is heightened, but only select information having to do with the task at hand enters into one's moment-to-moment consciousness. Nothing extraneous or irrelevant to the process seems to register.

There are a number of reasons why this type of heightened awareness and intense focus creates a joyous state. During periods of flow, we are not worried. All the "what-if" thoughts and anxieties that typically occupy our minds are temporarily kept at bay. They would only be a distraction, and we won't tolerate distractions. If a worry intrudes on a person in flow, it is swatted away like a fly.

We are not self-conscious during periods of flow. We are, for a time, able to transcend our preoccupation with our "image." What others have thought of us in the past, what kind of reactions we're eliciting in the present, or how we'll be judged in the future are irrelevant. A ballplayer who is in flow while at the plate is not concerned with cheers or boos. Later on, watching the video replay, he may smile or cringe at how his fans responded to his turn at bat. But while he has his bat in hand, only the game and his role in it exist.

When we're in flow, we lose track of time. Time is our external yardstick for measuring the duration of events. Time is allegedly objective, but we all know that time can subjectively seem to "drag" or "fly." Minutes can seem like hours when we are bored or filled with dread. But when we are happily in flow, hours can seem like minutes. People in flow often have no idea how much actual clock time they have devoted to their activity. A painter at her easel may tell herself she'll stop work at 8 P.M., only to find herself amazed that it's "suddenly" midnight. On the other hand, time in a particularly intense moment of the flow process can seem to be extended, or more accurately—*sus*pended. A basketball player taking a jump shot can perceive these few seconds in something like slow motion, his each mid-air micro-movement etching itself indelibly on his mind. This, too, represents a thrilling departure from our usual temporal reality.

The absence of worry, the suspension of self-consciousness, and the subjective reframing of clock time are all results of the intense allocation of attention. Naturally, when the chosen activity ends, consciousness returns to its more mundane mode. However, people who have been in flow have had what could be called a growth experience. They have expanded their concepts of who they are, of how they can feel, and of what is possible. And they are wiser and happier for it.

Finding Time to Flow

Of course, to pursue an activity where one can lose track of time, one first has to make time *for* it. Unfortunately, this is not the current trend in American society. For decades now, pollsters have been asking respondents in the United States how much time they spend at work and how much time they have available for leisure. And for the past three decades, the clear trend is that we are spending more time at work and *less* time at leisure. Women, it turns out, have even less time for leisure than men—especially if they have jobs and children. The explanation is that the bulk of child-rearing and housekeeping duties still seemingly fall to women, even in two-parent households.

Some fortunate souls are able to earn a living from their flow activities, or at least incorporate some flow activities into their daily work (more on this in Chapter 12). But anyone else interested in upping their potential for happiness might think about prioritizing "spare" time to pursue stimulating activities that offer the opportunity to focus intently and to rise to a challenge.

As for waiting until the day when you don't have to work any longer, studies indicate it's probably not a good idea to take an "I'll wait until I retire" approach. Retirees may have more time for leisure and recreation, but tend *not* to take up new interests after they exit the workforce. It's wiser to develop interests at a younger age and plan to expand your pursuit of them when you retire.

Helping Hand

If you find it difficult to devote even one day a week to leisure and play, consider the practice of "Saturday pennies." There are 52 Saturdays in a year and 75 years in the average life span. That means we each are allotted some 3,900 Saturdays. Take your own age, multiply by 52, and subtract that number from 3,900. (For example, if you are 39 years old you have already "spent" 2,028 Saturdays.) Put a penny in a clear glass jar representing every Saturday you have left until age 75. (For a 39-year-old, that's 1,872 pennies.) Every Saturday, take a penny out. As you "spend" your penny stash, ask yourself: have you spent your day in a way that brings you satisfaction?

By the way, when you reach 75, put a penny in the jar for every extra Saturday you've been given. And each week, ask yourself what you've done with that gift.

Do You Know Your Flow?

Making space for flow to occur might seem like putting the cart before the horse if you're not sure what your flow activity might be. Some people can pinpoint immediately the activity that allows them to combine play with passion. They'd love to have more time for making jewelry, or practicing the saxophone, or editing videos on their computer. But others may draw a blank.

If you are not sure what your potential flow activity is, start by answering the following questions:

◆ What activities do I enjoy that use my talents and capabilities?

◆ What subjects do I know a lot about?

◆ What pursuit do I find challenging and compelling—but never so challenging that I want to give up?

- What is an activity that I like at least as much for its own sake as for what I get out of it?

- Is there something I do where I look at the clock and cannot believe how much time has gone by?

- Is there an activity that I become so engaged in I sometimes even neglect to stop to eat?

- Is there an activity that I enjoy that, for me, has a mildly addictive quality to it?

- Is there an activity or subject that I am always eager to learn more about?

- Is there an activity or subject that I am always eager to talk about with people who do the same thing?

- Is there one pursuit that I always want to get better at?

If you are having trouble identifying a potential flow experience for yourself, try asking yourself what you most enjoyed playing when you were a child? Is there any way you can integrate that into your life as an adult? If you are still having difficulty, don't be afraid to experiment and try different activities on for size.

Happy Thought

"When you follow your bliss ... doors will open where you would not have thought there would be doors, and where there wouldn't be a door for anyone else."

—Joseph Campbell

If you are on a quest to find your flow, try to let go of any judgments you may have about what is an appropriate choice. Don't steer yourself toward one activity over another because you feel—or someone else feels—that is more highbrow, more suited to your age, or even more suitable for one gender or another. Go with whatever intrigues and engages you.

The following suggestions for starting places are only that: suggestions. Follow your instincts.

Art from the Heart

Making art—drawing, painting, sculpting, potting, and the like—enables many people to experience flow. What's more, artistic endeavors can be both physically and emotionally healing. As we focus completely on an artistic act, studies show heart rate and respiration slow, and blood pressure lowers. But art's healing ability also stems, in part, from the way it can express deep-seated feelings that we might believe is inappropriate to express directly.

The artistic process is also particularly effective in helping us suspend linear thought and objective "clock time." As we interact with paints, paper, clay, pen, or pencil, we lose our self-consciousness and, instead, begin to tap the power of our unconscious.

When the project in which we are engaged is complete, we have something to show for it. And even if the end product is not as important as the process, it can be rewarding to have created something—even if we choose not to show it to anyone.

If you are intrigued by the idea of creating art but don't know where to begin ...

- Try visiting an art museum (move through it *slowly* and pay close attention) or looking through art books for inspiration.

- Look for other venues that might offer visual inspiration—such as botanical gardens or bird sanctuaries, or even a farmer's market chock-full of lusciously colorful fruits and vegetables.

- Don't worry about buying the best materials—start with the basics.

- Don't be afraid of simplicity—try some fundamental exercises such as drawing basic shapes.

- Don't be afraid of abstraction—art does not have to be a literal re-creation of what already exists.

- Make a space in your home to work (even a small desk or fold-out table) and organize around it the things you will need—so you can slip away during quiet moments and dive right into the process.

Finally, try to think back to a time in your life when you were genuinely excited about making art. You might have to go as far back as kindergarten, because much of our later schooling does not allow a lot of time for original artistic expression. But childlike exuberance is exactly the feeling you are after.

Glory in the Garden

If you know any gardening buffs, you may have witnessed the joy they attain from kneeling on the earth and digging their hands in dirt. They probably were never so happy since making mud pies as children. But it's not the mere physicality of gardening that captivates them. Gardening is also about the joy and satisfaction of nurturing. The gardener's planting and tending brings the beginnings of life to fruition. Their intense, caring focus enables blossoms to grow and thrive. And their labor results in beauty that all can share.

Moreover, environmental psychologists believe that spending time in those beautiful, natural surroundings can positively influence our state of mind. So a garden seems like a perfect venue for pursuing a quest for happiness and flow.

Of course, not everyone believes they have the requisite green thumb for this horticultural pursuit. But plants are *meant* to grow, and even if you've had a bad experience with the odd houseplant here and there, you can probably stage a comeback.

If you're just starting, start small. Even if you have more land than the Ponderosa, cordon off a manageable plot. If you live in an apartment and have no outdoor space, you might want to look into the availability of public gardening space—often sponsored by schools, churches, and statewide environmental organizations. If that's not an option, you can plant a small, simple garden in a window box; just find out which kinds of plants thrive in such quarters.

> **Happy Thought**
>
> "Happiness held is the seed; happiness shared is the flower."
>
> —Anonymous

Next, find something to plant that is not as temperamental as, say, rare orchids. Some types of flora require more care and feeding than others, so visit a nursery and ask for hearty plants that are more or less foolproof. You can also find out about the relative hardiness of various plants by perusing gardening books and magazines—a potentially enriching and diverting pastime in itself.

The Satisfaction of Sports

Many people say they are happiest when they are playing a game of golf, basketball, soccer, softball, or whatever their sport of choice. Whether they realize it or not, if they are playing well against evenly matched opponents and using their skills optimally, they are probably enjoying a state of flow. Time passes without them realizing it, and they are focused intensely on what is happening in the moment.

If you are adept at a sport, or were at some point, consider setting yourself the goal of getting better at it. However, if you consider yourself "sports challenged," don't despair. This condition might also describe several of your friends. If you take up a sport together, you will be evenly matched and can enjoy the process of the game without feeling self-conscious. You'll get a workout, share camaraderie and commiseration, perfect your technique (such as it is)—and laugh! That's a lot of happiness to be mined from one new activity.

The Joy of Being a Beginner

One can be an expert at doing something and, in doing it, create flow. And one has expert *knowledge* of a field—such as an aficionado of opera, a devotee of foreign films, or a connoisseur of fine wine—that elevates the act of appreciation to a peak experience. But even experts must start somewhere. At a certain point, everyone was a beginner.

Beginners, too, can enter a state of flow as they manifest an attitude of awe and wonder coupled with the excitement of entering unexplored terrain. Allowing yourself to be surprised by new thoughts, new ideas, and new sensory input can help you recall the world as it seemed to you when you were a child—a child who loved to play.

When you begin any new pursuit, don't give in to the urge to overaccessorize or overspend. Focus on the process itself rather than the status implied by its accouterments. Do consider taking some classes. They'll help you with basic techniques, help you build confidence, and allow you to meet others with similar interests.

But when you feel comfortable with the basics, plunge in. If you found something that you enjoy, that's good. If you have found a potential gateway to flow, so much the better. If what you're doing turns out *not* to be for you, you can chalk any project up to a learning experience—and start something new!

The Least You Need to Know

♦ Research shows that one of the most significant predictors of an individual's life satisfaction is how much time that person spends engaged in leisure activities.

♦ Though the leisure activities we select tend to be pleasurable, those that bring the most lasting happiness are activities that create the state of mind known as "flow."

♦ Flow is a state of heightened awareness in which an individual is challenged (but not frustrated) and so intently focused that they suspend self-consciousness and lose track of time.

♦ To find a potential flow activity, ask yourself what pursuits utilize your skills and inspire your curiosity, as well as what pursuits you enjoy doing more for your own sake rather than for a result or reward.

♦ If you are still unsure of your flow activity, don't be afraid to dabble and experiment until you discover it—beginners as well as experts can enter into flow.

The Happy Path of Spiritual Seeking

In This Chapter

◆ Positive psychology's growing interest in religion

◆ Religious path and the spiritual path comparison

◆ Spiritual beliefs enhancing happiness

◆ The role of prayer in happiness

◆ The role of ritual in happiness

In recent years the biggest media story concerning the human mind and religion has been the lively debate about humanity's genetic predisposition to seek out the divine. Noted scientists have contended that we are all programmed with a so-called "God gene." We are neurochemically "wired," they say, to create soothing stories of a benevolent higher power and an eternal afterlife—the better to swallow the bitter pill of our mortality. Theologians, on the other hand, take a different view of spiritually inclined genes. If we have God-seeking DNA, they say, it is part of a divine plan—a preordained biochemical boost to jump-start us on a journey to unite with the Almighty.

This is not a debate likely to come to a definitive resolution. But for practical purposes, that doesn't matter. Because whatever the reasons for human spirituality, spirituality is widely recognized by scientists and theologians alike as generating well-being and happiness.

Positive Psychology Looks at Religion

For thousands of years, human beings have turned, in times of distress and unhappiness, to the person in our community—shaman, monk, rabbi, or mullah—with spiritual credentials. We have sought guidance on how to live a rewarding life from spiritual texts, from the Hindu Vedas to the Koran to the Old and New Testaments. We have searched what we refer to as our souls to summon the hope and strength to rebound from troubling emotional events and cope with physical infirmities. Yet, until recently, neither medicine nor psychology had devoted much study to the effect of spiritual belief and practice on our physical and mental state.

In the United States, two prominent early psychologists expressed interest in certain religious and spiritual phenomena. William James was particularly interested in esoteric elements such as mysticism and trance states. G. Stanly Hall—who actually published a journal devoted to the psychology of religion in the early part of the nineteenth century—was interested in the religious and moral training of young people. But after Hall's journal ceased publication in 1915, religion largely disappeared as a subject of psychological study for several decades. Neither behaviorism, which looked at immediate forms of reinforcement as determinants of human behavior, nor the Freudian school of thought, which dismissed the longing for God as a displaced longing for an elusive, perfect father figure, gave any credence to what the power of belief could accomplish.

In the 1960s and 1970s, however, things began to change. Publications such as the *Journal for the Scientific Study of Religion* were founded. Empirical research began to accrue. And in 1975, the American Psychological Association created a division devoted to the psychology of religion.

> **Happiness Trivia**
>
> Ninety-four percent of HMO professionals agree that spiritual practice can enhance medical treatment.

In the medical field, interest in the power of spiritual belief also burgeoned in the latter part of the twentieth century. After noting the role of religious or spiritual beliefs in helping people counter the debilitating physical effects of stress, modern healers were converted to the idea that something as ethereal as faith could have profound physiological consequences.

Harvard University Medical School, along with similarly prestigious institutions, began holding conferences bringing together renowned physicians and religious scholars. And by 2006, two-thirds of America's medical schools had adopted courses on spirituality and health.

Psychologists, too, were intrigued by all the data showing correlations between spirituality and stress reduction. They began to wonder what other domains were impacted by spirituality and religious practice. Thanks to the influence of positive psychology, there was special interest in the link between individuals' life satisfaction and their sense of connectedness to something beyond their immediate, earthly existence. The data began to accumulate. It shows that religious involvement among adults predicts well-being and happiness.

But what, exactly, constitutes religious involvement? Does being spiritual, but not religious per se, "count" in terms of enhancing personal happiness?

Religion and Spirituality: What's the Difference?

If you are one of the more than 40 percent of Americans who attend religious services weekly, you may well get a happiness boost from doing so. But what if you are someone who believes in some sort of divine force—perhaps with great conviction—yet you do not participate, or participate only minimally, in a formal, organized religion? Will this particular path to happiness elude you?

The answer: not at all. You are hardly alone if you consider yourself "spiritual but not religious." And you needn't fear that not attending a church, mosque, synagogue, or temple on a regular basis will exclude you from the ranks of the spiritually satisfied.

Many Americans desire and manifest a divine-oriented element in their lives, although without the traditional religious context. Demographic research shows that the baby boomer generation dropped out of organized religion in unprecedented numbers (and 32 million boomers remain unaffiliated today). But they, along with members of ensuing generations who continue the trend, often say that they did not drop out because they had lost interest in this aspect of life. Rather they were seeking more personal pathways to meet their needs.

Being unaffiliated does not mean being unbelieving. Being "informally" spiritual is a deep source of satisfaction for millions:

◆ The majority of Americans not affiliated with a religious tradition say that they believe in God or some higher power.

◆ Almost a third of those unaffiliated with an organized religion say they pray at least occasionally.

◆ At least 1 in 10 religiously unaffiliated Americans pray daily or even more frequently.

On the other side of the coin, merely going to religious services regularly—without, so to speak, practicing what is preached—is not necessarily a path to happiness. In 1950, Harvard psychologist Gordon Allport, one of the few psychologists displaying an interest in the study of religion during that period, made a distinction between what he called *extrinsic* and *intrinsic religiosity*. A purely extrinsic orientation means participating in an institutionalized religion strictly because doing so provides approval and status. An intrinsic orientation involves taking the credo of one's religion to heart and striving to bring one's behavior into harmony with it.

For the purposes of achieving happiness, going through the motions of religion without commitment won't do. The happiness that grows from the spiritual path does not result from outward conformity. Whether you go to church or not, what impacts your happiness is the effect your belief system has on your worldview, your character, and your personal behavior choices.

Helping Hand

Attending worship services does not guarantee a path to happiness, but it certainly does not preclude it. In fact, attending religious services is an excellent means of obtaining social support within your community—which is, in itself, a boon to happiness and well-being. If you are both religiously observant in a formal way *and* have internalized the teachings of your religion, you may reap the benefits of both orientations.

What Spirituality Offers

Back in the seventeenth century, renowned mathematician and philosopher Blaise Pascal became consumed with the question of God's existence. He applied the mathematical decision theory to the question and came up with a famous philosophical gambit known as Pascal's Wager. In it, Pascal argued that it is always a better "bet" to believe in a divine power because a positive bet would yield more "expected value" than a negative bet.

Since Pascal's time, that "expected value" has, in fact, been documented by psychology, even if divine existence itself has not. The "payoffs" of belief are among the variables that impact personal happiness.

Inherent Meaning

Those with a belief in divine power are apt to view the world and their place in it as a coherent system that follows some sort of logical order. Even when things seem incomprehensible on the surface, the faith that sustains believers instills in them the conviction that although they may not understand the grand plan, there is indeed a plan that will unfold exactly as it should.

Acting on the premise that their life has inherent meaning—as opposed to asserting that all events are random—serves to help believers find a sense of purpose that infuses them with energy. They feel connected to something larger than themselves and understand their individual role as one that honors that connection.

> **Happy Thought**
>
> "There is enough light for those whose only desire is to see, and enough darkness for those of the opposite disposition."
>
> —Blaise Pascal

Having faith that everything *is* as it should be and *will* be as it should be appears not to instill fatalism in believers, but rather to instill optimism. Believers maintain a high degree of faith that everything will work out for the best, and studies show they are less "thrown" by potentially traumatic events such as unemployment, divorce, illness, and even the death of a loved one. Their fortitude comes not from denying or ignoring their problems, but rather from accepting them and finding ways to cope with them. In the end, they feel, all will turn out for the best.

The more literally believers take the worldview offered by their chosen faith, the more optimistic they appear to be. According to research conducted by a University of Pennsylvania student who distributed questionnaires to believers and analyzed sermons and liturgy from 11 prominent religions, fundamentalists in any faith tend to be the most positive and hopeful believers. According to the study, Fundamental Christians and Muslims, along with Orthodox Jews, are more optimistic than Reform Jews and Unitarians.

However, it does bear mentioning that, as with optimism, religious faith and thoughts of the next life should be tempered with pragmatism and tolerance to generate satisfaction in this life. To generate happiness, faith must derive from sincere devotion, rather than from a desire to control others.

Virtuous Values

Those who internalize the teachings of a particular religion, or of a general spiritual orientation that incorporates the lessons of many religions, tend not only to live more meaningful lives but also more virtuous ones. The virtues they embrace, if put into action, can build and reinforce character strengths that contribute to happiness. Among the virtues extolled by virtually all major religions are the following:

- ◆ Compassion
- ◆ Gratitude
- ◆ Charity
- ◆ Honesty
- ◆ Tolerance
- ◆ Reverence for life

Having a religious orientation does not ensure that one will always act in accordance with such values, but most religions offer clear guidelines meant to help those who stray return to the path of virtue. Codes of behavior such as those comprised by the Ten Commandments or the Eightfold Path of Buddhism spell out expectations for acceptable behavior that should result in leading a "good life."

Helping Hand _____

If you are uncertain what spiritual direction might hold the most meaning for you, exploring spiritual perspectives through reading can be a satisfying activity itself. You might choose from among traditional scriptures such as the Bible, the Koran, and the Hindu Bhagavad-Gita. Or you might consider books by contemporary spiritual leaders and commentators, such as the Dalai Lama, Marianne Williamson, Thomas Moore, or Deepak Chopra.

An Attitude of Awe

Believers are also apt to approach the world with a sense of wonder and awe. They are predisposed to seek out and recognize the sacred in the ordinary—from a blade of grass to a starry night. They tend to appreciate nature and to recognize beauty throughout creation.

Spiritual faith can even predispose one to believe in miracles. The idea that anything is possible can be sustaining in one's darkest moments.

Enhanced Self-Care

Finally, those with spiritual beliefs are likely to consider *themselves* something of a miracle—and therefore worthy of care and tending. Most religions exhort moderation in bodily pleasures and preach refraining from self-destructive actions.

Not surprisingly, religious Americans are less apt to abuse drugs, commit crimes, or commit suicide. Research documents that they are physically healthier than nonbelievers and live longer.

Praying for Happiness

One of the most widespread spiritual practices is the practice of prayer. In America, a far greater number of people pray on a regular basis than attend religious services on a regular basis. So, in addition to the communal prayer that is a standard part of worship services, there's obviously quite a bit of "freelance" praying going on.

Nearly all world religions consider some form of prayer a central element of the spiritual life. But can prayer make us happier? The answer appears to be yes.

> **Happy Thought**
>
> "There is a miracle somewhere: At the point where two very large nothings have united to form a very little something."
> —Samuel Butler

Some prayers specifically address happiness, as does this one by Robert Louis Stevenson:

> *Grant to us, O Lord, the royalty of inward happiness, and the serenity which comes from living close to thee. Daily renew in us the sense of joy, and let the eternal spirit of the Father dwell in our souls and bodies, filling every corner of our hearts with light and grace; so that, bearing about with us the infection of good courage, we may be diffusers of life, and may meet all ills and cross accidents with gallant and high-hearted happiness, giving thee thanks always for all things.*

And as does this traditional Buddhist prayer:

> *May all beings have happiness and the causes of happiness;*
>
> *May all be free from sorrow and the causes of sorrow;*
>
> *May all never be separated from the sacred happiness, which is sorrowless;*
>
> *And may all live in equanimity, without too much attachment and too much aversion;*
>
> *And live believing in the equality of all that lives.*

And as does this traditional Irish blessing:

> *May there always be work for your hands to do.*
> *May your purse always hold a coin or two.*
> *May the sun always shine upon your window pane.*
> *May a rainbow be certain to follow each rain.*
> *May the hand of a friend always be near to you, and*
> *May God fill your heart with gladness to cheer you.*

But prayers come in many forms. And all prayer can induce happiness by instilling a sense of peace and purpose in the person who prays. In fact, many scientific studies have validated the health effects of prayer. Some researchers speculate this is no miracle per se, but rather a reflection of the effect that prayer can have on bodily systems by inducing a state of mental tranquility.

Helping Hand _____

In need of a prayer? At the World Prayers Prayer Archive (www.worldprayers.org) you can randomly select a sacred verse from among the thousands that have been collected, or you can search for prayers by category (such as prayers for peace and healing), textual source, or particular tradition. Spiritual traditions whose prayers are cited include Christianity, Judaism, Buddhism, Islam, Jainism, Sikhism, Sufism, Taoism, and the Native American tradition.

The Rewards of "Centering Prayer"

In addition to prayers of supplication and petition, there are prayers of adoration, praise, offering, and devotion. There are prayers of celebration, positive affirmation, and thanksgiving. And there are meditative prayers that comprise contemplation and reflection. The latter type of prayer, especially a type of it known as "centering prayer," has lately drawn a lot of attention as a means of creating a positive inner state.

Centering prayer is an ancient Judeo-Christian means of communicating with the divine. It has been rediscovered by Western seekers who are looking to merge an interest in Eastern-type techniques with their own religious philosophy. The method differs from the ritualized and conversational prayers of traditional Christianity, and has more in common with meditation techniques. In centering prayer sessions, participants attempt to avoid an intellectual analysis of their experience. They harbor no expectations or goals other than stilling the mind so that they may experience a spiritual presence within. The idea is, essentially, to "rest in God."

To engage in centering prayer:

◆ Sit in a relaxed and quiet place.

◆ Silently affirm your faith in the presence of divine presence at the core of your being.

◆ Visualize this center in a way that feels appropriate to you, perhaps with an image of a spiritual prophet or with a symbol of divinity that has personal resonance (for example, the Christian symbol of a crucifix).

◆ Choose a word that, to you, signifies a manifestation of the divine (such as grace, love, mercy, Jesus).

◆ Repeat the chosen word while focusing your warm feelings toward your "center."

◆ Bring your attention back to your chosen word whenever your mind wanders.

Centering prayer, as with meditation, seems extremely simple on the surface, but does take effort of concentration. And as with meditation (the benefits of which are described in Chapter 9), its rewards are commensurate with the potency of the concentration that is achieved.

Helping Hand

As with meditation, it is often recommended that people engage in centering prayer twice a day for a period of 20 minutes or so. But it is certainly beneficial to begin with any amount of time that you can allocate. In addition, you can engage in this practice even for a few moments whenever and wherever you find it helpful in quieting negative thoughts.

Done regularly, say researchers who have studied centering prayer at Johns Hopkins and Duke universities, the practice can instill a sense of hope and personal control and foster a positive belief system.

Happy Rituals

Another type of spiritual practice that can add a sense of peace and positivity to our daily lives is weaving some manner of sacred ritual into routine activities.

Rituals can encompass a broad range of small and simple activities. But at the same time they can be symbolically profound. They can infuse pleasure into seemingly mundane tasks, and they can also provide us with a greater sense of meaning in our day-to-day lives.

To enhance your daily happiness, consider trying some of these daily spiritual rituals:

- Start each morning by stepping outdoors, breathing deeply, and acknowledging the potential of the new day.

- Begin the day with a series of stretches that celebrate the power and grace of your body and that remind you to stay flexible in attitude.

- Once a day, place a fresh flower on your kitchen counter or dining table—stop momentarily to note its beauty and sweet aroma.

- Transition from work time to home and family time by turning the car radio news *off* and turning *on* an inspirational or devotional musical selection.

- Transition to bedtime by turning off the TV and lighting a candle.

- End each day by writing in a gratitude journal.

Rituals offer a respite from the ongoing barrage of thoughts, feelings, and worries that continually flow through our busy minds and resonate in our bodies. Rituals anchor us in the present moment, renew and restore us, and nourish our sense of awe. In short they can remind us to be happy.

The Least You Need to Know

- Modern psychology and medicine are embracing the ancient idea that spirituality can enhance emotional and physical well-being.

- Even those who do not participate in a formal religion or attend regular worship services can be deeply spiritual in their attitudes, outlook, and behavior.

- A spiritual perspective can enhance happiness by creating a sense of meaning and coherency, by instilling virtuous values and a sense of awe, and by inspiring believers to take good care of themselves.

- All types of prayer can engender positive emotions by creating a state of mental tranquility; centering prayer, in particular, can create many of the same happiness-related benefits as meditation.

- Spiritual rituals—pleasant breaks in the day that are simple on the surface but symbolically profound—can also lift our spirits by calming us and restoring perspective.

Part 4

Happy at Work

Some people think of work as a four-letter word; others view it simply as a means to accrue money or power. Yet work can also be a source of deep personal satisfaction. In this part of the book, you'll learn how the principles of positive psychology are being increasingly applied in the workplace. The goals of this new approach include increased employee involvement, constructive communication, and more creative thinking by individuals and teams.

Chapter 12

When Work Feels Like Play

In This Chapter

- ◆ Focusing on strengths at work
- ◆ Finding flow on the job
- ◆ Using social skills at work
- ◆ Being optimistic at work
- ◆ Relating work happiness to life happiness

Work can be a great source of satisfaction—or not. When we're fortunate enough to have work that brings pleasure, meaning, and purpose, our entire life takes on a more positive quality. That's not just because we spend so much time at work, but also because so much of our identity is wrapped up in our work.

Anyone who's ever worked a day knows, too, that work can be a great source of dissatisfaction and of high levels of stress. Of course we can't control everything that happens at work. But, as this chapter explores, to the extent we can control our approach to our work and our attitudes surrounding it, we will be happier on the job, and off.

Doing What You Do Best

A basic explanation of work is that it is something people do to make money. But if money were the only reason to work, then job satisfaction would go up as income goes up. We'd expect to find that the more you make, the happier you are—every lawyer would be happier than every teacher, and every investment banker would be happier than every hairdresser. But such is not necessarily the case. Job satisfaction has many determinants. Among those that figure prominently is that people want to feel they are doing something they are good at.

The Gallup polling organization decided it could learn a lot about how happy people were at work by asking the question, "Do you get to do what you do best every day?" But only 20 percent of the thousands of people surveyed answered yes. *Those* people loved their jobs. The implication is that if more people did what they did best when they were at work, more people would be enthusiastic about working.

After analyzing the results of their survey, the Gallup organization concluded that we can get more satisfaction from work by spending more time at work using our most potent skills and strengths. Positive psychologists agree. What we do well, we should find ways to do more of. That's a better use of our time than trying to make up for deficits in other areas. For example, if our job involves making client presentations (which we love and are good at) and cold calling prospective clients on the phone (which we loathe and aren't good at), we're better off honing our presentation skills than trying to improve our phone skills.

But positive psychologists are certainly mindful that work is about more than doing what feels good for the sake of the feeling. A strengths-based approach to one's work is also about measurable success. Research shows that, in many cases, capitalizing on strengths is a far more effective route to success than trying to shore up weaknesses.

Helping Hand _____

The Gallup organization offers an assessment called the StrengthsFinder to help organizations identify the strengths of their employees and harness their power. The StrengthsFinder measures an individual's talents as related to 34 central themes. The web-based questionnaire contains 180 items and takes about 40 minutes to complete. It can be purchased online at www.strengthsfinder.com.

Finding Flow on the Job

Suppose you are unsure what strengths to cultivate. A good first step in determining which of your skills might make you happier and more successful at work is considering what you do in other areas of your life that puts you into a state of flow. A flow state, as described in Chapter 10, is one in which you are fully focused and engaged in working to the height of your ability, often to the extent where hours spent on a particular activity can seem like mere minutes.

Look especially to areas where you exercise creativity in any manner. Do you like to write, for example? Look for opportunities to write more on the job. At first you might not imagine what writing reports at work might have in common with penning haiku in your spare time. But writing anything at all uses a skill set that involves the selection and ordering of words and the organization of information.

Do you enjoy building things and "puttering"? Look for opportunities where you can use this craftiness and inventiveness. Think about what tools or products you use or produce at work. Can you think of ways to improve upon them or use them more efficiently?

To enhance your potential for on-the-job flow, look for areas that you are interested in learning more about. Are these areas of interest applicable to your job? Is there any aspect of your job or industry you would be excited to learn more about? Or do you want to improve upon any of your work-related skills?

Stumbling Blocks

Flow is a very personal matter. One man's flow can be another man's phobia. One person might relish the idea of teaching a roomful of sixth-graders because they love the challenge of holding people's attention. Another might have a better time getting a root canal. One person might relish the daily roller coaster ride of an air traffic controller because they love employing spatial skills at a rapid pace. Another person might view such a job as heart attack fodder.

Don't wait for anyone to invite you to learn more. Being creative is partly about creating your own opportunities. Take a class, read a book, sign up for an online course. In this time of fast-paced change, employers reward people who are self-motivated to learn. Today, certain kinds of information can seemingly become obsolete in a heartbeat, but the love of learning itself will never be obsolete.

Helping Hand

For most people, the complete elimination of boredom or tedious tasks at work is an unrealistic dream. The trick is to look for positive aspects of the situation to neutralize negative aspects. For example: *I don't like filling out forms, but after I do this paperwork I'll have the resources to complete my project.*

Of course, looking for chances to flow at work is not a license to ignore the parts of a job that are necessary but perhaps not—for you—the most challenging or riveting. In the vast majority of cases, this wouldn't be very pragmatic. If you are a personal trainer who loves training but hates scheduling appointments, you'll quickly run out of clients to train.

However, if we use even 10 percent of our time at work each day exercising our strengths and talents in a way that contributes to flow, we will be ahead of the game, having gone a great way toward increasing our happiness and our effectiveness.

Eyes on the Prize

Using goal-oriented strengths is another way to increase personal satisfaction at work. While flow is about experiencing the joy of the moment, setting satisfying goals is about the positive anticipation of the future. Put another way, flow is about pleasure and meaning. Goals are about purpose.

Goals can be classified as intrinsic or extrinsic. The intrinsic ones have to do with our personal values (*I want to make this presentation so engaging that it will be my most effective talk ever*). The extrinsic ones have to do with meeting the expectations of others (*I have to get these slides done by Tuesday so my boss can approve them before Thursday's meeting*).

Meeting intrinsic goals is more likely to result in a sense of happiness and well-being than meeting extrinsic ones. But realistically, any work setting is going to involve meeting other people's goals as well as your own. If you can do both at the same time, your happiness will still be enhanced. So, for example, you can make it a goal to organize the best possible presentation you can by Tuesday—and make it so good that your boss won't want to change a thing.

Any goal-oriented strengths you may possess, such as conscientiousness and perseverance, can be brought to bear on any goal. No matter what you're doing, for example, make a point of doing it expertly and thoroughly, and stick with it until the job is complete. Using your goal-related strengths will be an expression of the values you hold dear, and will also contribute to accomplishment.

Workplace coaches, who use the principles of positive psychology to help their clients increase their success, satisfaction, and enjoyment at work, suggest some strategies when it comes to work-related goals.

The first is to set both short-term and long-term goals. Short-term goals help us continually hone our skills and remind us that we are capable of doing what we set out to do. But long-term goals fuel our hopes and dreams. It can help to use as role models for the latter those who have achieved long-term goals worth waiting for. For example, Walt Disney had the vision of Disneyland when he was a young father accompanying his daughters to what he considered subpar amusement parks. It took him 15 years to bring his dream park to fruition—but 30,000 people visited it on opening day.

Don't overfocus on material goals. Again and again, research shows that mere monetary success does not equate to life satisfaction. There's nothing inherently wrong with making money or working toward a goal of getting a bonus, a raise, a promotion— or all three! But people tend to be happier when material success is a by-product of an intrinsic goal, such as creating something innovative or providing a needed service to others.

Don't let passing emotions get in the way of your goals. It's easy to become distracted or unproductive because of anxiety, boredom, or even resentment of someone else's achievements. But drawing on valued character strengths such as personal reliability, commitment to excellence, and internal motivation can stabilize your attitude and get you over the ups and downs of frustrating days.

Apply your strengths most to what matters most. Work, being as busy and multi-faceted as it is, will often involve meeting numerous goals. With only so many hours in the day, it's necessary to prioritize. Examine the intrinsic and extrinsic value of your goals to determine which one gets the extra push—and when.

Finally, don't let insecurity divert you from your goals. The more goals someone achieves, the more goals they are likely to achieve in the future. To quote Body Shop founder Anita Roddick, "If you ever think you're too small to be effective, you've never been in bed with a mosquito."

 Happy Thought _____

"Excellence is the gradual result of always striving to do better."
—Pat Riley

"Doing the best at this moment puts you in the best place for the next moment."
—Oprah Winfrey

People Power

Interpersonal strengths—abilities that have to do with compassion, cooperation, and collaboration—are of paramount importance to people seeking satisfaction in the workplace. Positive and productive work relationships not only help the individuals who cultivate them but help the entire organization create and sustain a more positive culture.

Organizational psychologists who specialize in workplace dynamics note that organizations depend not only on the strengths of their individual members for success but also on the strengths of the interactions between workmates, team members, and supervisors and supervisees. High-quality personal connections don't just evolve by chance. They are the outgrowth of attitudes and actions by people who are good at developing and maintaining them.

Friendships That Work

Interpersonal strengths such as empathy, fairness, trust, kindness, loyalty, and genuineness all contribute to an individual's ability to forge and sustain workplace friendships. People strong in social skills have a way of connecting with co-workers. They can readily identify and bond with other individuals who are a "good fit" and nurture the relationships in ways that will be mutually beneficial.

Having friends, in general, is a significant contributor to happiness. But friends at work can play a special role. In addition to being a source of encouragement and camaraderie, work friends can be a kind of pressure release valve. When stressors pile up—as they do in even the best work environments—friends can take a break and share a quick laugh or engage in casual banter about anything from sports to shopping. They can also plan to duck out for lunch or get together when the day is done. Brief social forays such as this can make tedious tasks, cranky clients, and similar workplace pitfalls eminently easier to deal with. In fact, engaging in a few minutes of positive social contact is one of the best-known methods of relieving stress.

Helping Hand

Friendships at work are more sustainable when they are based on common interests and skills and a shared sense of humor than when they are based on gossip about others or about complaints about "common enemies." A continual diet of gripe sessions has been shown to make people angrier, not happier.

Workplace friends who are honest and genuine with one another can also serve as excellent sounding boards. They'll help each other do reality checks. They're a great resource for trying out ideas. And they'll also tell each other if they're overreacting to some minor frustration.

Becoming a Team Player

Whether or not you're officially designated as a member of a team, most work is, in some sense, teamwork. Unless you're a lighthouse keeper, most people's work requires pooling efforts and sharing ideas in a give-and-take process.

People with interpersonal strengths are adept when it comes to working collaboratively, even in situations when their teammates are not their friends or their favorite co-workers. There are several ways to sidestep negativity, even in tough situations.

Avoid black-and-white thinking. Few work-related decisions involve choosing between an all-good scenario and an all-bad one. If they did, work would be a piece of cake. Part of being a productive team member is being patient and open-minded enough to look at all the pros and cons, and flexible enough to synthesize solutions based on everyone's input.

Trust the people you work with. Even if you and your co-workers are not "best friends forever," approach your colleagues with an attitude of trust. Unless you have been given repeated, irrefutable evidence that someone is untrustworthy, offer them the benefit of the doubt. Trust is a calculated risk, but if you extend trust with the expectation of success, it will often produce success. Trust breeds trust; mistrust breeds mistrust.

> **Stumbling Blocks**
>
> Studies show that low-trust environments lead to low morale and unresolved conflict, not to mention dissatisfied customers. The bad experience for customers in turn has a negative effect on the bottom-line. And the lack of success can contribute to a vicious cycle of even *more* mistrust.

People with interpersonal strengths are good listeners. They listen with careful attention. They are sincerely curious and engaged when someone else is speaking. This sort of active listening gives them a chance to obtain valuable knowledge, and also make the person speaking feel more positively inclined toward the listener. Most of us have an inner radar system of sorts that can tell whether our words are falling on receptive ears or just getting the "nod treatment."

Don't jump to conclusions. Often the first response that occurs to us when we are feeling frustrated isn't the wisest or sanest one, or the one most likely to produce positive results. There is a reason why processes such as diplomatic negotiations and labor contract talks take a long time. People with interpersonal strengths still have very personal emotional responses to events, but they do not let impulsive feelings rule when there is a lot at stake. They allow time for rational thinking to prevail.

They also see the big picture and are willing to sacrifice short-term wins for long-term goals. Resist the temptation to "yes" others along and tell them what they want to hear just so they can come up with an easy fix. If your focus is on getting things right, you'll be able to tolerate intermittent uncertainty and even intermittent conflict.

Recognize and acknowledge the efforts and contributions of your colleagues and celebrate their accomplishments. Refrain from grandstanding and always give credit where credit is due.

Be ready and willing to mend fences, not only to forgive but also to ask forgiveness when necessary. If you know how open wounds can fester, you'll take personal responsibility and make amends when you've been at fault.

Happy Thought

"The most important measure of how good a game I played was how much better I'd made my teammates play."
—Bill Russell

Keep your sense of humor! People with interpersonal strengths often use humor to bond with others and to ease tension. They know better than to laugh at others or at the expense of others, however. They are especially apt to use self-deprecating humor. They know they won't offend anyone else if they are targeting their own foibles.

Perhaps most importantly, people with interpersonal character strengths refrain from trying to control other people. For one thing, they don't need to control others to feel positive about themselves. For another thing, they tend to be pragmatic. They understand that unless they have a bona fide magic wand, it would be impossible for them to change anyone other than themselves. They are, however, willing to modify their own behavior to alter the dynamics of their interactions for the better.

Optimism at Work

Having an optimistic disposition goes hand in hand with personal happiness. But is it a good idea to be optimistic at work? The answer appears to be yes, but with some caveats.

First, for the "yes" part. As in other areas of life, research tends to link optimism with increased success on the job. Martin Seligman notes that optimists tend to do better at work than their talents alone would suggest. And management literature abounds with case studies of optimistic leaders who brought their organizations to new heights.

Optimists are more likely to solve problems on the job because they see them as opportunities for bringing about beneficial change. Their desire to achieve positive outcomes, as opposed to the pessimist's desire to avoid negative ones, leads to greater persistence, greater flexibility in strategy, and increased creativity. And, yes, it also leads to more positive outcomes. Certainly optimists can fail, but if they succeed even part of the time, they're ahead of pessimists who never try.

Happiness Trivia

Optimism portends increased success in every field except law. When positive psychologist Martin Seligman surveyed law students at the University of Virginia, he found that pessimists got better grades, were more likely to make law review, and, upon graduation, received better job offers. Seligman offered no scientific reason. "In law," he noted, "pessimism is considered prudence."

But now for those caveats. Optimists, as *The Wall Street Journal* reports, sometimes don't come across so positively to people who work for them and with them. Employees who report to optimists sometimes say their bosses are denying unpleasant realities and falsely believe that more can be done with less. When someone counters the boss's optimistic credo, they are summarily labeled a pessimist, which has come to connote "an uncooperative nay-sayer" or, worse, "a slacker." (And because optimists get more promotions than pessimists, this label certainly does not bode well.)

In addition, some business commentators have linked optimism to disastrous business and fiscal policies. The subprime mortgage mess, it has been suggested, was an outgrowth of outrageous optimism on the part of mortgage lenders that housing prices would continue their exponential rise indefinitely.

As with almost anything, optimism in the workplace can be taken to unreasonable and unrealistic extremes. It's not hard to see why employees fail to get onboard with supervisors who set ill-considered goals and then expect their reports to put in all the effort to meet those goals—while they move on to envisioning even more unrealistic schemes. And it's easy to see how ill-advised policies can be conceived when cock-eyed optimism—tinged with greed—leads professionals who should know better than to refrain from seeking knowledge and to vastly underestimate legitimate risk.

People in the workplace who fly the banner of optimism to justify a lack of account-ability give genuine, realistic optimists a bad name. But this is no reason for sincerely optimistic workers to abandon their personal realistic optimism. Realistic optimism is associated with a *greater* desire to obtain information about how to reach goals and with selection of more attainable aspirations. It's also associated with greater internal motivation rather than pass-the-buck delegation.

The bottom line: if you are a realistic optimist, take your optimistic attitude to work every day. Your upbeat disposition will help you mobilize all your other strengths, will lessen your stress, will help you focus on the most positive elements of your environment, and will help you make meaningful contributions.

If anyone around you seems irritated by your optimism, use your empathic social skills and try to see the world from their vantage point for a minute. It could be they are just not in the mood right now to look on the bright side. Maybe they just need to feel bad for a little while, so they can feel better later. In the meantime, you can have all the optimistic thoughts you like.

How Happy Can Work Make You?

This chapter began by stating that when we are fortunate enough to have work that brings us pleasure, meaning, and purpose, our entire life takes on a more positive quality. But just how happy can our work make us?

Work as a Percentage of Life Satisfaction

Research confirms what we might intuitively suspect: that there is a reciprocal influence between job satisfaction and life satisfaction. In other words, satisfaction with one's work tends to make one's life happier overall, and those satisfied with their life overall tend to be happier at work. As in many fields of research, however, investigators disagree about the degree to which job happiness affects life happiness and vice versa.

A study by the Russell Sage Foundation on American quality of life attempted to quantify the relationship. It concluded that work satisfaction accounted for 20 to 25 percent of overall life satisfaction. Although on the face of it this might not seem like a high number, one can appreciate its relative magnitude by considering the many other variables that can impact our happiness—including marital status, social support, health, and so on.

Of course not everyone will have the same proportion of ingredients in their personal happiness recipe.

Job, Career, or Calling?

One factor that could make work more or less significant to someone than the estimated percentage is whether they consider their work a job, a career, or a calling. A study identifying attitudes toward work noted that these are the three primary ways in which individuals in the Western world view what they do for a living:

A job is something one does to earn money. The compensation is of primary interest and the main motivation.

A career is a vocational path with an upward trajectory. The focus is on development, advancement, promotions—in general, on getting to the next level.

A calling is something people feel they were meant to do. Those who see their work as a calling also feel that in doing it they are contributing to the greater good. People who view their work as a calling ascribe the highest degree of meaning to their work. They affiliate it with a higher purpose. And compared to those who see themselves as having jobs, or even careers, they see their work as a great source of joy.

Not everyone may feel they have a calling. That does not mean they cannot be happy at work. People can make friends and use their skills at a job. People can accomplish a great many goals and do a great deal of good in the course of their careers. But even considering what one's calling might be can increase one's potential for happiness.

To do so, return to considering your character strengths and your talents. Ask yourself how you can employ your traits and skills to help others, to further a cause you believe in, or to make the world a better place in some way.

The Least You Need to Know

♦ Increasing the amount of time spent doing what we do best on the job, and cultivating "flow" at work, will increase satisfaction.

♦ Setting and meeting goals is a way to continually improve skills and to keep work-related aspirations alive—but to truly increase happiness, goals should offer more than monetary ends.

♦ Using social strengths at work helps improve the work experience by building stress-relieving friendships and enabling successful collaboration even with those who are not necessarily friends.

◆ In general, optimists are more successful at work than pessimists—but workplace optimism must be grounded in realism to be effective.

◆ Research shows that work can account for as much as a fifth to a quarter of our overall life satisfaction—we tend to take the most satisfaction from work we consider to be our true calling.

Chapter 13

Positivity and Productivity

In This Chapter

- ◆ Expressing gratitude in the workplace
- ◆ Building positive cultures through trust
- ◆ Benefiting from organizational honesty
- ◆ Having leaders as character role models
- ◆ Learning positive responses to organizational crisis

Positive psychology is extremely concerned with the issue of individual character. But organizations also have character. When an organization embodies positive attributes and positive values, that's good for its workforce, good for its customers, and—as savvy business leaders have not failed to notice—good for the bottom-line.

This chapter looks at some key organizational values and examines how they're being put into action to make the workplace more emotionally satisfying *and* more profitable.

Acknowledging What Goes Right

Organizations typically expend a good deal of effort examining how and why things go wrong. Organizational leaders routinely diagnose problems and search for prescriptive measures to counter them. They ask, "Why was our forecast off? Why did we not win that contract? Why aren't we getting better recruits?" It's all an effort to avoid the same problems in the future.

This is certainly a sensible approach to self-scrutiny. After all, it would be foolhardy for forward-looking organizations to repeat past mistakes.

But in recent years, many progressive organizations have borrowed a page from positive psychology's book, expanding their self-examination to ask, "What are we doing right?" And they have initiated efforts to recognize employees who have contributed to their successes. In doing these things, organizations have begun to tap the power of gratitude.

Appreciative Inquiry

Appreciative inquiry (*AI*) is a positive practice that is becoming increasingly common in businesses, health-care systems, educational institutions, local governments, and religious institutions. It's a method of examining an organization to see what works well and what its *life-giving forces* (*LGFs*) consist of. The idea is that every organization must be doing *some* things right. By identifying those things through appreciative inquiry, its future can be brighter.

def•i•ni•tion

Appreciative inquiry (AI) is an organizational development strategy that was originally the brainchild of David Cooperrider and Suresh Srivastva of Case Western University's Weatherhead School of Management. The AI process focuses on what things an organization does best.

Life-giving forces (LGFs) refers to the unique structure and processes of an organization that makes its very existence possible. LGFs can be ideas, beliefs, or values.

Appreciative inquiry uses a four-stage process:

1. **Discovery:** Identifying the organizational processes that work best.

2. **Dreaming:** Envisioning of processes that would work well in the future.

3. **Design:** Planning and prioritizing processes that would work well.

4. **Delivery:** Implementing the positive processes.

Appreciative inquiry is a highly inclusive process. It is based on the value of equality and acknowledges the importance of community. During the course of the inquiry process, hundreds or even thousands of people involved with the organization in various capacities were asked about their vision of what is positive and what is possible. Ideally, the process itself fosters positive relationships and inspires people to creatively build on the strengths and goodness already in the system.

But appreciative inquiry is as much about unique individuals as it is about the community they form. AI also seeks to discover each person's exceptionality. What are their gifts and their outstanding qualities? The process actively recognizes people for their achievements and for their contributions.

The Power of Praise

In general, today's employers praise their employees more in the belief that positive recognition enhances performance and increases loyalty. Studies show that saying "thank you" works. And for those to whom the expression of gratitude at work does not come so easily, there are even management consulting services specifically designed to teach the finer points of praise.

In recognition of the positive power of gratitude, many companies have implemented creative praise programs. Some require their managers to write a certain number of praise or thank-you notes to underlings every year. Universal Studios Orlando, with 13,000 employees, has a program in which managers give out "Applause Notes," praising employees for work well done. Universal workers can also give each other peer-to-peer "S.A.Y. It!" cards, which stand for "Someone Appreciates You!" The notes are redeemed for free movie tickets or other gifts, but the sentiment carries emotional weight.

A caveat when it come to praise: positive psychologists stipulate that at work, as in school and at home, praise that is baseless, highly exaggerated, or disproportionate will not lead to personal satisfaction nor translate into motivation to develop one's strengths. Praise must be tied to actual achievement to generate happiness and an increased sense of self-efficacy. When praise is earned, the person who earned it will feel that what they've done is significant and meaningful.

Nevertheless, organizations are learning the potency inherent in offering positive feedback for a job genuinely well-done. Even a simple text message that says, "Your presentation was great," can have lasting positive repercussions. When positive behavior is recognized, more of the same tends to follow.

Stumbling Blocks _____

Different age groups appear to have different expectations for praise. In some cases, praise has become an intergenerational sticking spot. Some older employees have been reluctant to praise in the workplace because they themselves were not praised for their efforts. As one 60-year-old law firm partner told *The Wall Street Journal*, when he was a young attorney, "If you weren't getting yelled at, you felt like that was praise."

Some positive psychologists believe that this resistance to praise can be overcome if supervisors are coached to avoid loading their praise with emotional content. Their advice: comment strictly on behavior and its outcomes. Don't overpersonalize workplace praise.

Trust: Empowering Employees

Trusting employees to evaluate options and make decisions is another practice increasingly favored by successful organizations. Positive psychologists believe that when employees are empowered to make decisions about aspects of their work that directly affect them, they feel a sense of belonging, competence, and control—all of which are highly motivating. In addition, research shows that people feel more positively about any decision that is ultimately made if they believe they have had a voice in it.

Happy Thought _____

"Organizations are more likely to instill 'want to' attitudes in people if they nurture three factors, namely 'I belong' feelings, 'can do' beliefs, and an 'I'm responsible' or 'I'm allowed' mindset."

—Alan McLean, educational psychologist

Some managers are more inclined to trust than others. According to prevailing leadership theory, whether managers take a participative-democratic approach or a directive "hand down the edicts" approach depends on the assumptions they make about human nature. According to this theory, managers can be categorized as either Theory X managers or Theory Y managers:

- Theory X managers assume that workers are lazy, prone to mistakes, and motivated predominantly by money.

- Theory Y managers assume that people are inherently motivated to work for reasons that go beyond financial—for self-fulfillment and because they enjoy satisfying relationships with their co-workers.

In short, Theory Y managers take a more positive view of humanity. They're far more likely to give employees direct control over work procedures and welcome their participation in decision-making. They believe that when employees are given challenges and the discretion to meet those challenges however they see fit, they will demonstrate their competence and their creativity.

Theory X managers, as an outgrowth of their assumptions, closely monitor those who report to them. They assign tasks they feel are relatively simple to complete as opposed to those that might pose a challenge. And their idea of incentivizing people begins and ends with the prospect of monetary reward.

The outcomes of these differing attitudes have been clearly demonstrated time and again. Theory Y managers have employees who are more creative and more satisfied. Theory Y is now the guiding force behind the contemporary movement by many organizations to empower employees and to trust the decisions they make.

Happiness Trivia

Harley Davidson's success story is frequently cited in business literature as an example of a company that increased profitability by abandoning a command-and-control style of management and by pushing planning and strategizing down through the organization. In the mid-1990s Harley signed a cooperative agreement with unions assuring worker input in decision-making in virtually every aspect of the business. Every $1 worth of Harley Davidson stock purchased in 1987 was worth $150 by the end of 2002.

The Culture of Open Communication

Nowadays one hears a great deal about *transparency* in organizations. The term connotes an open informational structure in which policies and practices are visible to all interested parties. Transparency in the workplace is in part an outgrowth of technology. Even if those in positions of power wanted to hoard information, it is increasingly difficult to do so, given the ubiquity of online forums, blogs, and chat rooms, not to mention universal and instant electronic access to financial reports.

But for organizations with positive character, transparency is more than a necessary reaction to technology. It is also a proactive philosophy, an outgrowth of a value system that embraces honesty. The more honest and open the communications within an organization, the more trusting employees are—and the better they perform.

Happy Thought _____

"When the world is opaque and you can't see beyond people's personal proxies, there is a Certainty Gap in your interactions with them. But when active transparency is in the room and people show you what's behind the curtain, it raises the floor, the Gap is smaller, and the conditions that breed the trust you need to fill it rush in."

—Dov Seidman, chairman and CEO, LRN

Communicating the "Why"

One significant factor in an individual's satisfaction at work is the sense that they are actively working toward some known purpose (other than the pragmatic purpose of getting a paycheck). Workers want to know *why* they are being asked to do what they are being asked to do in the way they are being asked to do it.

In the best-case scenario, employees participate in decisions that impact what they do on a daily basis. Some decisions about larger organizational matters will still inevitably be made at higher levels, but if universal participation in a decision is not feasible, the next best thing is for decision-makers to be forthright not only about what was decided but why.

A study conducted by Phillip G. Clampitt, a consultant and communications professor at the University of Wisconsin at Green Bay, surveyed some 300 managers and employees at more than 100 U.S. employers, asking what they knew of decisions and how supportive they were of them. The study concluded that employees of companies that more fully explained decisions were more than twice as likely to support those decisions as workers who got less information.

Stumbling Blocks _____

Although transparency about motives and rationales behind decisions has been shown to create positive employee attitudes, some executives feel they are too busy to explain their thinking—or that their reasons should be obvious. Nonetheless, time devoted to open discussion of "why" is time well spent, because positive attitudes translate to productive performance.

Professor Clampitt suggests that decision-makers explain new initiatives to workers by telling them …

- How the decision was reached.

- The reasons underlying it.

- What alternatives were considered and rejected.

- How the decision fits into the organization's overall vision and mission.

- What changes it will mean for the organization.

- How it will directly affect employees.

Satisfaction blossoms when purpose is clear. And the most effective organizations know that honesty about motive and means must not only be genuine, but also specific. To generate positive attitudes and positive outcomes, it's not enough to link a decision to a value in name only. Saying, "We are changing your compensation to drive innovation," or, "We are reorganizing your department to improve quality," is not exactly inspiring. To embrace a united purpose, people want to see how A connects to B.

Keeping Daily Tasks Relevant

In the most effective organizations, honesty from the top also drives interpersonal honesty at every level. On a daily basis, positive, productive employees want to know not only "why" but "how." *How will we be working together? How can what I do each day further the greater goal?*

When daily tasks seem mindless and meaningless, demoralization sets in. Management consultants employing a positive-psychology approach believe that, ideally, every direct supervisor in an organization should, within reason, tie daily tasks to the big picture. They should also be honest about the expectations surrounding those tasks: what's needed and when?

Nearly everyone in the workplace can tell tales about the boss who repeatedly insisted they needed a particular piece of business on their desk by noon, only to ignore it for days—if they ever acknowledged it at all. These artificial deadlines—essentially a form of crying wolf—have been shown to drive lethargy and apathy. They create undue stress and spark a "can't do" attitude. Employees typically approach a falsely urgent task by determining what *cannot* be accomplished rather than what can.

Helping Hand

Organizations can boost employee satisfaction by spelling out expectations. At Intuit, the California-based maker of Quicken, TurboTax, and other money-management software, CEO Steve Bennett urges his managers to create a "psychological contract" with every employee, spelling out what is expected of them, how well they are performing, and precisely what they need to do to advance.

The bottom line: a lack of transparency about the purpose of tasks and their relative urgency dilutes meaning. Positive organizations attempt to avoid communication patterns that lead to the triumph of the "urgent" over the "important."

Bad News Beats No News

Creating active engagement can also be facilitated when knowledge is not only shared, but also shared in a timely manner. Research shows that work and work attitudes suffer during periods of extended waiting and uncertainty. Whether it is waiting to learn about key decisions affecting the fate of the organization or waiting for feedback with regard to one's own actions, drawn-out periods devoid of meaningful information lead to boredom, frustration, and rumormongering.

Studies show that when it comes to an individual's level of happiness, it's apparently better to receive bad news than no news at all. People given bad news can begin to adjust; people facing uncertain outcomes have nothing to adjust *to*. They may feel paralyzed and resist taking any action on any matters whatsoever while their uncertain waiting endures. Or they might do something destructive rather than constructive—simply for the sake of doing *anything* at all.

Happiness Trivia

Long waits have been shown to compel people to make impulsive decisions with negative consequences. In a study conducted by Gregory Burns, associate professor of psychiatry and behavioral sciences at Emory University, subjects were given a choice of receiving an electric shock now or a lesser shock after waiting. Roughly a third opted for more voltage sooner. This urge to put potential pain behind us is the same impulse that causes some employees to "fire themselves" at the mere possibility that they might be laid off.

Leadership: Character in Motion

The character of an organization depends on its community and its culture. But its character is *embodied* by its leader. All leaders lead by example, whether they mean to or not. Leaders set the standards for individuals in their organizations to emulate.

Strengths of Positive Leaders

When leaders are detached, intimidating, or self-serving, their behavior sends negative emotional messages that take their toll on the organization. Those who work for such bosses say they have learned to be extremely self-protective. They are reluctant to share knowledge or to generate new ideas. According to psychologist Daniel Goleman, an expert in the areas of social and emotional intelligence, leaders with these characteristics can cause "emotional distress that impairs the brain's mechanism to learn and think clearly."

But when leaders make a conscious effort to imbue positive values in their organization, those values create a ripple effect. They resonate exponentially, making what's good about the organization even better.

Although not every positive leader has been exposed to positive psychology per se, many positive psychologists who specialize in organizational coaching stipulate that the best way to spread positive psychology-based practices throughout an organization is to start with a leader who is innately positive.

Positive leaders model and instill positive values by …

- Sharing information rather than hoarding it.
- Having transparent motives rather than hidden agendas.
- Empowering individuals to make decisions.
- Communicating clearly about goals and expectations.
- Acknowledging and rewarding achievement.
- Conveying a sense of enthusiasm and optimism.
- Building relationships and conveying a sense of connection.
- Fostering a sense of positive purpose.

None of this is to say, however, that effective leaders coddle those who work for them. As with effective parents and teachers, they don't squander praise and they are not afraid to offer constructive corrections. They know that one of their most important jobs is to continually challenge everyone in their organization to improve.

Reputation and Social Responsibility

Positive leaders also help an organization by enhancing its reputation in the world at large. A company's reputation, the most commonly held perception of an organization's values and character, is an intangible but invaluable commodity. A form of psychological capital, it impacts virtually every level of a decision about whether or

Happy Thought

"I start with the premise that the function of leadership is to produce more leaders, not more followers."

—Ralph Nader

not people outside the organization want to interact with it: do they want to be its employees, its customers, its business partners, or stakeholders of any kind? That depends on its reputation.

Research shows that a leader who embodies an attitude of altruism is especially effective in boosting an organization's reputation. Social responsibility, as *The Wall Street Journal* notes, "is becoming an ever more critical component of corporate reputation." For example, Microsoft's ascension to the topmost rank in the 2007 *Harris Interactive/The Wall Street Journal* ranking of the world's best and worst corporate reputations was ascribed to Bill Gates' increasing involvement in his philanthropic foundation.

Most people find it difficult to separate the qualities of leaders from the qualities of their organizations. A socially responsible leader inevitably translates into the perception of an organization as a caring, character-driven entity. Just as an attitude of altruism turns out to be its own reward in private life, where it generates enhanced personal well-being, so it does in public life. In the wider world, altruism not only does genuine good—it also translates into a competitive edge.

Positive Actions in Crisis

Individuals who are positive and character-driven are not immune to crisis, and neither are organizations. In the past, most research on organizational crisis focused on negative outcomes. But positive psychologists involved in organizational research point out that even in crisis, organizations can take positive actions that speed their recovery process and enhance their resilience and overall stability.

Organizational crisis is characterized as "low probability, high impact" events. Whether an organization's crisis is externally generated (*We sell widgets, but the demand for widgets is down*), internally generated (*We sell whatzits, but our last batch of whatzits was defective*), or caused by multiple overlapping factors (*We sell whozits, and our operating costs were already skyrocketing when the hurricane struck*), it is the organization's *response* to the crisis that counts.

Facing a challenge or a setback, a positive organization will mobilize its strengths. Good communicators will become better communicators, working to offer transparency as opposed to hiding behind closed doors and keeping the rank and file waiting and guessing. Creative solutions will be solicited and logically considered. Flexibility will be paramount.

In a crisis, positive leaders will lead—as opposed to doubting their abilities or pointing fingers. They will not waste time or energy denying the existence of problems or shirking responsibility. Their commitment will be to get the organization back on track *by doing* the best thing and right thing.

In the aftermath of a crisis, an organization can flourish. According to positive psychology research, among the benefits it may reap are the following:

♦ Heightened attention to its relationships with all of its stakeholders

♦ Deeper organizational identity

♦ Increased mindfulness of vulnerabilities

♦ Enhanced reputation

♦ Enhanced sensitivity to the emotional needs of its members

Although some organizations are inclined to sweep a bygone crisis under the carpet, others—even while resuming standard operating procedures—take pride in their battle scars. Having faced adversity and survived with dignity, such organizations, and the many individuals that comprise them, know they are better prepared for future challenges—and future success.

The Least You Need to Know

♦ As with positive psychology itself, positive organizations have begun asking "What do we do that works?"—and expressing gratitude to individuals who contribute.

♦ Organizations express trust in their employees by empowering them to participate in decisions that affect them.

♦ Transparently honest organizations make for more satisfied and motivated employees who understand the meaning and purpose of what they are doing.

♦ Leaders embody the character of an organization; they impact the emotions and perceptions of people within the organization and outside of it.

♦ As with individuals, an organization's true test of character is revealed in crisis—and, similar to each of us, organizations can flourish as a result of having experienced crisis.

Chapter 14

Happy Workplaces and Work-Life Balance

In This Chapter

- ◆ Juggling work and "real life"
- ◆ Commuting affects happiness
- ◆ Having fun in the workplace
- ◆ Setting boundaries around work

Thanks to the body of research that positive psychologists and positive-psychology coaches have been amassing, many organizations are doing a great deal to promote a sense of meaning and purpose among their employees. But let's not forget that happiness is also about "the pleasant life."

As this chapter shows, organizations have a far greater chance of keeping their employees happy—and keeping them around—by making the workplace more flexible and more fun.

Happy Life, Balanced Life

One of the main reasons organizations are invested in employee satisfaction is that they want their workforce to stick around. A happy employee is a loyal employee—and a loyal employee is good for the bottom line. In many industries, it costs a company one and a half times an employee's yearly salary to replace them.

In addition to being loyal, happy employees are willing to go the extra mile. They are willing to help co-workers, ready to take initiative, and eager to promote the company outside of work. All this adds up to what human resource professionals call *employee engagement*.

In recent years, an increasing number of employers have been surveying workers in an attempt to find out what would make them happier and more "engaged" on a daily basis. Responses show that in addition to wanting work that employs their strengths and managers who respect their opinions, employees want one other key thing: they want their employer to acknowledge that employees have a life outside of work, and they want job flexibility that enables them to enjoy that life. When employers do this, they contribute to their employees' *perceived organizational support* (POS), an important metric when it comes to measuring work-related happiness.

def•i•ni•tion

Employee engagement is the degree to which employees feel pride in their organizations, are loyal to them, and feel they are an important and respected part of them.

Perceived organizational support (POS), an important determinant of employees' well-being and satisfaction in organizations, is a measure of how well employees feel organizations assist them in moderating the negative effect of stressors in the workplace.

An interweaving of work life with outside-of-work life is, according to Harvard sociobiologist Edward O. Wilson, not a radical new concept but a natural arrangement for humankind. For most of history, work and family life were intertwined. Hunting and gathering, farming, and craft skills were passed from one generation to the next. The way many people work today—out the door before breakfast, home for a late dinner—dates back to the nineteenth century's Industrial Revolution, when we switched from home-based manufacturing to factory work.

Now employees want that dawn-to-dusk model reexamined. And many companies are obliging by offering various options, including the following:

◆ Telecommuting, in which employees work from home or a close-to-home satellite office for some of their dedicated work hours.

◆ Flextime, in which full-time employees are able to craft their own daily schedule (although they are sometimes required to work onsite for certain "core hours").

◆ Compressed workweeks, which allow employees to condense a 40-hour work week into fewer than five days.

◆ Permanent part time, in which employees, up to and including high-level managers, work less than a 40-hour week.

◆ Job sharing, in which two part-time employees share responsibility for one job that requires full-time coverage.

Each of these options provides employees with increased discretionary time to spend with friends and family or pursuing hobbies and recreational activities. Because all of these have been shown to increase happiness, employees who avail themselves of such opportunities are likely to report for work with a better mood and attitude. They're also apt to be less drained from one of the greatest happiness-sappers of our time: the daily commute.

Commuting: The Happiness Crusher

Sometimes it is the seemingly little things in life that make us happy, or unhappy. Most of us don't think of commuting as a significant aspect of our existence. It's just an "in-between" time when nothing much happens. Yet a growing body of evidence shows incontrovertibly that people with long journeys to and from work report having significantly lower subjective well-being.

Their unhappiness has to do not only with what happens during their daily travel time, but what does *not* happen.

The Paradox of Commuting

People consistently rank commuting as one of the unhappiest times of their day, yet many people accept longer commutes to jobs farther away if the jobs offer more money or if they can afford a bigger house in a more distant locale. Apparently, this is a faulty strategy as far as personal happiness is concerned. Two economists at the University of Zurich, Bruno Frey and Alois Stutzer, released a study called "Stress That Doesn't Pay: The Commuting Paradox." They found that someone whose commute is an hour each way would have to make *40 percent more* in salary to be as "satisfied" with life as a noncommuter is. Most are far from adequately compensated.

Why does commuting make people so miserable? Because it is unpredictable, for one thing. Humans have a way of adapting to stressors—even very serious ones, such as accommodating a physical handicap. When the adaptation is complete, our happiness level reverts to where it was before. But, as any commuter can attest, it is virtually impossible to predict with certainty how long a supposed one-hour commute will *actually* take. Accidents, bad weather, road construction, politicians' motorcades, and countless other random and uncontrollable factors can prolong behind-the-wheel angst—with no way to tell, while actually sitting in traffic, when it will end. Every time commuters get into the driver's seat, they are playing a game of chance with a potentially negative outcome—similar to Russian roulette.

But there is another major reason why commuting is so hard on people. According to Frey and Stutzer, and others who have studied the problem, commuting takes an enormous toll on happiness because the time devoted to this activity cannot be devoted to happiness-promoting activities—such as exercise, sleep, and socializing.

Happiness Trivia

When Nobel laureate Daniel Kahneman and economist Alan Krueger asked 900 working women in Texas to rate their daily activities, according to how much they enjoyed them, commuting came in last. (Sex came in first.)

In a study conducted at the University of California at Irvine, researchers found that the stress of commuting has direct physiological effects of raising blood pressure and releasing stress hormones into the body. Commutes of more than 18 miles each way may also increase the likelihood of having a heart attack due to exposure to high levels of air pollutants, which appears to be a risk factor for heart disease.

Robert Putnam, a Harvard political scientist, calls commuting "a robust predictor of social isolation," and notes that social isolation directly causes unhappiness. Putnam has even quantified the negative; every 10 minutes of commuting, he says, result in 10 percent fewer social connections.

Putnam advises each person who will potentially commute to work to visualize a triangle comprising where they sleep, where they work, and where they shop and socialize. In many American cities, you can spend an hour or two traveling along each side of that triangle. However, the smaller the triangle, the happier the person. The happiest people of all would be able to walk everywhere.

Easing Commuting Pain

With commuting creating unhappy consequences for workers and for the environment, and with globalization creating a need for varied employee availability, it's likely that even resistant organizations may become increasingly inspired to offer more flexible work arrangements. Until then, not everyone will be able shrink their commuting triangle. Nevertheless, commuters can take some actions to lessen commuting stress.

If you're among the unhappy commuting cadre:

- **Get ready the night before.** Lay out clothes and briefcases and even pack your lunch at night. It can buy you time in the morning to have a few quality family moments, not to mention a nutritious breakfast.

- **Stock your car with entertainment— and knowledge.** Order audio versions of all the books you've been wanting to read. Keep your favorite music CDs on hand as well, so you will never lack for entertainment.

Helping Hand

To add greater purpose to your travel time, consider learning a new language—or brushing up on your high school French while you're in *l'automobile.*

- **Work out after work.** If your boss won't flex your schedule, flex it yourself— along with your muscles. Join a gym near work and spend some time there in the evening before hitting the road. The time you spend on the treadmill should cut the time you spend in traffic if you have been habitually leaving at rush hour.

- **Change your routine now and again.** To keep boredom at bay, vary your route or, better yet, vary your method of commuting. Try public transportation or, if at all possible, see if you can bicycle on a fine day.

- **Ride with a friend.** Because this eases social isolation, it is perhaps the best way to diminish commuting's anti-happiness effects. Studies show that ride sharing lowers commuter stress significantly, and also that it is easier to relax while someone else does the driving.

Finally, anyone faced with an arduous commute should be certain to get a good night's sleep to restore body, mind, and mood (see Chapter 19 for more on sleep benefits). If their employer is one of the growing number who are providing time and space for naps at work, they should take advantage of the perk—preferably some time between the hours of 1 and 3 P.M., when research shows that most of us could use a biological boost. Adequate sleep not only decreases the likelihood of flaring tempers and road rage, but also promotes safety behind the wheel. That's good, because nothing compounds the unhappiness of commuting like a car accident.

Having Fun on the Job

When it comes to keeping employees around, keeping them happy, and keeping their relationships with one another on a positive note, effective organizations have another strategy up their sleeves. It does not necessarily require a lot of money; nevertheless, it does require time, thought, and attention. It is—simply enough—making sure employees have more fun on the job.

When Fun Works

Some people think of "work" and "fun" as antithetical concepts (and it's a pretty sure bet that those people aren't happy at work). Lots of other people think of fun on the job as something that happens only "accidentally"—for example, a spontaneous outburst of laughter that relieves tension but is quickly suppressed to avoid drawing a supervisor's attention. Still others think of fun on the job as something they can only have with their good friends—so they grab lunch and swap stories in small groups.

But recently, many organizations have begun to intentionally create opportunities for employees to play and have fun at work. Proponents of systemized fun say that a little fun doesn't hurt—and, in fact, really helps to up the level of retention. People bond when they have fun together, and want to stay on a job when they are close to their colleagues.

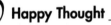 **Happy Thought**

"Time you enjoyed wasting is not wasted time."

—T. S. Eliot

Moreover, fun at work also helps people to take breaks, relieve stress, and even become more creative. As anyone who's ever tried to tackle a knotty problem can attest, it's often easier to view a challenge with a fresh perspective and a burst of energy after a little rest and recreation.

Employers can also attest that fun, in addition to bolstering individual happiness, is a good team builder and a catalyst for company pride. As for customer relations, employees are more likely to provide service with a smile when their smiles are genuine.

There are some caveats, however, to attempting to inject fun into the work environment. Psychologists and management consultants who specialize in the matter (yes, fun consulting is becoming something of a specialty) caution that employers should think about what their staff might actually consider to *be* fun. One man's fun—be it square dancing, squash, or Scrabble—might be another man's full-blown misery. It's a good idea to find out what employees typically do for fun in their free time and then take cues from those preferences.

Fun at work also works best when people at all levels of the organizational hierarchy participate. Enjoyable events won't be enjoyable if they're seen as an indulgence for the "little people." Employees take their emotional and behavioral cues from leaders. When leaders loosen up, they do as well.

Finally, it's important to remember that planning a game or party is not a cure-all for a dysfunctional environment. Any change, even for the better, takes some getting used to. People need to be given the message that it's safe to have fun, and that the fun represents a sincere commitment to building morale and creating an organization that not only likes to celebrate itself but is worthy of doing so.

Some Fun Ideas

At a New York ad-sales company where most employees are recent college graduates, the sales force participates in group activities with a competitive element—such as city-wide scavenger hunts organized by a team-building and adventure company. At a Columbus, Ohio, industrial-design firm, designers compete against other firms in an annual miniature derby car race, often tinkering with their own automotive entries on a practice racetrack prominently installed in their office. And at a Chicago recruiting firm, employees periodically attend concerts outside the office, and even have performers come in to serenade them.

These are just some of the creative events that organizations have come up with to spread fun and good cheer. Others include the following:

- Paper airplane tournaments
- Company T-shirt design contests
- Crossword puzzle competitions
- Weekly lunchtime pizza parties
- "Silly hat" or "horrid tie" contests
- "Guess whose baby picture?" (or high school yearbook picture) bulletin boards
- Anniversary parties celebrating employees' "hire days"

Companies are also looking for ways to add pizzazz to regularly recurring events to keep them fresh and drudgery-free. Business trips might be supplemented with a detour to a state park. Sales conferences might be punctuated with bingo games, with prizes being those aforementioned self-designed company wearables.

Stumbling Blocks

An annual holiday office party can seem like an awkward affair if it's the only "fun event" of the year, and it can make employees more socially anxious than happy. It's best to spread fun at work throughout the seasons. If holiday parties, or any festivities, include groups of employees who barely know each other, it's a good idea to plan ice-breaker games.

Finally, although it's great to have fun during the good times, it's also important for organizations not to lose their sense of humor or their ability to have fun during the less-than-perfect times. During the down times people most need to feel supported. If "pizza Wednesday" is eliminated at the first sign of a lackluster financial quarter, employees will feel punished. If the camaraderie persists, they will remember the many positive reasons why they actually like getting out of bed and going to work each day.

When Happiness Means Saying No to Work

This chapter began by discussing the importance of work-life balance in a happy life. But employers are not the only ones responsible for creating that balance. Employees are responsible, too.

Regardless of how much we enjoy our work and our work colleagues, it's important to know when to stop working.

Knowing When to Quit

Although positive psychology keeps reminding us about the rich psychic rewards of family time, volunteering, and "extracurricular" hobbies, many of us are still in jeopardy of giving our entire lives over to work. Ironically, if work and other parts of life can't peacefully coexist, then all of them—including work—will suffer.

It used to be that only a select few of us could properly be labeled "workaholics." It was said that workaholics chose to work all or much of the time to keep from dwelling on unwanted emotions or to avoid intimacy in relationships. Workaholic-type addiction certainly still exists today. Those who have it would likely exhibit extreme signs of work addiction:

- Talking about work a vast majority of the time

- Having friends and family who've given up expecting them at important events

- Working during meals

- Taking work to bed

- Becoming irritable when people ask them to stop working

- Becoming impatient with people who don't work as hard as they do

- Taking on the work of others in the belief that no one else can ever do it as well as they can

Helping Hand

Workaholics Anonymous offers a free 12-step program for anyone who desires to stop working compulsively. Information about meeting and materials can be found at www.workaholicsanonymous.org.

However, workaholism is not the main thing that keeps a great many of us tethered to work more or less around the clock nowadays. For that we can thank—or curse—technology that makes us continually accessible, a global economy and global financial markets, and round-the-clock Internet commerce. All these things drive expectations—our own and other people's—that we need to be on the job, or at least on call, 24/7.

But if we are to maintain a happy balance, there are times when we have to be unavailable. Sometimes we have to say "no," or at least "not now."

Whatever our work is, and even if we like it enormously, we must trust that we know it well enough to discriminate between which matters need instant attention, which ones can wait, and which ones *should* wait because they will benefit from some more time and consideration.

If the Thrill Is Gone

Everyone has an optimum work pace that feels appropriate. It is one where they can accomplish a lot and be creative and productive without crossing that fine line into unbalanced burnout. It's important to know when enough is enough. And the tip-off may be that work you once really loved to do now feels like a grim habit. When the thrill is gone from work, you may just need to do less work to get it back.

It's not always easy to slow down, but these strategies can help:

- **Continually reevaluate your "to-do" list.** Delete any task that has been on the list more than a week or month with no progress. You are probably not going to do it, so don't let it haunt you.

- **Set time and space boundaries.** For example, have an e-mail cut-off time when you arrive at home. Pledge to turn off your cell phone (yes, the vibrator, too) during dinner. Announce your intention to be off-line in a nicely phrased automated e-mail reply and cell phone message.

- **Shut the home office door.** If you work in a home office, you are theoretically able to spend more time with loved ones—but do you? Don't forget to come out of that office at a regular time, and turn off the light and the computer. It will all be there in the morning.

- **Take your vacation time.** Count the days you have coming and plan to take them off. If you're afraid of pressure build-up while you're gone, take long weekends before building up to weeks.

Happiness Trivia

If you're impairing your happiness by not taking all your vacation time, you're not alone. Thirty percent of employed adults give up vacation time they have earned, resulting in a total of 415 million unused vacation days in 2004, according to a survey by *Harris Interactive*. The United States is one of the only modern countries without vacation-time minimums mandated by law.

- **Forget the multi-tasking myth.** Studies show we are actually most effective when we do one thing at a time. Besides, you'll never get into a flow state unless you focus. (To this end, try turning off your e-mail alert "ping." Check your e-mail at times of your choosing.)

- **Ask for help.** Use your network. Tap into the expertise of colleagues and co-workers. (Let them know you'll do the same for them.)

- **Prepare for peak cycles.** Many occupations have their busiest seasons. Short of changing professions, there is nothing to do to prevent a busy season, so spend the months beforehand making sure that your mind and body are in the soundest possible shape. Eating right, getting enough rest and exercise, and tending to your social and spiritual needs will enable you to create a reservoir of energy to draw on when the going gets tough.

Finally, hold on to your long-term goals. Remember the meaning and purpose of what you are trying to accomplish. Then ask yourself what you can do to put the fun back into your fundamental vision.

The Least You Need to Know

- ◆ Employees are happier when their employers acknowledge that they have a life outside of work and offer job flexibility that enables them to live that life.

- ◆ Commuting is one of the biggest daily drains on happiness because it is unpredictable (and therefore stressful), and causes social isolation—depriving drivers of time they could spend in pleasant company or pursuing meaningful activities.

- ◆ Although some think of "work" and "fun" as opposites, many organizations are making a concerted effort to up employees' satisfaction and commitment by intentionally creating opportunities to have fun on the job.

- ◆ Regardless of how much satisfaction work provides, living a happy, balanced life requires setting some boundaries around work time and pursuing other enjoyments.

Part 5

Happy Together

Spouses, children, and friends might not always seem like sources of happiness. There are days when they can be downright irritating, to be sure. Yet those in relationships where positive actions outnumber negative ones tend to be more satisfied with their lives. This part looks at the dynamics of strong marriages, positive parenting, and supportive friendships.

Chapter 15

Wedded Bliss?

In This Chapter

- Learning why the married are happier
- Determining the typical marital happiness pattern
- Having sex and happiness
- Communicating positively in marriage
- Handling divorce and unhappiness

Social psychologists have long been interested in studying marriage and its effects, and an enormous number of surveys of married people have been conducted. The single most striking fact from all of them is that married people report being happier than anyone else. Marriage is a more significant happiness factor than job satisfaction, money, or community. In fact, there are few more reliable predictors of happiness than a stable, long-term, intimate relationship.

But not all marriages are equally happy, and wedded bliss is not a given. As this chapter shows, lasting happiness is not a result of simply putting on a wedding band. It has more to do with what we give and receive every day.

The Cause and Effect Conundrum

For a long time it seemed that, for every social scientist who pointed out that happiness correlates with marriage, another one noted that maybe it wasn't marriage per se that caused satisfaction. Perhaps we were confusing cause and effect—maybe happier people were the ones who tended to get married in the first place, and the more sanguine, optimistic people were more willing to overlook the minor bumps in marriage and stick with their relationships.

But newer evidence suggests that committed relationships are not simply correlates of well-being, but may have what's called "causal force." It may indeed be happier people who tend to marry, but marriage—a good marriage, that is—makes them even happier.

> **Happiness Trivia**
>
> In the United States, 95 percent of the adult population marries at some point. Of married adults, 40 percent call themselves "very happy," whereas only 23 percent of never-married adults describe themselves that way. This holds true across every ethnic group and across data collected from 17 nations.

Married people are less depressed than unmarried people, whereas the end of a marriage due to divorce or death of a spouse corresponds strongly with depressive episodes. Married people are also healthier than unmarried people and live longer—quite possibly, scientists now think, because close positive relationships have a directly beneficial effect on the immune system.

Close personal relationships of some sort appear to be *necessary* for happiness. And when a marriage is strong, there is arguably no closer relationship than the bond between two partners who have decided to navigate through life side by side, supporting and caring for one another.

The Life Cycle of Marital Happiness

Each marriage is its own unique relationship, but overall, marriages tend to start out with both parties very happy. Marital happiness then reaches a low point when a couple has adolescent children. But among couples who remain married, satisfaction rises again when the children leave home.

Of course, not all marriages will last long enough for partners to reap the benefits of happiness's later life upswing. One thing that differentiates those couples who remain happily united is their ability to transition successfully from the initial "falling in love" phase to the less dramatic but potentially rewarding state of deep intimacy and enduring commitment.

The Falling Phase

Falling in love with someone can create intense feelings of ecstasy—or agony, should one's passionate stirrings be unrequited. But for those fortunate souls for whom falling is a reciprocal plunge, the sense of ebullience is intense and pervasive. Signs of affection and approval from one's beloved can create the feeling of "walking on air." And for a time we can imagine that, so long as our beloved remains drawn to us, we will never experience a moment of unhappiness, self-doubt, or even boredom again.

What happens to us during the passionate attraction phase of love is as intense on a neurochemical level as it is on an emotional level. Behind the scenes, powerful brain chemicals are fuelling our euphoria. A group of neurotransmitters called *monoamines* play an important role. These monoamines include the following:

◆ **Dopamine:** This chemical stimulates our "desire and reward" response by triggering an intense rush of pleasure, increasing energy, lessening our need for sleep and food, and focusing our attention. It has the same addiction-generating effect on the brain as nicotine or cocaine.

◆ **Adrenaline:** Otherwise known as norepinephrine, this chemical starts us sweating and gets our heart racing, contributing to the physical sensations of emotional free fall.

◆ **Serotonin:** One of love's most important "feel-good" chemicals, this one contributes to the near obsessive-compulsive nature of falling in love, allowing us to fixate delightedly on the smallest details of our novel, budding relationship.

However, the biochemical effect of falling in love doesn't last forever. When smitten subjects are tested in the lab in the early phases of attraction, their chemical cocktail is in full flow. But after their relationship is a year old, their levels return to normal. Something has to happen to keep love alive and to create a lasting bond.

Happiness Trivia

A formula for creating romance has actually been created in the lab. Psychologist Arthur Arun, who has studied why people fall in love, asked subjects to choose a total stranger, spend half an hour sharing intimate life details with that person, and then spend four minutes gazing into their eyes. Many of his couples felt deeply attracted after those 34 minutes.

Companionate Love

Most couples who move toward marriage start their romantic "screening process" the same way. They evaluate one another largely on the basis of physical appearance and observable behavior—pleasing personality traits, such as being "funny" or "sweet."

But this level of evaluation is fairly superficial. Couples who will be successful in a long-term relationship move on to a phase of deeper exploration of one another's beliefs and attitudes, upon which it is important that they fundamentally agree. Do they share spiritual or religious convictions? Are they socially liberal or conservative?

From there, they will move on to evaluate one another as prospective lifelong mates by considering how well their individuals needs and goals mesh. Do they want to live in the city or the country? Do they want to have a family, and of what size? Are they both committed to careers and can those careers coexist?

def•i•ni•tion

Companionate love, the basis of long-term relationships that outlasts the first blush of passion, is defined by positive psychologist Christopher Peterson as the unshakeable affection shared by two people whose lives have become intertwined.

No two people will agree on everything. But partners who are mutually honest about beliefs, attitudes, and goals, and pragmatic enough to consider whether their similarities outweigh their differences, have a good start on making the leap from passionate love to *companionate love*.

Although companionate love is not accompanied by the same exhilaration as initial attraction, it is a sound basis for happiness. For within the framework of such love, one gives and receives the following:

- ◆ Emotional security
- ◆ Respect
- ◆ Loyalty
- ◆ Admiration

- ◆ Acceptance
- ◆ Guidance
- ◆ Understanding
- ◆ Comfort

Last but not least, they get companionship—someone with whom to enjoy all the good, pleasant, meaningful things in life.

If companionable love sounds a lot like friendship, that's because love and friendship actually have a great deal in common. In good marriages it can be difficult to distinguish between the two—and there is probably no need to do so. Indeed, some speculate that marriage makes so many people so happy because, boiled down to its essence, it offers a combination of two very pleasing things: friendship and sex.

What's Sex Got to Do with It?

It would be a mistake to think of the progression from passion to companionate love as being linear. In strong marriages, the passion component may wax and wane, and sexual desire may be stronger at some times than at others. But even though it may never reach the frenzied heights it did when the relationship was new, sex is an important element in a happy marriage.

Physical intimacy, research has shown, is a key contributor to happiness. On a purely physical level, having an orgasm can release feel-good endorphins into the bloodstream. And on an emotional level, lovemaking can make a close couple feel even closer, serving as a way to reaffirm their lasting affection and, yes, attraction—even after the "falling" phase is a happy memory.

But do married people really have more sex than single people? Popular culture might have us believe the answer is no. But research shows the answer is yes, yes, yes. They have 30 percent more sex than single people.

To say happy marriages are rich in sex is no exaggeration. "Happiness economics" researchers have found that sex is better for one's happiness than money. After analyzing data on the self-reported levels of sexual activity and happiness in 16,000 people, Dartmouth College economist David Blachflower and Andrew Oswald of the University of Warwick in England concluded that sex "enters so strongly (and) positively in happiness equations" that they estimate increasing intercourse from once a month to once a week is equivalent to the amount of happiness generated by getting an additional $50,000 in income for the average American.

> **Happiness Trivia**
>
> Money itself not only won't buy you happiness, it also won't buy you more sex. Despite popular opinion, there's no correlation between an individual's having a high income and having a high frequency of sex.

In fact, economists calculate that a lasting marriage equates to happiness generated by getting an extra $100,000 each year. (Divorce, meanwhile, translates to a happiness depletion of $66,000 annually.)

Communication Counts

"Friendship plus sex equals good marriage, which equals happiness" may sound like a relatively simple equation. But because not all marriages are equally happy, we have to conclude that there are a lot of factors that must contribute to a relationship where friendship and sex are sustainable. Key among those factors is strong positive communication.

If You Can't Say Something Nice: The 5-to-1 Rule

Researchers who have looked closely at the elements of a good marriage are apt to give a modified version of some advice your mother may have given you: *If you can't say something nice, don't say anything at all.*

It's not realistic to imagine that married people—even the happiest ones—will never argue, criticize their partners, or voice a complaint. What makes a marriage happy, however, is that positive communications outweigh negative communications—and they do so by a five-to-one ratio.

Helping Hand

The five-to-one rule is bound to vary with circumstances, and no truly happy couple will sit around and count compliments. But as a general rule, couples thrive when spouses—over time—have many more good things to say to one another than bad things. It's also important that the positive communications be very explicit, so they can be clearly registered as positive.

Psychologist John Gottman determined this ratio after he and his colleagues studied numerous marriages over time. Gottman reached the conclusion that disagreement and even anger are not necessarily destructive to marriage. What is important is that couples find ways to handle discord. Even during disputes, which typically—and understandably—include stubborn statements and defensive postures, couples can manifest empathy, affection, and even humor. The couples whose positive statements comprised the bulk of their communications flourished.

Active-Constructive Responding

According to positive psychologists, another way to ensure happiness in marriage and to make good marriages even better is for spouses to notice how they respond to one another when one of them shares news.

Shelly Gable, a UCLA-based psychologist who works on the positive psychology of love and marriage, was less interested in how a couple responds when one mate criticizes the other or how they talk to one another when something bad happens than how they react when something *good* happens. She noted that there are four possible response styles to a spouse's news. For example, if one partner came home and said they got a call from a headhunter and are now going to interview for their dream job, the other might respond in a manner that is …

- ◆ **Active/Constructive**—*Wow, that is great. You deserve it. I know you'll get it.* Enthusiasm is obvious and the spouse sharing the news will feel that her spouse is as excited as she is—maybe more so!

- ◆ **Passive/Constructive**—*Hey, good for you.* The response is low-key, but the spouse with news still feels supported.

- ◆ **Active/Destructive**—*Won't that be a lot more work? Aren't you a little old to take this on at this point in your life?* The response is negative. The killjoy partner feels compelled to point out potential problems and downsides.

- ◆ **Passive/Destructive**—*Wait, there's something on TV I want to hear.* The response is disinterested, and the responding partner seems not to care much about the news one way or the other.

Gable refers to the active/constructive category as *capitalizing.* In happy marriages, each partner knows how to magnify the pleasure of a good situation and thus initiate an upward spiral of positive emotion. Capitalizing turns out to be a critical factor in strong relationships. Couples who attest that they have an active/constructive mate also say they are more in love, more committed, and have more marital satisfaction throughout their marriage.

Helping Hand

A spouse can also exhibit active and constructive interest in her partner's news by displaying curiosity and asking lots of questions. Asking a spouse to elaborate lets her know you are listening carefully and that you care enough to want details.

Fighting Fair

Tolerance and patience during interaction is another factor in long-term relationships. No one can expect a spouse to be a model communicator all the time. Inevitably, there will be moments when communication is not at its most constructive. In other words, everyone fights—even happy couples.

Avoiding fights, while seemingly offering a short-term benefit (peace), can actually pose a danger if taken to extremes. Everyone needs to blow off steam now and then, and repressing all anger in the short term can result in blow-ups where the stakes are far too high.

An occasional argument can actually strengthen a bond by instilling trust that even an angry spouse is not going to lose control. To this end, marital therapists have noted that couples who fight well do so because they fight fair:

- ◆ They stick to the topic at hand and don't make "you always" statements, cite every infraction, or bring in everything but the kitchen sink.

- ◆ They speak in "I" statements, describing how they feel and avoiding the accusatory "*you* did this or that."

- ◆ They avoid threats and ultimatums, refusing to imply they are about to take drastic and impulsive steps.

- ◆ They don't interpret their partner's behavior—resisting the temptation to play amateur psychiatrist, they refrain from speculating on the deeper meaning of *why* their spouse did this or that.

- ◆ They leave third parties out of the mix and never ask a friend or family member to take sides.

- ◆ They modulate their volume and watch their tone, understanding that it is not only what one says that can hurt, but also how one says it.

Momentary anger need not undermine lasting happiness. Even in conflict, fundamentally satisfied spouses remember how much their partners have contributed to their happiness. They get mad, but they don't become insensitive. They keep their wits about them, say their piece, and move on—forgiving both themselves and their partner for any transgressions committed in the heat of battle.

Living Happily Ever After

Happily married couples also do not make the mistake of taking one another or their relationship for granted. Even the best marriages can suffer from lack of attention. To this end, positive psychologists and marital therapists are today focusing on many things happy couples can do to stay happy and perhaps become even happier.

Time Together

The amount of time a couple spends together is positively related to marital happiness, as well as to overall life happiness. Spending time together helps to build mutually warm feelings; but, interestingly, it helps even more to dissipate any negative feelings. It's easier to nurse a grudge when you aren't in direct contact with someone. Just having a partner around can remind you of all the things you like about them.

That said, there is also the question of what you can be doing during time together to enhance the relationship even further. Physical intimacy is a happiness booster, as we've seen. But so is trying new activities together, traveling to new places together, learning new skills, or brushing up on old ones together.

> **Stumbling Blocks**
>
> Many couples are partly drawn together because they share enjoyment in a par-
> ticular activity, from scuba diving to tango dancing. But during the course of their
> marriage they may abandon that activity, and say they are too rusty and out of practice
> to return to it. Yet refreshing your interest and brushing up your skills as a duo will pack
> a double happiness punch—it can spark up the relationship and rekindle each partner's
> confidence in their own abilities.

A Giving Attitude

We know that to do good is to feel good, so it makes sense that doing good for a spouse can be good for the relationship. Few things build love and trust like an attitude of care, consideration, and thoughtfulness toward one's mate. Before asking, "Will this or that make me happy?" a partner in a happy marriage is apt to ask, "Will this make my husband or wife happy?"

It's important to note that this recommendation is not a recipe for martyrdom. Naturally there will be times when individuals need to do things for themselves. But if *each* partner puts the other's needs first the *majority* of the time, the result will be a most happy collusion.

Positive Focus

Realistically speaking, no one likes every single aspect of their spouse's personality, appearance, or behavior all of the time. To be human is to have an annoying habit or two. In unhappy marriages partners fixate on the negative, and even a relatively small peccadillo (perhaps failure to floss or a propensity for eating the last cookie in the cookie jar) can take on immense proportions.

Happily married partners, however, develop the ability to notice the annoying things less. They are skillful "screeners." In the big picture, they remind themselves, tiny quirks are no big deal.

Happy Thought _____

"What counts in making a happy marriage is not so much how compatible you are, but how you deal with incompatibility."
—Leo Tolstoy

"I got gaps; you got gaps; we fill each other's gaps."
—Rocky

Active Reminiscence

Happy people look back on their lives and tell their stories with retrospective optimism, focusing on good aspects, or on how seemingly bad situations turned out well. Happily married people do much the same. They enjoy telling and retelling the stories of their relationship: how they met, how they struggled early on to make ends meet, how they raised their family, how they made decisions large and small, how they laughed and cried and fought and made up.

Reminiscing together is a sign that couples value their shared history. Those who do it frequently will likely have a lot more history to make.

Addressing Personal Issues

Someone who is married and unhappy may not be unhappy because of the marriage itself. People can be unhappy for numerous reasons that have little or nothing to do with their relationship—including stress and lack of fulfillment at work, health or age-related concerns, concerns about weight and physical appearance, and concerns about other relationships in their lives (for example with their parents, siblings, colleagues, or friends). But sometimes it's all too convenient to make a spouse a scapegoat:

I'm overweight because you buy junk food.

I'm unsuccessful at work because you don't like it when I spend time working.

My mother is mad at me because you aren't nice to her.

The marriage is more apt to endure, and to endure happily, if partners are willing to examine any dissatisfaction from a personal standpoint before jumping

Helping Hand _____

Many couples that at one time chose to remain in what they described as unhappy marriages end up describing themselves as happy five years later—even though nothing in the marriage itself had changed. Whatever changes did occur were on a personal level.

to place blame. It's not always easy to differentiate the source of problems when one is entwined in a close relationship that affects many aspects of life. Nevertheless, it's a good idea for spouses to try to make distinctions and to take responsibility for issues that fall largely in their corner.

When Divorce Happens

Not all married couples will live happily ever after. And most people are familiar with the oft-cited statistic that more than half of today's marriages end in divorce. There is, however, some happy news when it comes to divorce: that sad statistic has now been shown to be incorrect.

As a 2005 *New York Times* article explained, "The figure is based on a simple—and flawed—calculation: the annual marriage rate per 1,000 people compared with the annual divorce rate .... But researchers now say that this is misleading because the people who are divorcing in any given year are not the same as those who are marrying." Contrary to popular belief, studies find that the divorce rate in the United States actually never reached one out of two marriages. And because divorce rates are now declining (they peaked in the 1970s), it probably never will.

Nevertheless, one piece of popular wisdom about divorce does hold true: divorce is not a happy event. Regardless of what causes it, the dissolution of a marriage is an emotionally painful episode. In the immediate wake of divorce there is increased risk of depression, alcohol abuse, and even physical illness. However, not all divorced individuals suffer from these conditions, and most people who divorce make a successful adjustment within two years.

> **Happiness Trivia**
>
> About 60 percent of all marriages that eventually end in divorce do so within the first 10 years. According to the National Survey of Families and Households, the median duration of first marriages that end in divorce is seven years.

In addition, most people who divorce remarry, and this is especially true if their divorce occurred relatively early in their adult life. That marriage is a happier state than being single evidently rings true even for those whose first marriages did not have staying power. Hope prevails that committed love will bring satisfaction the second time around.

The Least You Need to Know

♦ A good marriage is a more significant happiness factor than job satisfaction, money, or community.

♦ Married people have 30 percent more sex than single people—and sex is a greater source of happiness than a big boost in income.

♦ Positive communication is essential to a happy marriage—overall, the number of positive communications, such as praise and enthusiasm, should far outweigh the number of criticisms or complaints.

♦ Happy marriages can be made even happier when couples spend time together, put their spouse's needs first, overlook negative aspects of their partner, refrain from blaming their marriage for personal unhappiness, and retell positive stories of their life together.

♦ Happily, the frequently cited statistic that one out of two marriages end in divorce is untrue; but when divorce does occur, happiness diminishes—although most people adjust within two years.

Chapter 16

Positive Parenting

In This Chapter

- ◆ Learning the effect of parenting on happiness
- ◆ Fostering positive emotion in children
- ◆ Modeling character strength
- ◆ Helping children be optimistic
- ◆ Determining children's happiness at school

Biologically, we're programmed to want to procreate. Culturally, we're sent the message that parenting is something we should want to do—our obligation to society. But is becoming a parent a guarantee of happiness, and if so, what kind of happiness will that be? This chapter addresses this issue. It will also explore the recommendations of positive psychology for parents who want to help their children realize their own potential for happiness.

Does Parenting Make Us Happy?

Ask parents to name the source of some of the greatest joys in their life and, chances are, they will mention their children. They might tell you what a wonderful person a child of theirs has turned out to be, or cite instances when their offspring's actions have made them proud, or recall times when they shared family fun. Based on this, you might conclude that parenting is an altogether happy process. However, available research might cast some doubt on your original conclusion.

As mentioned in Chapter 15, marital happiness tends to start out high, but sinks to a nadir when a couple has adolescent children. Marital happiness also ebbs significantly when a couple has very young children in the "diaper phase." The reason for these dips is most likely that parenting is stressful, a source of worry and anxiety. And parenting needy, helpless infants and unpredictable teenagers comprise two particularly stressful times.

In addition, psychologists who have measured how people feel as they go about their daily chores and activities have discovered that people report being *less* happy when interacting with their children than they are when doing numerous other things. They feel happier, in fact, when they are shopping, eating, exercising, or watching television. This, too, is easily explainable. Parenting is demanding; it requires mental, emotional, and physical exertion. Who wouldn't agree that, moment by moment, it can be more pleasant to watch a sitcom than to chase a toddler, help with math homework, or talk a fussy eater into downing—rather than flinging—her peas.

Finally, economists who have modeled the impact of many variables on people's happiness have concluded that parenting has a small effect on personal happiness—a small, *negative* effect, not a positive one. Surprising? Not from an economic standpoint. The costs of raising children are high—not just emotionally and physically but also financially. Raising children often means deferring the happy prospect of that snazzy two-seater convertible or that dream cruise to the Hawaiian Islands.

As Harvard psychology professor Daniel Gilbert has summed it up, "Our children give us many things, but an increase in our average daily happiness is probably not among them." Still, most parents are happy that they had their children. The vast majority of parents report that if they had the chance to live their lives over again, they would still choose to parent. Moreover, parents tend to remember most vividly the *rewards* of parenting, rather than the stress, the drudgery, or the expense.

That we are, by and large, happy to have children even when they don't enhance our immediate pleasure at each moment speaks to the components of happiness that children *do* add to our lives. Parenting is unquestionably a source of meaning and purpose. Most parents feel the purpose of parenting is less about being given something than about giving to their children. And the thing most parents would like to give their children is a happy life.

Happiness Trivia
In their study, "The Macroeconomics of Happiness," Rafael DiTella (Harvard Business School), Robert J. MacCulloch (Princeton University), and Andrew J. Oswald (University of Warwick) say that parents value children precisely because they pay so high a price for them. We have a tendency, say the researchers, to assume that anything that costs us a great deal and that involves sacrifice must make us happy.

Raising Happy Children

Parents have profound influences on their children's lives. Bearing such a large responsibility is by no means easy, and parents frequently turn to psychology for input and assistance when it comes to effective parenting.

In times past, much psychological literature on parenting focused on how parents should handle children's negative, or potentially negative, behaviors or emotions. Such topics are still of great importance, but positive psychology is especially interested in looking at the ways parents can help their children cultivate and broaden *positive* emotions. And today's psychologists, overall, are paying increased attention to the art of positive parenting.

An Authoritative Style

One element of parenting that has garnered a lot of attention in recent years is the concept of parental style. Virtually all parents want to encourage certain behaviors in their children and discourage others. Parenting style basically refers to how they go about doing this.

In the United States, researchers have identified three predominant styles of parenting:

- Authoritarian parenting is a rigid child-rearing style in which parents issue strict guidelines for what is right and wrong and demand unquestioning obedience.

- Permissive parenting is a lax parenting style in which parents are unrestrictive and exert very little control over their children.

- Authoritative parenting is a style in which parents set restrictions and have high standards for their children's behavior, yet are communicative, warm, and supportive.

These differing styles affect the social and emotional development of children. Children of authoritarian parents tend to be conflicted, anxious, irritable, socially uncomfortable, and generally unhappy. Children of permissive parents may be friendly and sociable but also tend to be immature, impulsive, and aggressive (and those whose parents' "permissiveness" is actually neglectfulness rather than indulgence tend to be depressed).

> **Stumbling Blocks**
>
> Most people tend to parent in the style in which *they* were parented. However, they can consciously alter their style if they are knowledgeable and motivated.

Of these styles, authoritative parenting is the most likely to produce children with positive attitudes and behaviors. Compared to children of parents who embrace other styles, children of authoritative parents are more curious, more outgoing, and more socially competent.

Praise and Discipline

Parenting style is only one factor that may influence children's development. Another is how parents punish and praise. With regard to both praise and punishment, moderation is the wisest course for parents who want children to be able to ultimately develop self-mastery.

It's easy to see how excessive or inappropriate punishment can be detrimental to a child's developing positive traits. Children who are punished unjustly and who are not given a clear sense of which infractions lead to which consequences will feel powerless to control events. Their relationship with the punitive parent will suffer and the parent will be unable to leverage the relationship to model desirable behavior in the future.

But even positive psychologists believe that fair and effective punishment—punishment that "fits the crime" and that is clearly linked to a specific behavior rather than to an indictment of the child's character—has its place in discouraging behavior that is genuinely dangerous or offensive.

> **Helping Hand**
>
> Punishment can have positive effects in deterring negative behavior provided it's reasonable and proportionate. The child must not perceive it as a withdrawal of parental love. Punishment should also be administered with consistency so that the same misbehaviors reliably meet the same consequences. (*Share your toys with your brother or the toys get put away.*)

As for praise, one might think that the "positive" thing to do would be to praise one's children all of the time. But positive psychologists point out that this would actually produce very negative consequences. As Martin Seligman notes, giving a child love, warmth, and affection unconditionally will produce positive emotion. But lavishing praise unconditionally—that is, without linking the praise to a genuine accomplishment—will backfire.

Children who are praised without achieving anything can become passive rather than proactive, because they have learned that *anything* they do will be lauded. In addition, such children will be unable to recognize their true successes in the future because they are unable to distinguish sincere praise from fluff. Parents who want to raise a child who will be motivated to explore and achieve mastery would do best to wait until the child does something praise*worthy* before telling them what a wonderful job they've done.

Stumbling Blocks

Although parental interactions with children impact children's self-image, they are not the only determinant. In general, children's self-regard actually *declines* during childhood, because their initial self-concepts were unrealistic. Self-regard typically reaches a low point at age 12 or 13, then increases during adolescence as teens make more realistic comparisons between their abilities and those of other people.

Positive Play

Parents can also contribute to the development of positive emotions in their children by playing with them in a responsive way from an early age. Playing simple games in which the child's actions have a demonstrable impact (the child claps and the parent claps back) teaches the child the basic premises of cause and effect: do something and something else happens. *What you do matters.*

Parents should also select toys that require the child to actively *do* something rather than be a passive spectator. For example, stacking blocks teaches spatial skills and encourages decision-making and creativity. When the blocks fall over the child learns about frustration and about coping with frustration in a resilient way—by building yet another tower of blocks.

It's important, too, to pick toys and encourage activities that match the child's developing capacities. The concept of *flow* applies to children as well as adults, and children will enter that highly gratifying state of focused engagement where "time flies" when their capabilities are employed and, to some degree, stretched. Activities that require a skill set well beyond their abilities will prove frustrating; activities that are too easy will prove boring.

> **Helping Hand** _____
>
> Young children's capabilities develop and change rapidly, so today's highly engaging toy or game can be tomorrow's ho-hum pastime. This doesn't mean you have to rush out to the nearest toy store for a new stash of amusements, however. Be creative—look around the house to see what diversions can be crafted from what's already there. Can you and your child construct a telescope from cardboard tubes using colorful bits of cut-up catalogs?

Gratitude Prompts

Children and adults alike can cultivate positive emotions by actively appreciating the good things in their lives. Dinnertime and bedtime are two opportune occasions to review the day together and enumerate what's made you happy, what's gone right, and what you've found to treasure in the course of the day.

Parents can prompt their children toward an attitude of gratitude by creating rituals that reinforce thankfulness. Family dinners, for example, can begin with each family member telling something positive that's happened to them since the last time the family gathered. Bedtime preludes can include a minute for acknowledging the things for which a child is grateful. This can certainly take the form of a formal prayer, but it can also be handled in a more informal, secular way depending on the family's beliefs and traditions.

Nurturing Character Strengths in Children

When it comes to instilling thankfulness or any positive character strength in a child, the very best thing a parent can do is be a positive role model. Children are born with an innate gift for imitation and they will re-create a parent's behaviors:

- ♦ If you want your child to express thankfulness to others, set the example of saying "thank you" when others help you.

- ♦ If you want your child to be creative, turn off the TV and do something active and inventive yourself.

- If you want your child to be courageous, stand up for what you believe and for those in whom you believe.

- If you want your child to be kind, be conscious of how you treat others—and make an effort to treat them as you would like to be treated.

- If you want your child to be conscientious, don't be a quitter.

- If you want your child to be curious, make sure you are open-minded and that you never stop learning.

- If you want your child to be empathic, listen to their point of view and imagine seeing the world through their eyes.

- If you want your child to be trusting, offer them guidance and then trust them to do the right thing.

- If you want your child to have a sense of humor, lighten up and laugh along with them.

- If you want your child to have hope, have faith that they will turn out well.

"Do as I say, not as I do" is *not* positive role modeling. Children will pay far more attention to your deeds than your words. If your instructions are congruent with positive deeds, they will resonate. If they are incongruent, they will only serve to raise a red flag.

Happy Thought _____

"We are apt to forget that children watch examples better than they listen to preaching."
—Roy L. Smith

"My father didn't tell me how to live; he lived, and let me watch him do it."
—Clarence Budinton Kelland

Helping Children Develop Optimism

As with most traits, a tendency toward optimism probably has both *nature* and *nurture* components. Studies of twins raised apart indicate about a 25 percent heritability factor for optimism and pessimism. However, the fact that identical twins reared together have a higher correlation of optimism or pessimism speaks to the influence of the *way* in which children are reared.

Setting an Example

Many people other than parents can influence a child's sense of optimism. These include teachers, coaches, and even peers. But parents are the first role models for optimism or pessimism, as they are the first role models for so many things.

Children see their parents in all kinds of emotional circumstances, reacting to good events and not-so-good ones. They pay particular attention to how their parents behave when they are upset, because an upset parent is a destabilizing factor in their familiar world.

Parents have every right to all of their emotions, of course. And there is little point in trying to conceal upsets from children, who have keen emotional radar where their parents are concerned. But if parents overreact to negative events with a pessimistic mindset, they can unwittingly be setting their child up to respond to life's wrinkles with gloom and doom.

Stumbling Blocks

Humor is a wonderful coping mechanism, but some forms of humor can backfire and send the wrong message to children. A parent who continually notes that "it rains every time you wash the car" and that "there's always a windstorm after you rake the leaves," may simply be making some wry observations about the randomness of the weather. Just be sure your child knows you don't really take the weather personally or believe that you actually *cause* rain and wind by attending to your chores. A smile and a comment that you're "only kidding" can help a young child avoid misunderstanding.

As detailed in Chapter 8, optimists see negative events as temporary; pessimists see them as permanent. If it's your habit to say things such as, "I'll never get anywhere at that company" after a hard day at the office, you may feel as though you are just blowing off some steam. But consider the message you are sending to a child who happens to overhear you.

Likewise, optimists see negative events as specific and limited; pessimists see them as global. If you're surprised by an astronomical electric bill when you open the mail, it's fine to note that the cost of energy is high—and altogether reasonable to request that your kids turn off the lights and the television when they leave the room. But taking the occasion to launch into a diatribe about the escalating economic squeeze on the middle class won't lower your bill and won't teach your children anything about pro-activity and perspective.

Positive psychologists note that it's especially important not to take a pessimistic bent when commenting on an action of your child's. If your child's behavior merits criti-cism, be specific about what they did that was wrong and what they need to change in the future. Never say or imply that the fault inherently lies within them or that the blameworthy behavior is an unalterable or permanent condition.

Criticism is not anyone's favorite thing to hear, but optimistic criticism can serve a constructive purpose, whereas pessimistic criticism will prove ineffective and most likely just worsen the problem. What's the difference? A child who doesn't clean their room after repeated requests might be told, "You are lazy and sloppy." But this is a pessimistic criticism because it describes a global, permanent, internally caused condi-tion. Now the child has been defined as a lazy slob *so why should they clean their room?*

On the other hand, a child who is told, "Your room is a mess, stop stalling and straighten it up," has been told what the problem is and how it can be resolved. It's unlikely they'll be delighted to hear this (they'd still rather play video games), but the criticism is still optimistic—and effective—because it assumes that the condition of the child's room is temporary and that the child has the power to improve the situa-tion by altering their behavior.

Reinforcing the Skills of Optimism

Parents who observe that a child is continually interpreting events negatively can get proactive. Optimism may have a heritable component but it is still largely a skill set that can be taught. Apart from honestly evaluating and making changes to their own style, a concerned parent can ask questions that prompt their child to stop catastroph-izing and to consider the true scope of problems.

A pessimistic child who fails to block an opposing team's soccer goal may contend, "I'm a loser and the coach will never play me again." But a parent can help the child dispute this assumption by asking, "Doesn't every good athlete have bad days some-times?" and, "What do you think you should do differently the next time you are on the field?"

A pessimistic adolescent who gets a poor grade on a term paper may contend, "I'll never pass this class." But a parent can help the child evaluate the realistic impact of one poor grade on one assignment by asking "What percentage of your grade does the paper count for?" and, "How can you prepare better for future tests and assignments?"

Note that interventions such as these are not meant to instill pie-in-the sky attitudes. They are meant to instill a sense of realistic optimism. Parents won't help their kids by implying that problems will magically disappear of their own accord, but they can help them meet challenges and cultivate resilience by taking positive action.

Are They Happy at School?

From the time most children are very young, they spend a large part of each day at school. In many cases they spend more waking time at school than they spend in the company of their parents. It stands to reason, therefore, that a child's school will have any impact on their emotional state.

The Self-Esteem School Movement

Although schools have always and inevitably influenced the emotional life of students, in recent decades many schools decided to address this influence in a more systematized manner. One way they have attempted to do this is through programs that purport to build children's self-esteem. But positive psychology cofounder Martin Seligman has been a vocal critic of self-esteem curriculum elements that put the cart before the horse.

Seligman notes that although self-esteem correlates with success, it is not the cause of success. In fact, it is the other way around: mastery, achievement, and persistence cause self-esteem. Feeling good is not the same as doing well, and Seligman contends that the latter is being sacrificed to the former when schools engage in practices such as grade inflation (so that no one feels bad about his grades) and devote time better spent learning exercises such as fill-in-the-blank games where children list reasons why they are special.

In his book, *The Optimistic Child*, Seligman says, "By emphasizing how a child *feels*, at the expense of what the child *does*—mastery, persistence, overcoming frustration and boredom, and meeting a challenge—parents and teachers are making this generation more vulnerable to depression." The depression he cites could result from a perceived sense of helplessness, a sense that the child is powerless to exercise control over events.

None of this is to say that parents should be upset if a teacher occasionally intervenes to simply make a child feel better in the face of a disappointment. However, parents who want to ensure that their children develop happiness-linked skills such as diligence, persistence, and tolerance for frustration might work with their child's school to ensure that goal-oriented learning is not sacrificed.

Character Education

Another recent development in schools—and yet another acknowledgement that schools contribute to the areas of development apart from the strictly academic—has been the integration of what is called character education. Character education programs were put in place to formally instruct children in values. Although part of character education curricula usually involves deterring children from such social ills as violence and substance abuse, more of an emphasis has recently been placed on positive values-based development.

But as with self-esteem, it is difficult to instill character simply by talking about it. As positive psychology cofounder Christopher Petersen writes, "Reciting the Pledge of Allegiance every morning is not an automatic route to good citizenship, and viewing the Ten Commandments on the wall of a classroom is no guarantee that the exposed students will become moral adults. After all, I stared for years at the periodic table of elements at the front of a classroom, and I certainly did not become a chemist."

For a child's school to truly contribute to the development of positive character traits, it needs to practice what it preaches. It can do this by offering the following:

- A safe environment

- Tolerance for difference and diversity

- A forum for discussion and debate on civic issues

- A clear definition of the school's goals and purpose

- Good role models and strong leadership in the school's administration

- Policies that encourage respectful dialogue among students and between students and teachers

- Disciplinary policies that are clear and that are enforced with fairness and consistency

- Recognition of student achievement

In the end, children are most likely to become positive, productive, and capable of meeting their full potential for happiness when schools and parents work hand in hand. Children who head off to school each morning with a positive mindset are able to make the most of their education. Children who leave school each day with a sense of accomplishment are likely to transport their positive attitude home.

The Least You Need to Know

◆ Although parenting children is not always pleasurable on a day-to-day basis, it adds meaning and purpose to life—and the vast majority of parents say they would do it all again.

◆ Parents can foster positive emotion in children by developing a firm but supportive authoritative style, doling out appropriate praise and discipline, choosing play activities that require a child to be active and engaged, and encouraging them to appreciate the good things in life.

◆ Children are natural mimics, so the most effective way to instill positive character strengths in children is for parents to embody those traits themselves.

◆ Parents can model optimism for their children and encourage them in the skills of optimism—which involve reassessing events in a less dramatic, all-or-nothing way.

◆ Schools can also contribute to the development of positive emotion in children; they can do this best by embodying the values, not simply talking about them.

Chapter 17

The Friendship Factor

In This Chapter

- The happiness friendship brings
- The benefits of social networks
- The reason optimists have more friends
- The advantages of befriending positive people
- The pleasures of having pets

You are probably familiar with the song lyric, "People who need people are the luckiest people in the world." But what's truer is that people who *have* people are the lucky ones—or, at least, the happy ones.

The evidence is extensive and incontrovertible: people whose lives are enriched by strong social ties feel more satisfied, more content, and more secure. When people who describe themselves as "extraordinarily happy" are surveyed, they invariably attest that they have meaningful social bonds.

And friendships are not only boons in the good times. People with social support are better able to face life's not-so-good times. When the going gets tough, their friendships empower them with a more positive perspective and a greater degree of resilience.

The Happy Rewards of Friendship

One of the most interesting aspects of human beings is that we are truly "social animals." Friendship was no doubt an enormous evolutionary advantage. There's safety in numbers. Joining forces and sharing resources gave everyone a leg up in the survival sweepstakes.

To help us out in this regard, Mother Nature even equipped us with a hormonal reaction known as the *tend-and-befriend response*. When faced with immediate and acute threats (say, being chased by a hungry wolf), we might choose to fight or flee—both of which correlate with the release of adrenaline into our systems. But if the threats are long term and chronic (say, a pack of wolves that is continually prowling about the outskirts of our village), we might choose instead to join forces with others, share duties and responsibilities, look out for one another, and "hold down the fort." In such cases, the driving hormone in our systems would be *oxytocin*, a chemical that instigates bonding behavior, sometimes jokingly referred to as the "hug hormone."

def•i•ni•tion

The **tend-and-befriend response** is an alternative to the fight-or-flight response, and involves reacting to threats by forming social alliances. The term was coined by psychologist Shelley Taylor.

Oxytocin is a hormone secreted by the pituitary gland that contributes to bonding behavior. Oxytocin is sometimes thought of as a female hormone because it is released during breastfeeding, but both men and women produce it.

But forming friendships was never solely about practical necessities. It was, and is, about emotional necessities as well. People who are socially isolated, study after study shows, are apt to suffer poorer moods and to exhibit and report less satisfaction than those who have friends.

Friends—people we trust, with whom we reciprocate good turns, and toward whom we feel warmly—offer a cornucopia of happiness-inducing benefits:

◆ **They offer moral support.** Their mere presence calms us because it reminds us someone is in our corner, and that someone would defend us if we needed defending.

◆ **They provide shoulders to cry on.** A friend's understanding and acceptance helps us tolerate events and emotions that might have felt intolerable.

- **They—literally—give us hands to hold.** Their "attaboy" pats on the back and their reassuring bear hugs offer us the balm of positive touch.

- **They provide receptive ears.** Sharing good news with a friend makes the news seem that much sweeter. Confiding bad news to a friend can calm and cheer us (and may even earn us some good advice).

- **They give us a chance to yuck it up.** Providing opportunities to share a joke or tell a funny story is one of the services friends cheerfully provide. You are 30 times more apt to laugh in the company of someone than you are to laugh alone.

- **They give us a sense of purpose.** It's nice when our friends do things for us, but sometimes even nicer when we get a chance to do something nice for them.

Happiness Trivia
Does catching a cold drain your happiness? You might assume you're more likely to get a cold if you're social, but you're actually *less* apt to do so because the immune systems of social people produce a higher number of anti-bodies than those of nonsocial people.

- **They boost our confidence in our abilities.** In a number of studies, subjects were asked to perform an anxiety-provoking task such as giving a public talk or performing mental math. When they did these things in the presence of a supportive friend, their cardiovascular stress response was significantly lower than when they did them alone.

Having friends makes us feel better about ourselves overall. Our self-esteem gets a boost when we know people voluntarily choose our company—no bribes, booty, or blood ties necessary! In addition to helping us feel better about ourselves, it appears that friends just make us feel better in general. People with a circle of friendships are apt to stay healthier and take better care of themselves.

The Power of Social Capital

One-on-one friendships are important to happiness. But so is belonging to social networks, which increases what's known as our *social capital*. Social capital is measured by our involvement in groups, organizations, and communities that allow us to feel a part of something greater than ourselves.

The Participation Principle

Social capital directly correlates with happiness. The more capital we spend, the better we feel and the more meaning we ascribe to our existence. We can up our social capital by participating in the following:

◆ A recreational group (such as the office softball team, a bowling league, a bridge foursome)

◆ A performing group (the church choir, a poetry workshop, a community theatrical group)

◆ A faith-based group

◆ An exercise-oriented group (such as a running, hiking, or cycling club)

◆ A meditation group

◆ A group concerned with philanthropy, community service, or any kind of community betterment

◆ A self-improvement group (such as Weight Watchers, Toastmasters, or any 12-step program)

◆ An environmental action group

◆ A group concerned with public issues

◆ A group concerned with children (Girl Scouts, Boy Scouts, Big Bothers and Sisters, the PTA)

◆ A political party or club

◆ A labor union or professional group

It's not how many organizations you belong to that matters, though—it's how involved in them you are. When it comes to social capital, quality matters more than quantity.

Just being a member of an organization in name only—maybe you're on their mailing list, or carry their card in your wallet—is not apt to create a great sense of belongingness and meaning in your life. Nor is it apt to offer you increased opportunities for meeting kindred souls. But if you attend meetings, contribute time, or are involved in planning group activities, you should reap happiness in proportion to the effort you expend.

Do Online Communities Count?

With the advent of the Internet and vast success of online social sites such as Facebook and MySpace, it's only natural to wonder whether interacting with large numbers of people in cyberspace "communities" is also apt to contribute to happiness. Social scientists considering that question often cite something known as the *Dunbar number*, 150, as a ceiling on how many personal contacts the human mind can effectively deal with.

The researcher who came up with the number in the first place is not so sure, however, that new technology won't alter our capacity for social contacts. Robin Dunbar has said that, "in principle" at least, we may push past the limit because technology could conceivably increase our memory capacity. The question is whether or not interacting with vast numbers of people we've never met in person can be meaningful enough to boost our life-satisfaction levels and provide the benefits of "real-life" friendships and communities.

def•i•ni•tion

The **Dunbar number** posits a natural upper limit (150) for the social contacts the human brain can manage. It arose as a result of research done in 1993 by Oxford anthropologist Robin Dunbar. The limit was derived by extrapolating from social groups in nonhuman primates, and then crediting people with greater capacity because of our higher capacity for conscious thought and language.

Cyber-friendships that remain online-only relationships are certainly not going to provide any warm hugs or pats on the shoulder, and the "touchy-feely" aspect, those studying the cyber-friend phenomenon say, are important. As for meaningful interaction, once again, quality matters more than quantity. If, say, you belong to an online community that is united for a purpose—for example, mobilizing public opinion on a social issue—and you play a role, such as creating content for the group's website, that might be a level of involvement that brings emotional satisfaction. But if you are simply swapping astrological signs and exchanging opinions on YouTube videos, you probably should not expect more than an amusing diversion.

Researchers at England's Hallam University who have surveyed young people on the topic of online relationships point out that, despite the preponderance of social networking sites, most friendships still usually begin off-line. There is something about making friends "the old-fashioned way" that still appeals to even the most enthusiastic web surfers.

On the plus side, when you do have a "real live" friend, the Internet offers a wonderful opportunity to stay in touch, even if that person lives or moves far away. It also offers a chance to track down old friends with whom you already share a positive history—perhaps the college roommate or former work friend you lost track of—and reestablish ties. And when you are back in touch, you can communicate very conveniently and inexpensively.

Stumbling Blocks

> Trying to keep in "virtual" touch with hundreds of online acquaintances is time-consuming. Be careful not to pursue this activity at the expense of your closest relationships, those people you can turn to in times of distress, or to the detriment of your involvement in your actual community. If you're too much of a mouse potato (that is, tethered to your computer) you can actually diminish your social capital and the happiness that comes with it.

The Optimist's Friendship Advantage

Making and keeping friends is a skill. And, as with any skill, some people are more naturally inclined toward it than others. Optimists, it turns out, are better at making friends and maintaining relationships than pessimists. Happiness researchers say the reason can be summarized in one word: *leniency*.

def•i•ni•tion

> **Leniency** is the tendency to classify a larger set of outcomes, events, and characteristics as subjectively positive. Leniency can also correspond to the adoption of relatively modest thresholds of minimum acceptability.

Optimists are very good at looking for—and finding—the positive aspects of people and situations. What's more, they are more willing than pessimists to use the positive aspects to balance or neutralize any negative aspects they perceive. In other words, optimists excel when it comes to giving people the benefit of the doubt.

A pessimist typically can be quick to rule out someone as a potential friend, or to terminate a friendship with someone after it has begun, because they see the other person as exhibiting some sort of flaw. *I can't be Stan's friend—he's so arrogant. I can't be Emily's friend—she talks too much.*

An optimist, on the other hand, would tend to reframe such so-called flaws:

Stan's a bit full of himself, but he's so smart and funny and interesting that maybe he deserves to be a little vain. One thing about Stan—he's never boring!

Emily sure can go on, and that can be annoying if I'm in a mellow mood. But there is no one like Emily to drop everything and help you when you've got a problem.

Of course, just because optimists are willing to "give a guy a break" doesn't mean all their relationships will be predominantly positive. Where friendship is concerned, we see once again the importance of tempering optimism with realism. No friendship is apt to generate true happiness if one party is deeply deluded as to the other's character strengths or flaws, nor will a relationship work if one party does all the giving and one does all the taking.

For the optimistic approach to friendship to work, it's important for optimists to recognize that their opinion is, in fact, subjective. They have to be aware of the fact that they *choose* to make allowances for their friend, and that it is their choice to continue that practice or to modify it as necessary.

That said, we'd likely all have more friendships—and more rewarding ones—if we allowed for the fact that no one, not even our very best friend, is capable of being perfect, and that's okay.

Hanging Out with the Happy

Understanding the benefits of friendship may make you want to go out and make some additional friends. But when it comes to helping you be happy, not all friends are created equal. If you really want a happiness boost, spend your time with people who think positively and who say positive things.

Catching a Positive Vibe

When Dr. John Suler of Rider University wants to prove to his psychology students that expressing positive thoughts can impact the moods of other people, he conducts an on-the-spot demonstration. He polls the students as to who is in a positive mood and who is in a negative mood. He writes the numerical tallies on his chalkboard—labeling both positive and negative totals "before." Then he instructs everyone in the room to shake hands with five people and genuinely wish them health and happiness. Afterward, he tallies up the positive and negative moods again, and labels those results "after." According to Suler, every time he conducts this exercise, the intervention works to create an increase in the number of positive moods.

Although this exercise has not been done as a large-scale experiment, chances are you have experienced a similar phenomenon in your own life. When we are around upbeat people, we feel happier. And when we are around those who wish us well, we feel better. Any emotion can be contagious. Being around angry people can make us feel angry. Being around glum people can make us feel glum. Although no one is apt to be, nor obligated to be, in a good humor all the time, choosing to be around those who are predominantly positive is a sound happiness-enhancing strategy.

Attracting Positive People

If we want to attract positive people, we need to do our part. Even the most upbeat and outgoing person in the world is not apt to befriend us if we give off signals that say "go away." If we want someone to be friendly toward us, we need to communicate that we'll be receptive to them. We need to be approachable.

Approachability is hard to quantify. It's an attitude and an "energy" we exude when we're feeling curious and trusting, and when we are not on the defensive. Most of us can just sense when someone is open to interaction as opposed to when they are totally preoccupied or self-absorbed. Not surprisingly, others can intuit the same things about us.

That said, there are times when we appear closed-off to others without even realizing that we appear this way. If you feel as though no great new people ever enter your life, it may be because you are sending nonverbal messages that ask them not to.

To signal the fact that you are approachable:

- **Make eye contact.** Staring isn't necessary, but don't dart your gaze away too quickly. Don't walk around eyeballing your shoes, or continually glancing at your watch or the wall clock. Eye contact indicates that you register the presence of others and are not averse to a friendly "hello."

- **Smile.** A mere upturn of the lips can make all the difference in how people respond to you. If you feel there's nothing to smile about, then here's your chance to try out your optimism and gratitude skills: *think* of something worth smiling about.

- **Avoid closed-off body language.** Folding your arms across your chest, clasping your hands, crossing your legs or ankles, and turning your body away from someone are ways of signaling, "I'm unapproachable." People sense that you are likely to reject friendly overtures. Conversely, when you face someone fully, with open hands and with feet planted forward, you signal emotional availability.

Stumbling Blocks _____

If you want to attract friends, prioritize the people around you over the people on the other end of your cell phone. No one is apt to approach you if you're already in mid-conversation.

You might also consider taking a break from your electronic stash of music. If you go everywhere with headphones in your ears, don't be surprised if you're not meeting anyone. Even if people are shouting warm and cheerful greetings at you, you won't hear them.

Unplug. Notice who's around and try communicating face-to-face.

If you do these things, you might suddenly find yourself striking up conversations with positive people left and right. Obviously not every encounter will result in a budding friendship, but some could. If not, you'll be none the worse—and indeed probably much better—for your positive exchange.

After you do start attracting positive new friends, don't take them for granted. Nurture your ties and you will strengthen them. Remember to express your gratitude to your friends for all they bring to your life. Gratitude, as we've seen, is its own reward. Beyond that, acknowledging the comfort and joy that your friends bring to you will reinforce their positive behavior, build up a reservoir of good feelings, and make them feel smart and proud that they have chosen you to hang around with.

Positive About Pets

As much as we value the comfort and companionship that our friends provide, let's not overlook some other important companions: pets. Virtually anyone who's ever cared for a pet can vouch that the company of cats, dogs, and other furry, finned, or feathered creatures can be emotionally uplifting and also provide an enhanced sense of meaning and purpose in one's life. This intuitive knowledge is now supported by research.

Pets brighten our spirits and even help us respond better to our fellow humans. Bringing a pet into a nursing home or hospital has been shown to boost peoples' moods and enhance their social interaction.

Pets calm us down. In a UCLA study, dog owners were found to require less medical care for stress-related conditions than nondog owners. When we are ailing or feeling blue, pets give us a reason to keep on keeping on. In a study from City Hospital in

New York, heart patients who owned pets were more likely to survive the first year after a heart procedure than those who did not own pets.

Stumbling Blocks

Some people cannot keep a pet for practical or financial reasons. But you can still spend time with and enjoy other people's pets or volunteer at an animal shelter. Merely being in the presence of animal life can be relaxing. In one study, dental patients awaiting oral surgery spent a few minutes before the procedure watching a tank of tropical fish. Their stress level at the time of surgery was found to be less than those who had not watched the tropical fish, as measured by the patients' blood pressure, muscle tension, and behavior.

When it comes to boosting happiness, what, exactly, do pets provide?

◆ **Unconditional love and acceptance.** Pets accept us for who we are. We never have to worry about impressing them. If we care for them they repay us with abundant affection.

◆ **A chance to nurture.** Pets bring out our nurturing instincts. They induce empathy in us, and this alone can be a happiness booster.

◆ **A reason to take care of *ourselves*.** Our pets depend on us. They give us an incentive to tend to our own well-being. We need to stick around because we don't want to abandon them.

◆ **An other-oriented focus.** Caring for and interacting with animals can help us obsess less on ourselves. Rather than thinking and talking about our problems, we watch and talk to and about our beloved animals.

◆ **A link to the natural world.** Pets remind us that we are part of a delicate ecosystem and that we share the planet with many beings. In some cases they cause us to spend more time outdoors, which itself can be a source of contentment—not to mention a chance to exercise.

◆ **Touch.** Many pets give us a chance to cuddle, nuzzle, and hug. Having an animal to hold and stroke can make a world of difference to anyone, especially people who would otherwise have no positive physical contact.

◆ **Communication.** Most pet owners routinely talk to their pets, and many feel there is some level of comprehension and reciprocation going on. Even if you're no Dr. Doolittle, almost everyone who cares for a pet feels they can communicate to their animals through body language.

◆ **Laughter.** Most pet owners thoroughly enjoy watching their animals' playful antics. There is nothing like a frisky, mischievous pet to evoke a spontaneous laugh.

Finally, pets can help us meet other people with whom we have something significant in common. Walking your dog in the park, for example, is a great way to meet a new friend. Most pet owners tend to feel positive toward other people who have opened up their hearts and their homes to a loving creature.

Helping Hand

Don't know what kind of pet to get? Find an animal that suits your temperament. Pets have personalities: some are shy, some are boisterous, and some are more demanding of attention. Consider what type of animal will work best with your own personality. Emotional chemistry is as important with pets as it is among people.

Also, make sure the pet's needs are suited to your schedule, your budget, and your living space.

The Least You Need to Know

◆ Humans are social creatures, and friendship helps us not only survive, but also thrive.

◆ Happiness accrues to those who are actively involved in purposeful social organizations that make them feel connected to something greater than themselves.

◆ Optimists are skilled at making and keeping friends because they are lenient in their evaluations of people: even when they notice a negative aspect of a person, they tend to see it is balanced out by a positive aspect.

◆ Happiness is contagious, so it pays to spend your time with upbeat people—remain open to new encounters and you'll be surprised how many you encounter.

◆ Relationships with pets can add pleasure, meaning, and purpose to your life. They offer us reasons to touch, communicate, laugh, and nurture.

Part **6**

Wellness and Happiness

Both body and mind play a role in generating happiness. And happiness, in turn, can play a profound role in keeping the body healthy and the brain pliant and agile—even as we age. This part of the book looks at how practices such as regular aerobic exercise, yoga, and meditation can positively impact the mind-body system; how hope can help healing; and how happiness may impact longevity.

Chapter 18

Exercise for Happiness

In This Chapter

♦ How exercise impacts feel-good brain chemistry

♦ Why exercise boosts attitude and self-image

♦ How to start exercising in spite of excuses

♦ Why yoga is known for its positive nature

♦ How the link between posture and positive attitude is made

When we think about how to be happy, we tend to think of psychological, social, and even spiritual pathways. But science, medicine, and psychology all agree that a profound mind-body connection exists, and what happens on the physical plane resonates in the psychological arena.

We can undertake physical activities that have a proven impact in creating a positive frame of mind. A landslide of research shows that getting regular exercise is among the best things we can do for our body *and* will up our happiness quotient. Exercise works so well to improve mood and outlook that many find it, in effect, a golden ticket to happiness.

Active Body, Happy Mind

Unless you've been living under a rock for the past 30 years, you probably know that exercise is good for your body. It can lower blood pressure, strengthen the heart, increase lung capacity, regulate blood sugar, maintain strong bones, increase muscle strength and suppleness, and increase the functioning of our immune system—to name just some of its many benefits. But fewer of us are aware that exercise can also provide a significant psychological "lift," not only in the short term but also the long term.

Studies indicate that the 3 in 10 Americans who exercise regularly handle stressful events better and feel more vitality and self-confidence than their couch potato counterparts. They also experience less anxiety, less depression, and less fatigue. In a 2002 Gallup survey, those who did not exercise were twice as likely as those who did exercise to report being "not happy."

> **Happy Thought**
>
> "It is exercise alone that supports the spirits, and keeps the mind in vigor."
>
> —Cicero

For a time, researchers wondered if a positive correlation between exercise and self-reported happy feelings was enough to go on. Did the exercise engender the positive feelings, or was it perhaps that depressed people just didn't bother to exercise? Experiments were designed to clear up any ambiguity. In one, a third of a group of mildly depressed college coeds were assigned a program of aerobic exercise, another third were assigned relaxation exercises, and the remaining third made no change in behavior. At the end of 10 weeks, the women in the aerobic exercise program reported the greatest decrease in depression. Today, more than 150 studies have confirmed that exercise is as effective as certain prescription drugs in reducing anxiety and depression. In fact it can be even better than drugs because exercise is better at preventing the recurrence of symptoms.

In a sense, exercise employs drugs—not pharmaceuticals, but natural, endogenous (meaning "produced within") chemicals. Two primary chemicals involved in making exercise feel good are cortisol and endorphins. Cortisol is a hormone produced by our bodies when we are under stress. It ultimately inflames and damages our organs. Exercise burns cortisol, and thereby makes us feel calmer and happier.

Exercise also prompts the brain's pituitary gland to release endorphins into the bloodstream. Endorphins are morphine-like hormone molecules that enter the brain's neurons and attach to receptors that normally send pain-signaling molecules back to other parts of the brain. Some say endorphins are more potent and create a more euphoric feeling than opiate drugs such as morphine and opium, which attach to the same receptors when introduced to the body.

How much and what type of exercise does it take to tap our internal feel-good pharmacy? Various researchers give varying answers. A general rule of thumb offered by Robert G. McMurray of the University of Carolina at Chapel Hill is that 20 to 30 minutes of exercise during which you are working at 80 percent of your heart and lung capacity brings on endorphin release. But renowned mood researcher Robert Thayer says that even a 10-minute walk stimulates two hours of increased feelings of well-being by reducing tension and increasing energy.

Stumbling Blocks

Some scientists contend that significant endorphin release occurs only with heavy weightlifting or anaerobic exercise—that is, exercise involving short energy bursts that cause the body to temporarily run out of oxygen. But you are the best judge of what makes you feel good from within. Experiment for yourself, and don't let a quest for the "perfect workout" prevent you from getting a workout that is good enough.

Exercise and the Well-Lived Life

It's easy to see how exercise can contribute to the kind of happiness that Martin Seligman calls the pleasant life. But it can contribute to the good life and the meaningful life as well.

In addition to giving us a physiological mood boost, exercise can give us a mental edge. For one thing, it actually helps create new brain cells—the better to stay alert, alive, curious, and creative. For another thing, exercise tends to instill what is known as "the mastery effect," engendering a sense of personal achievement as we master new skills or get better at old ones. The resulting self-confidence inspires us to tackle new challenges and seek new opportunities.

Exercise can also promote more social interaction, which in itself can promote happiness. Joining a gym or participating in a dance class or a running or hiking group means finding potential friends with similar interests. (Not to mention creating a social-reinforcement network that will make it harder to make excuses for not showing up.)

Not a joiner? That might change after you begin shaping up. Exercise not only makes us feel and look better, but also makes us feel better about the way we look. Armed with a trimmed-down waistline, glowing skin, and the enhanced self-image such improvements can instigate, exercisers might find they are more interested than ever in becoming part of a group.

Happiness Trivia

According to a 2007 Harvard study, the mere belief that we are getting a workout affects our physiology as much as the workout itself. That is, exercise may impact health in part through the placebo effect: you believe you are doing your body good, and that belief leads to some of the well-documented benefits of exercise—both physiological and psychological.

The study followed a number of hotel housekeepers—some of whom were told that their job provided a good workout, and some of whom were told nothing. Those who believed they were getting a workout reported feeling better, even though the amount of movement done by each group was the same. Amazingly, the informed group also lost weight and lowered their blood pressure.

Moving Toward Movement

Getting started with a fitness program need not be a complicated or costly affair. There are usually more mental hurdles than logistical or financial ones. But all hurdles can be overcome in the name of happiness.

Simple First Steps

It doesn't take much more than a comfortable pair of shoes and a little determination to get started on a walking program. You can enjoy the outdoors, say hello to your neighbors (racking up some additional social contact), and vary your route to avoid boredom.

If there's a bicycle gathering dust in your garage, check the air in the tires and spray the gears with some oil. Then find your helmet, or buy a new one, and pedal away to instantly experience some of the fun and freedom you felt in childhood when you were independently mobile. Remember, this is not the Tour de France, so you needn't seek out the highest hill in town. Pick a destination that's a quarter of an hour away, get there, turn around and come back. Next time you can go further if you like.

Dancing is also great exercise. You can sign up for classes, of course, but you can also do a private (or semi-private) Tom Cruise *Risky Business* imitation. Draw the shades, strip down to your skivvies, and improvise.

Swimming promotes strength, stamina, and mobility along with cardiovascular fitness—and immersion in water can have a soothing effect. Access to a swimming pool is probably more readily available than you think. Call your local "Y" or municipal pool and inquire.

Other excellent aerobic choices include the following:

- Ice skating

- In-line skating

- Rowing

- Racquet sports such as tennis or squash

- Downhill or cross-country skiing

- Snowshoeing

If you're just starting out or giving one of these activities a tentative try, don't buy equipment. Rent it instead and see if it is an activity that you enjoy. If it is, you can invest later; if not, you can move on to new movements.

Moving Beyond Excuses

Now that you know you don't have to spend a fortune to exercise, what other excuses do you have? Not enough time? Exercise is boring? No companion to work out with? Too embarrassed about the shape you're in now? Most people who have not yet been bitten by the exercise bug can come up with lots of these. But—as with all things—for every negative reaction, there is a positive response:

"Not enough time." Fair enough. If necessary, combine exercise with another activity you do daily. If, for example, you watch a half hour of financial news on television each morning, consider doing so while you walk on a treadmill. Alternatively, consider swapping exercise for an activity that brings you little joy. Perhaps you can bike to the office and avoid sitting in traffic. Finally, consider that regular exercise adds an average of two years to your life. You get all the time spent exercising back in the end.

"Exercise is boring." Not all exercise regimes are for all people. The trick is to find some things you like to do, then mix those things up. Altering your exercise regime prevents monotony and gooses the endorphins again. From time to time, vary your intensity, cross train, take up a new sport, or sign up for a few sessions with a trainer. Keeping your exercise fresh is as important as keeping your love life fresh.

"No companion." After you start exercising you'll likely run (perhaps literally) into others who do the same thing at the same time. It's a great opportunity to "buddy up." However, if you want to leave nothing to chance, sign up for a class or join a gym where you can fraternize with other workout devotees or fellow novices. Find a gym with convenient hours and a nearby location so you do not generate additional excuses.

"Embarrassed about my shape." Not working out because you are embarrassed about not being in shape is like not going to the dentist because you are embarrassed about having a cavity. You have to start somewhere! That said, it's reasonable to avoid situations where you will be thrown in with only hardcore veterans or exercisers with "attitude." Look for a venue that clearly welcomes people at all levels of fitness. If you're self-conscious about your body in front of the opposite sex, consider joining a gym that is gender-specific.

Helping Hand

Many people find exercise more engaging and get an even more intense mood boost when they combine a workout with music. Consider an exercise class where the instructor incorporates music into the routine. Or strap on your iPod and do it yourself. Choose up-tempo songs that inspire you to keep going and give it your all.

Some people work so hard at coming up with excuses they'd actually expend less effort exercising than stalling. If you count yourself among this number, it's time to stop moving your lips and try putting one foot in front of the other. You'll undoubtedly be happy you did.

Yoga: Thousands of Years of Happiness Training

The practice of *hatha yoga*, an exercise discipline that has thrived around the world for thousands of years, can also be a way of moving toward happiness. As mentioned in Chapter 2, the foundational texts of *yoga* refer repeatedly to the cultivation of bliss. Contemporary research backs up the yoga-happiness connection. In fact, many studies suggest that yoga can bring about and maintain positive states of mind to those who practice it, in spite of life's ups and downs. As practiced yogis might say, yoga can induce *ananda*—a state of delight.

def•i•ni•tion

Yoga, from a Sanskrit word referring to the binding of opposites, is actually comprised of eight interrelated practices, some of which have to do with purifying the body and some with purifying the mind.

Hatha yoga is the aspect of yoga that focuses on physical postures, and here in the West is the typical entry point to yoga practice. *Ha* means "sun" and *tha* means "moon"—thus, the word itself incorporates the concept of natural balance.

When a British research team compared the effects of two relaxation techniques—chair sitting and visualization—with yoga, the team found that yoga resulted in the greatest increase in alertness, mental and physical energy, and what they termed "lust for life." Similarly, a German study, which compared a group of women practicing hatha yoga to a control group that did not, found that the yoga practitioners showed markedly higher scores in life satisfaction and lower scores in aggressiveness, emotionality, and sleep problems.

Most recently, scientists from the Boston University School of Medicine reported the results of a long-term study of yoga using the latest brain-scanning technology. They found that practicing yoga appeared to elevate brain levels of gamma-aminobutyric (GABA), the brain's primary inhibitory neurotransmitter. The findings, which appear in the *Journal of Alternative and Complementary Medicine,* suggest that the practice of yoga be explored as a possible treatment for depression and anxiety—both disorders associated with low GABA levels. The study's lead author, Chris Streeter M.D., an assistant professor of psychiatry and neurology at BUSM said, "Our findings clearly demonstrate that in experienced yoga practitioners, brain GABA levels increase after a session of yoga."

The Yogic State: More Than Poses

Because anti-depressant drugs work in part by boosting a patient's GABA levels, the fact that yoga might be doing this without pharmaceuticals is significant. Moreover, it does so without negative side effects. Of course hatha yoga does have many positive effects, apart from its impact on brain chemistry, like the following:

It induces better breathing. While holding each posture, practitioners are taught to lengthen their stretches by deep, slow breathing. This is the sort of breathing that naturally counters stress and tension as it stimulates the body's natural relaxation response.

It engenders increased flexibility, agility, and balance. Even those who consider themselves "klutzes" often report feeling more graceful and more in control of their bodies after they take up yoga. This can lead to an enhanced self-image and even to a greater self-confidence at other physical activities.

It can lead to sounder sleeping. As you'll see in Chapter 19, getting enough good-quality sleep is an integral part of overall happiness. Many who have taken up yoga report that it has become easier for them to fall asleep and that they sleep more soundly. Some contend they can substitute 30 to 60 minutes of yoga for 30 to 60 minutes of sleep and feel even better.

It increases focus and present-moment awareness. The practice of yoga does not require a great deal of physical strength or know-how from the beginner, but it does require focus. The postures—called *asanas*—can be held comfortably for increasing lengths of time as one progresses, provided you keep your mind on the activity at hand. This kind of mindfulness—and the corresponding freedom from the nagging chatter of anxious thoughts—is also conducive to creating a sense of contentment and inner peace.

Finally, the long-term effects of yoga practice can include a decrease in self-judgment and self-criticism. Good teachers encourage their students to honor and value their bodies and to respect their current limitations as they *gently* progress to doing more. With the proper guidance, students can take this positive attitude with them and apply it outside the yoga studio as well.

> **Helping Hand**
>
> Most yoga classes, no matter how active, conclude with a period of time spent in the restorative pose known as *shavasana*, or "corpse pose." This feels better than it sounds! It allows you to fully absorb the benefits of the practice as you lie flat on your back with your arms and legs spread apart. As you feel yourself sinking into the earth, scan the body for signs of any residual tension and consciously relax those spots. Avoid the temptation to leave class early. This part "counts" as much as the rest of class, if not more.

First Steps on the Yogic Path

If you have never attempted yoga, it might seem as though it is a strange ritual of twisting yourself into a pretzel, perhaps in a semi-darkened room, perhaps with some Eastern-style music in the background. Can this sort of thing really make you happier if the very idea makes you uncomfortable? Is it really for you? As with anything, you will never know until you give it a try. That said, it is true that newcomers to yoga can be intimidated if they don't keep a few things in mind.

Don't be put off by any glossy magazine covers featuring Hollywood stars doing their daily yoga routines or flawless models performing gravity-defying backbends. Everyone has to start somewhere and you can be sure this is not how they started. Even if you never come close to achieving such feats, you can still do yoga and get a great deal out of it.

Also, don't worry that, "I can't do yoga because I'm not flexible." That is just like worrying, "I can't get in shape because I'm not in shape." Bit by bit, yoga will limber and strengthen you, and you'll start stretching not only your body but also your confidence.

As with any exercise activity, you can spend quite a bit of money on yoga-related items. But you can also choose not to. A pair of leggings and a fitted T-shirt will do fine for a wardrobe. Happily, you don't need special shoes because yoga is done in bare feet. As for accouterments such as straps and blocks, any good yoga studio should be equipped with all you need. After a while you might want to buy and bring your own mat, but that's a preference rather than a necessity—and in any case you should wait until you're sure you're going to become a yoga regular.

Yoga's Not a Competitive Sport

Perhaps the most important thing to remember about yoga is that it's not a competition. Don't overdo it in the beginning in the attempt to keep up with fellow practitioners. In fact, don't overdo it *ever*. Your body can have a different tolerance for various postures on various days. It's not about forcing but rather about expanding.

If you find yourself in a class that you feel is too advanced for you, look for a class with a greater number of beginners. There you will receive more detailed step-by-step instruction and, most likely, feel less self-conscious.

Also, be aware that there are many different styles of practice that fall under the general umbrella of hatha yoga. All offer physical benefits as well as the potential to simultaneously relax and energize you. But some take a more vigorous approach, whereas others are slower and more meditative.

Among the approaches you may choose to sample:

Iyengar is one of the most popular styles of yoga. It is all about attention to detail, with focus on the subtleties of each posture. Iyengar makes use of props, including belts, chairs, blocks, and blankets, to help accommodate beginners or those with any special needs, such as injuries or structural imbalances.

Ashtanga is a fast, flowing series of sequential postures that offers an aerobic challenge—and thus gives you a chance to generate extra endorphins. Ashtanga practitioners can be very zealous and classes quite rigorous. If you are a novice, be sure to find a teacher who welcomes beginners.

Sivananda is a fairly gentle style of yoga that promotes physical strength and flexibility while incorporating specialized breath work. It is very focused on stress release and on removing energy blockages. Classes tend to include a mild spiritual dimension and might include a little *"Om"* chanting.

The focus in *Kundalini* yoga is to liberate the energy at the base of the spine and draw it upward through the body's energy centers. This is a very energetic style of yoga, and includes a lot of dynamic breathing and quickly repeated postures. It can provide quite a workout.

Sometimes called "hot yoga," *Bikram* yoga is conducted in studios where room temperatures push or even exceed 100 degrees Fahrenheit. Practitioners say its sauna-like effect is cleansing. This style of yoga was designed by Bikram Choudhury, who sequenced a series of 26 traditional hatha postures to enhance the optimal functioning of every bodily system. Be prepared to perspire your way to happiness.

Ananda yoga offers a system for enhancing spiritual growth while releasing unwanted tensions. The unique part is the use of silent positive affirmations while holding poses. Class also focuses on mindful posture and controlled breathing.

Anusara means "to step into the current of divine will." A newer system of hatha yoga, it focuses not only on body mechanics but also on cultivating a transformative attitude. Practitioners aim to awaken their true inner nature. Each pose is conceived of as not only an exercise, but also an artistic expression of the benevolent spirit in one's heart.

In *Kripalu* yoga, practitioners are asked to hold postures to the level of tolerance— and gradually push that level. This deepening concentration and focus is said to result in complete release of the body's internal tensions as well as enhancement of self-confidence and mental tenacity.

Many yoga classes—often those that are simply billed as yoga or hatha yoga—offer a blend of styles suited to the students who regularly attend. The instructor will assess the students' abilities and goals and then work accordingly.

In general, finding an instructor with whom you are comfortable is more important than what the class is called. Trust your instincts. You will know the right teacher when you find someone who makes you feel not only happy about taking yoga in the moment, but happier about yourself as a result.

Helping Hand

After you take a number of yoga classes, you might choose to bring some aspects of your yoga home. Many practitioners put together a personal practice and they take about 20 minutes to do it on a daily basis, wherever they are. Yoga is extremely portable. If you've got your body and a floor, you can do it.

The Effect of Positive Posture

Even if there is no chance of your fitting aerobic exercise or yoga into your life, there is one thing you can do physically that will take but a moment and will change your outlook significantly: straighten up.

Your mother may have always told you to stand up straight, but chances are she did so in order for you to look good. What she probably did not know, but the field of *embodied cognitive science* has now discovered, is that standing tall can also help you maintain a positive attitude. According to the principles of embodied cognition, manipulating one's stance can causally affect how emotional information is processed.

In one study, participants were divided into two groups: one adopted a posture in which the head and shoulders slumped; the other adopted a posture in which the shoulders were held back and high. Both groups were informed they had been successful on an achievement test completed earlier. Those who received the good news while in a slumped posture reported feeling less proud and being in a worse mood than did those who were standing tall. The subjects with good posture literally embodied happiness.

def•i•ni•tion

Embodied cognitive science is an interdisciplinary field of research whose aim is to explain the mechanisms underlying intelligent behavior. It evaluates psychological and biological systems in a holistic manner that considers the mind and body as a single entity.

Helping Hand _____

As long as you're standing up straight, you can take your mother's other classic piece of advice and put a smile on your face. Even when you don't feel like smiling, studies show that forming a grin can lift your spirits and make you perceive communications from others as more positive. If you need help raising the corners of your mouth, try holding a pencil between your teeth.

The Least You Need to Know

♦ Exercise stimulates the body's internal pharmacy—it triggers the release of feel-good endorphins and inhibits cortisol, a chemical that accompanies stress.

♦ Exercise further contributes to happiness by making us feel a sense of mastery, by boosting self-esteem, and by providing potential opportunities for social contact.

♦ Beginning an exercise program can be as simple as getting into the habit of taking walks—the important thing is to overcome habitual excuses.

♦ The practice of hatha yoga as an exercise discipline has been shown to correlate with happiness—the breathing, relaxation, and mental focus techniques that accompany the postures likely play a role.

♦ If all else fails, stand up straight—studies show that ergonomically correct posture improves mood and attitude and literally helps us "embody" happiness.

Chapter 19

Sublime Sleep

In This Chapter

- Linking sleep and happiness
- Discovering our sleep-deprived society
- Finding sound sleeping strategies
- Sleep-inducing relaxations and visualizations
- Enjoying the happy effects of napping

Imagine that, on a given day, you've done everything you can, based on what you know, to go to bed happy. You spent part of the day using your strengths at work and in your personal life. You spent quality time with friends and family. You shared a good laugh, did a good deed, and had a good workout. You even took a few moments before bedtime to be consciously grateful for all the positive things in your life. But then it happens: you just can't sleep.

Maybe you're tossing and turning because of noise; maybe it's because of a late-night cappuccino you enjoyed; maybe it's because there's something on your mind. Whatever the reason, one thing is for certain: you won't start the next day in an especially happy frame of mind, nor feel well-equipped to continue to do the things that you know keep you satisfied, unless you've gotten a good night's sleep.

The Sleep/Happiness Connection

Getting consistent high-quality sleep is strongly correlated to being happy and productive and feeling emotionally and mentally healthy. The analysis of comprehensive Center for Disease Control (CDC) data that examined the behaviors and attitudes of more than half a million Americans found a strong correlation between an individual's level of happiness and the amount of sleep or rest they get each day.

At first this might seem odd. Why should eight hours of "nothingness" have such an impact one way or the other? But it makes sense if we really look at what, exactly, sleep is for. It is, in fact, *not* for nothing.

On a physical level, sleep restores bodily energy supplies that have been depleted during the course of the day. Sleep is also the time when our body repairs muscle tissue by secreting a human growth hormone, which our tissues require even after we are "grown." Sleep improves muscle tone, enabling us to run faster, jump higher, and in general, be agile rather than slow and clumsy. Sleep also appears to boost the body's immune system and helps prevent us from being sick.

On a cognitive level, sleep recharges our mental batteries and keeps the mind sharp. Although the adult human brain accounts for only 3 percent of body weight, it consumes 25 percent of body energy. Thinking, creating, and problem solving require lots of "juice," provided by a molecule called glycogen. The slow, steady brain waves of sleep restock our glycogen stores. Some sleep experts also believe that sleep detoxifies the brain by lowering its temperature. And although the jury is still out in terms of the exact purpose of dreams, there is no doubt that the REM (rapid eye movement) stage of sleep that indicates dreaming is essential for optimal mental functioning. Keep us from our REM sleep, and we can quickly go to pieces under the slightest pressure.

> **Happy Thought**
>
> "A good laugh and a long sleep are the best cures in the doctor's book."
>
> —Irish proverb

Another reason we feel less emotionally stable with diminished sleep is that restorative, slow-wave sleep (not the REM type, but the type in which we spend most of our sleep time) decreases the amount of stress hormones in our system. A poor night's sleep, let alone several in a row, actually increases the levels of such hormones. Now, little irritants and setbacks that might not ordinarily bother us (especially if we've resolved to keep an optimistic outlook and remember our sense of humor) can suddenly seem overwhelming.

In short, a sleep-deprived person will greet each day with a fatigued body, a fuzzy mind, and a propensity for negative emotional overreaction—three clear happiness handicaps. Physical pleasures will seem dulled, making the pleasant life elusive. Mental tasks will feel harder, making it harder to stretch and challenge ourselves in ways that offer personal satisfaction. As for interpersonal relations, they're bound to suffer casualties. It's hard to feel loving, compassionate, or altruistic when we're in a perennial state of crankiness. Instead of lending a helping hand to those in need, we'd be more likely to bite their heads off.

Cutting into Our Happiness

How much sleep is optimal for a happy life? To some extent, that varies from one individual to another. Factors such as physical size, muscle mass, and other variables that affect metabolic rate can vary. But on the whole, if you're in the seven- to eight-hour range, you're in the ballpark.

For much of human history, worrying about how much sleep we got was not an issue. We simply slept when it was dark. With the advent of artificial light, we had more options. But even as recently as the start of the twentieth century, the average American slept nine hours a night. Now we are faced with an epidemic of sleep debt. By 2001, only 38 percent of American adults got eight hours of sleep a night. By 2007, according to the National Sleep Foundation, that number had dropped to 26 percent.

We Americans say we crave more sleep. According to a Yankelovich Inc. poll, 43 percent of working people claim they'd take an extra hour of sleep during an hour of free time. But the statistics just don't back this up.

Some sleep loss is the result of sleep disorders and other medical problems. But for the most part, not sleeping enough is a self-inflicted condition. Sleep experts say we make excuses to rationalize our lack of sleep. We say …

- ◆ We are exceptions who can "handle" lack of sleep.
- ◆ Life's too short and we don't want to "waste time" sleeping.
- ◆ We're too busy and too in-demand.
- ◆ We're not sleepy.
- ◆ We'll catch up on sleep later.

But these excuses don't hold up. No one performs up to their potential when they don't get enough rest. The life we are trying to squeeze more out of actually becomes less rewarding. And all those commitments we think we should keep are actually harder to keep as we lose our energy and focus.

As for those who are "not sleepy," chances are they're tanked up on caffeine or sugar, or both. And as for those who say they'll catch up, they're probably fooling themselves. If you need eight hours of sleep and you sleep for five hours, three nights a week, you'd have to spend nine additional hours sleeping during the weekend to catch up. In other words, you'd have to lose most of one waking day. And that's certainly not a happy prospect.

Stumbling Blocks

You might not think you're sleep-deprived, but stay alert for signs that you could be. These include increased daytime grogginess, frequent yawning, sleeping through an alarm, a tendency to doze off as soon as you stop moving around (when you're reading or watching TV), decreased motivation and initiative, wandering attention and flagging memory, decreased decision-making ability, or increased moodiness and irritability.

Secrets of Happy Sleeping

The bottom line is that anyone who is not getting enough sleep is not getting the most out of life, no matter what they think. To up our capacity for happiness, we have to take the time to refuel. Sadly, however, some of us have developed some very counterproductive sleep habits and need to teach ourselves to sleep again.

A Serene Sleep Space

If you want to embark on a worthy project, acknowledging your ongoing quest for happiness, consider re-creating your bedroom into a simple space designed for sleeping and not too much else (okay, one other bed-related activity—but that adds to happiness as well).

If you have a computer in your bedroom, you will be tempted to work, answer e-mails, do some online shopping, or engage in myriad web-entangling experiences. Because cyberspace never sleeps, neither will you. If you have a television in the bedroom, you'll watch it ... and watch it. But although watching TV seems like a passive activity, it is actually stimulating. You'll stay up later than you otherwise might, and when you do fall asleep, the TV might still be blaring. If so, the quality of your slumber will be poorer than it ought to be.

Of course, there are things you should have in your sleep space. One of those is a firm mattress—the better to support your spine. The mattress should be big enough to spread out on, but not so big you feel lost. If you like touching your partner during sleep for a reassuring sense of "home base," a full or queen size might suit you better than a king (but the reverse is true if your partner routinely wakes you by tossing, turning, flailing, or inadvertently kicking you in the shins). Keep your bed free of clutter. Rolling over into a crackly newspaper or a crunchy bag of chips can lead to a rude awakening.

Money can't buy happiness per se, but splurging a little might enhance your sleep experience. If you want to feel like you're sleeping on a cloud, invest in a fluffy goose-down comforter. Also try one of those Tempur-Pedic pillows that mold themselves to your neck and head shape. Many sleepers grow so fond of their personalized pillows that they pack them when they travel.

Another way you should tend to your sleep space is to keep it at the proper temperature. To facilitate sleep, the bedroom should be between 60 and 65 degrees. If it feels a bit chilly before you get under the covers, you're doing it right. You can always adjust your own temperature after you're in bed by adding blankets or wearing cozy long silk underwear. Keep the room well-ventilated with an open window or two—unless doing so creates a noise factor.

Happiness Trivia

A "Sleep in the City" study conducted by researcher Bert Sperling (known for his national "Best Places" studies) in conjunction with the manufacturers of a prescription sleep aid evaluated the 10 best and worst cities in America for getting a restful night's sleep. Minneapolis, Anaheim, and San Diego were the top three cities with well-rested inhabitants. Detroit, Cleveland, and Nashville were the cities where inhabitants reported not getting enough sleep or not waking up refreshed.

The study was based on analysis of recent Centers for Disease Control and Prevention (CDC) data, along with data from the Bureau of Labor Statistics and the U.S. Census Bureau.

It's also wise to keep the lights in your bedroom low—especially for half an hour to an hour before you plan on turning them off altogether. When you're in bed, the darker it is, the better you'll sleep. Even an illuminated alarm clock or telephone dial can be an annoyance when you're having trouble drifting off. If you want to be able to check the time during the night, opt for the kind of alarm clock that lights only when you press on it.

A Regular Routine

A few changes in your schedule can increase your chances of getting enough quality sleep to keep your stress in check and your happiness potential high. Even if your personality resists regular routines, your body likes them, so modifying your behavior will cheer you up in the long run.

It's a good idea to get up at around the same time each day (yes, even on weekends and vacations), to eat at more or less the same intervals, and to get to bed at around the same time each night, even if you don't feel especially sleepy when the hour arrives.

def•i•ni•tion

A **circadian rhythm** is a roughly 24-hour cycle in the physiological processes of living beings. The term "circadian," comes from the Latin *circa*, "around," and *dies*, "day." Although circadian rhythms are internally generated, they can be influenced by external cues, such as sunlight and temperature.

If you're worried about not being tired enough at bedtime, give serious thought to getting up about a half hour earlier than you have been. If it helps, you can adjust this in 10-minute increments during the course of a week or two. Getting up earlier will help you wind down earlier and it will expose you to more natural sunlight, which can improve your mood and help regulate your *circadian rhythms*.

Also, after you're awake, get up. There's an old joke that goes, "If we were meant to pop out of bed in the morning we'd all sleep in toasters." But lolling about between the sheets, unless perhaps for some active morning romance, is not conducive to falling back to sleep later on. (If you really need help getting up, consider getting a cat. As cat-lovers have pointed out, there's no such thing as a snooze alarm on a cat who wants breakfast.)

At first, altering your schedule might cause some mental stress or some social glitches, but your body will be grateful and will show its gratitude by sleeping long and well. This should more than compensate for any initial sense of inconvenience.

Helping Hand

If you've been sleeping poorly for a while, try keeping a sleep diary, and record the time you awoke, the time you got out of bed, the time you went to bed, and about how long it took you to fall asleep. See if you notice any patterns that could be sapping your shut-eye. For example, do you sleep in on Sunday mornings only to find you lie awake for hours on Sunday nights?

Bedtime Cooldowns

If you have difficulty getting to sleep, getting ready for bed takes on a whole new meaning beyond brushing your teeth and putting on your pajamas. A little preplanned unwinding ritual or two can help get you in the right frame of mind to switch gears. Here are some things you can try:

- **A warm bath.** There was a reason your Mom gave you a bath before bedtime when you were small. It calms you down and signals that the energetic part of the day is done. Throw in a few drops of calming aromatherapy oil—a lavender fragrance is a wonderful choice—for extra help.

- **Soft, soothing music.** Music can help ease you toward sleep, and if you don't already have your own favorites there are a number of collections designed for this purpose. If you put the music on your iPod, you can program it to turn off after a set number of minutes. Also consider trying "white noise" machines that re-create calming natural sounds such as waves or a forest rainfall.

- **Sip some soothing tea.** A number of herbal teas are said to have sleep-inducing properties. Experiment with valerian tea, chamomile, catnip, anise, or fennel tea. Most health-food stores also have special blends designed to help you slumber.

- **Get some L-tryptophan.** If you like milk, drinking a warm glass of it about a quarter of an hour before bedtime soothes the nervous system, thanks to its calcium and an amino acid called L-tryptophan. L-tryptophan is also found in turkey, chicken, cashews, beans, yogurt, and fresh cheeses such as ricotta, but keep your snacking small and light in the hours before bed.

- **Gentle evening exercise.** Doing 15 to 20 minutes of gentle exercise (yoga, t'ai chi, or walking) in the evening can provide your body with the oxygen it needs to sleep well. The trick is not to overdo it; stop exercising long enough before bedtime to allow your body to slow down. This slowdown period could take half an hour, but might take up to several hours. See what works best for you.

When it comes to bedtime cooldowns, different solutions vary in their effectiveness for different people. You might have to play around to come up with one that works for you, but when you find one you like, you may well find it works consistently. Your brain will begin to associate your chosen technique with the onset of sleepiness.

Stumbling Blocks _____

Caffeine can keep you awake, sometimes even if you drink it six or seven hours before bedtime. Caffeine is found not only in coffee but also in black tea, chocolate, cola drinks, and a number of so-called "energy drinks."

Alcohol can also interfere with your sleep. Its aftereffects can wake you up in the wee hours, preventing you from getting a deep rest. Although a glass of wine at dinner may not impact you too much, it's best to avoid drinking two to three hours before bedtime.

Don't Just Lie There

If you're already in bed and feeling as if you have ants in your pants, is it time to count sheep? In a manner of speaking, yes. Counting sheep—or visualizing any benign, repetitive imagery (puppies, goldfish, or whatever you like) while counting—can make you pleasantly drowsy. If that doesn't do the trick, try one of these relaxation and visualization techniques:

- **Tummy circles.** Lying on your back, place your right palm on your navel, making tiny clockwise circles as you gently glide your hand. Let the circles gradually increase in size until they cover your stomach area. Then decrease the size of the circle again until you are right over your navel. Now transition to counterclockwise circles and do the same thing. Do this several times and you'll soothe yourself to sleep.

- **Toe twirls.** While lying on your back and keeping your feet still, turn your toes in a twirling motion—first clockwise, then counterclockwise, 10 times in each direction. Repeat. This simple exercise relaxes your entire body because, according to reflexologists, bodily energy channels called *meridians* converge there. Twirling the toes first stimulates then relaxes the meridians in your feet and, in so doing, relaxes every internal organ.

def•i•ni•tion _____

Meridians are one of the pillars of traditional Chinese medicine, and therefore of acupuncture and acupressure. They are the channels said to distribute vital energy throughout the body. Although meridians have no discernible physical structure, they are likened to the wiring in a house or the veins through which blood flows.

- **Progressive relaxation.** Close your eyes while lying on your back and begin to feel each part of your body in turn sinking into the mattress as it grows heavier and heavier. Begin with your feet, then follow in an upward-moving sequence with your ankles, calves, upper legs, abdomen, chest, arms, neck, jaw, eyes, and forehead—if you last that long!

- **Blow out the candles.** This sleep-inducer combines a calming visual stimulus with breath-based relaxation. Imagine a large round birthday cake with 100 glowing candles. Breathe in and think "100." Breathe out, as if blowing out a candle and think "99." Take another breath and repeat, counting backward until you count yourself among those who are happily sleeping.

- **Listen to your inner ocean.** Lying on your back, place your hands behind your head with fingers—except thumbs—interlocked. Now use your thumbs to press gently on your lower ear lobes so that they fold over the entrance to the ear canal. As you lie quietly, you will notice a deep, ocean-like sound inside your head. The sound will ebb and flow as you naturally breathe in and out. Simply focus on the noise—it's like creating your own personal "white noise" machine in your head.

- **Cast your eyes down.** A simple yoga technique for inducing sleep is to keep your eyes closed and aim them downward, as if you were looking down at the base of your nose. This signals the body that it's time to sleep. When eyes are focused straight ahead, the body is more alert.

- **Elevate your feet.** Take two pillows and place them under your feet. Yes, your feet. This posture signals your heart to slow down. It can also remind you of the way you feel when drifting off to sleep in a backyard hammock, swaying in the gentle breeze on a lazy afternoon.

- **Imagine a snow day.** If you enjoy the feeling of "stealing" a few more minutes of slumber after you hit your snooze alarm on a workday morning, use this predilection to your advantage. Pretend it's your usual get-up time, but that you've just heard everything is closed due to an overnight blizzard. You've been given a reprieve to sleep in—enjoy it!

If you keep experimenting, you should be able to find a technique that works to help you get to sleep most nights. If there is a night when it is not working, try another. However, if there is an occasional night where nothing works and 30 minutes have passed, you will experience diminishing returns. Get up and pursue some quiet, non-stimulating activity such as inspirational reading (no news magazines or page-turning mysteries, please) or meditation. When you start to feel tired, go back to bed.

Happy Napping

If getting eight hours a night does not seem feasible for you, or even if it does, you might want to consider adding to your happiness potential by catching a nap. Scientists are discovering more and more evidence that a midday rest can improve mood; alertness; memory; and visual, motor, and spatial skills. As a study of 24,000 subjects showed, it can even improve cardiac health.

Naps of 20 minutes are typically recommended if one is seeking these benefits. But some researchers believe that even a five-minute midday nap can have a salutary effect. Although you might fear waking up groggy and inert after sleeping for such brief lengths of time, chances are you won't, because the short duration will prevent you from entering the deep state of sleep known as slow-wave sleep.

Many of us say we "can't nap," but scientists would argue that we are naturally pro-grammed to nap. The first modern evidence for this came from a German doctor named Jürgen Aschoff, who performed sleep habit studies in the 1960s. He furnished abandoned World War II bunkers with all the amenities of small apartments, except without any clocks, calendars, or even whether it was light or dark outside, Aschoff simply instructed his subjects to choose their own schedule for eating and sleeping. When they did, he observed that they generally experienced a large drop in energy in the middle of the "night," during which they would sleep for six to seven hours. Then, roughly 12 hours later, a smaller dip drove them back to bed for a shorter period of sleep. In other words, when people are free from environmental cues and follow their own internal rhythms, napping quickly materializes as part of their everyday behavior.

So why have so many of us "forgotten" how to nap? One answer is that we've gotten out of the habit because our schedule is not conducive to napping. Another is that we live in a culture where napping can be considered morally suspect. Only the "lazy" and "shiftless" nap, we may tell ourselves.

But social and moral perspectives on napping are changing, thanks, at least in part, to a linguistic switchover. Where we once spoke of catnaps—the sort of thing one indulged in on the sofa on a Sunday afternoon—we now hear of *power naps*. Power naps sound permissible even to high achievers, as they imply that a midday snooze is now an activity not for losers but for winners. And the stereotype of

def•i•ni•tion

The term **power nap**, coined by Cornell University social psycholo-gist James Maas, refers to a short (about 20 minute) workday nap that leaves nappers refreshed and more productive. Power naps are associated not with slackers, but with go-getters who wish to maximize their waking time.

nappers eschewing the work ethic is now under such serious revision that many major corporations are providing time and quiet spaces for employees to take naps during the workday.

With the stigma of napping rapidly becoming a thing of the past in our culture, it's a great time to give the practice a try. There is, however, one caveat. If you are seriously sleep-deprived, you might quickly fall into a deep sleep from which it is difficult to reorient. The power nap works best as a complement to adequate nighttime slumber, not as compensation for chronic deprivation. The bottom line: to fulfill your happiness potential, it's best to get a good night's sleep and then some.

The Least You Need to Know

- Studies have found a strong correlation between an individual's level of happiness and the amount of sleep or rest they get each day.

- Only 26 percent of American adults get an optimum eight hours of sleep a night—we give many other activities priority, which ultimately lowers our quality of life.

- Strategies for inducing sound sleep include simplifying your sleep space, sticking with a regular schedule seven days a week, and indulging in a little prebedtime winding down time so you don't shift gears too quickly.

- If you're in bed and can't sleep, practice a relaxation or visualization exercise in lieu of tossing and turning—but if you can't fall asleep after 30 minutes, get up and try again later.

- Napping can contribute to a happy, productive day by improving mood, skills, memory, alertness, and health.

Chapter 20

Meditation and Positive Emotion

In This Chapter

- ◆ Discovering meditation's growing acceptance in modern Western culture
- ◆ Changing the brain with meditation
- ◆ Making meditation part of your life
- ◆ Trying a sampling of meditation methods
- ◆ Achieving gradual change through practice

If you have ever encountered someone who has a regular meditation practice, you may have had the sense that they project an air of calm and contentment, and that they seem to be able to maintain that air come what may. As it happens, that "sense" you had about such people has been scientifically validated.

The practice of meditation has been clearly linked with the generation of positive emotion. In fact, meditation can actually alter the brain and perhaps permanently raise the setting on our internal happiness thermostat. The good news is that it's not necessary to go off to a mountaintop or to live in a cave or to devote hours a day to "contemplating your navel" to integrate meditation into your life and to accrue its benefits. As with physical exercise, it is a path accessible to most anyone willing to devote some consistent time and effort.

Meditation Off the Mountaintop

Meditation is a contemplative practice that has been around for thousands of years. It involves stilling the mind and resting one's mental focus on a single, simple phenomenon, such as the breath or the repetition of one word or sound. Although it may look like someone deep in meditation is doing "nothing," meditation requires the systematic cultivation of will and attention.

Meditation can seem mysterious and even off-putting to those who are unfamiliar with the ancient mental discipline. But because it can be such a valuable tool in allowing happiness to blossom, it is well worth understanding what meditation is and how and why its practice has endured and spread.

For as long as humans have been cognizant of and curious about consciousness, numerous cultures have—through slightly different styles, but with the same goals— explored the profound impact of meditative states. Meditation has been practiced in Christian monasteries and by Native American shamans, but we primarily think of it as an Eastern practice hailing from such faraway and exotic lands as India and Tibet. And indeed, until the 1970s most Westerners had no notion, or only the most vague idea, of what meditation is.

By the late 1960s, photographs of the Beatles sitting at the feet of Mahareshi Mahesh Yogi, whom they referred to as their *guru*, had captured the interest of the public. At the same time, Western scientists became intrigued with meditation not for its celebrity proponents but for its potential to create physical well-being—for example, by lowering blood pressure and mitigating other health conditions linked to stress.

In 1975, the publication of a landmark book of research, *The Relaxation Response* by Harvard Medical School's Dr. Herbert Benson, documented the benefits of a simple form of *mantra* meditation in treating patients with heart conditions, chronic pain, insomnia, and other medical conditions. Benson emphasized that meditation could provide physical benefits even in the absence of the devotional or metaphysical elements we typically associated with it. In other words, meditation, even as a strictly secular rather than spiritual practice, did a lot of good.

def•i•ni•tion

The word **guru,** from the Hindi language, refers to a spiritual teacher, counselor, or leader. Some think of a guru as an awakener of consciousness, or someone who can bring a pupil or follower from "darkness to light."

A **mantra** is a simple word or sound—such as *Om* or *peace* or *one*—that becomes the point of meditative focus.

By the 1980s, the general public had become familiar, at least in a general way, with the notion that meditation could help us relax and, in so doing, better our health. To some extent, meditation has been demystified and popularized. Still, many more people knew of it than tried it.

Recently, however, researchers have come up with another compelling reason to consider giving meditation a go. Backing up anecdotal advice that has accrued for millennia, scientists are proving that meditation can alter neural circuitry, in effect rewiring us to be happier.

Meditation and the Brain

By the late 1980s, great strides in medical research technology allowed scientists to study meditators by taking detailed photos (and, later, videos) of activity in various brain regions. Using functional MRIs (magnetic resonance imaging) and EEGs (electroencephalographs) they accumulated a wealth of hard data illuminating the effects of meditation on brain activity. What they learned was startling—and highly encouraging for happiness seekers. But their findings are more easily understood if we first detour briefly to understand some other fascinating brain research developments.

The "Plastic" Brain

Human infants are born with 100 billion or so neurons, or brain cells. Each individual neuron connects to about 2,500 other neurons, to start. For the first two or three years of life the brain continues to make connections at an astonishing rate, forming an average of 15,000 *synapses* per cell by the time we reach the age of two or three.

After age two, the brain starts reducing—or pruning—its number of synapses. We lose about half the connections we originally made. This is not as dire as it sounds, because what we are probably eliminating are redundant connections. The brain goes on a second connectivity binge just before puberty.

For a long time, however, it was thought that the adult brain was out of luck when it came to either generating new brain cells (*neurogenesis*) or making new connections in response to new input (*neuroplasticity*). Except for the fact that brain cells die as we age, the adult brain, it was assumed, was fixed and nonmalleable. There would be no new tricks for old dogs.

Happily, neuroscience has now proven—much to its own surprise—that the adult brain actually *does* generate new brain cells and is still quite "plastic." In fact, our brains can change under the influence of experience well into our eighth decade.

Among the things researchers now wanted to know: Was meditation the kind of experience that could literally alter the brain? And if so, how would those alterations affect those who meditated?

def•i•ni•tion

A **synapse** is a junction between two brain cells, where fibers are close enough to transmit signals across a small gap.

Neurogenesis refers to the birth of new brain cells.

Neuroplasticity refers to the ability of brain systems—including visual and auditory systems, attentional systems, and language systems—to change with experience and input from the environment.

Happy Meditators in the Lab

At the vanguard of scientists asking such questions was Richard Davidson, director of Neuroscience at the University of Wisconsin at Madison. Davidson and others crafted experiments involving meditation and brain imaging, the subjects of which were initially Buddhist monks, a.k.a. "the Olympian athletes of meditation." Because the researchers wanted to begin by looking at the upper limits of potential brain plasticity, they chose monks who had undertaken tens of thousands of hours of meditation.

MRIs and EEGs of the monks produced some amazing results. These subjects consistently showed intense activity (some of the highest ever recorded) in the left prefrontal context of the brain. That is the area associated with the generation of positive emotion. When activity in the left prefrontal cortex is notably higher than that in the right, people report feeling alert, energetic, joyous, and enthusiastic. In short, they enjoy life more. They are happier. (Conversely, when there is greater activity in the right prefrontal cortex, people report experiencing negative emotions, such as sadness, worry, and anxiety.)

Obviously, however, the average person interested in cultivating happiness is not—no matter *how* interested—going to be willing or able to devote thousands of hours to meditative practice. Can ordinary people willing to carve out a brief time each day for meditation expect a surge in positive feelings?

Wanting to know this, Davidson and colleague Jon Kabat-Zinn undertook a study of employees at a high-tech company who took a two-month meditation training program. Their brain imaging also showed substantial changes in brain activity, accompanied by beneficial mood changes and a decline in anxiety. It seemed that the average Joe could indeed enhance happiness and well-being through regular—but not extreme—meditation practice.

Happiness Trivia
In 2001, researchers at the University of Wisconsin fitted 256 electrodes to a Tibetan Buddhist monk known as the "happy *geshe*," who was known for his infectious aura of joy and contentment. During the time the monk was meditating on compassion—unbiased, benevolent feelings toward all beings—he registered left prefrontal cortex activity that was more than 99.7 percent of everyone ever measured.

Resetting the Happiness Set Point

Feeling calm and content during or immediately following meditation is a good thing. But Davidson and others are now coming to believe that the regular practice of meditation may do much more. It may actually reset our happiness set point.

The happiness set point, as mentioned in Chapter 1, is akin to a "default setting" for happiness. It's a benchmark to which we tend to return even after experiencing relative highs and lows. In part, the set point is genetically predetermined (as is, say, our blood pressure or our resting heart rate) but in part it is self-determined by what we choose to do (in the way that we can permanently impact our resting heart rate or blood pressure through regular exercise).

Of course, meditation won't change our genetic make-up. However, Davidson hypothesizes that, over time, mental training such as that involved in meditation could produce changes in the brain by taking advantage of its neuroplasticity. It could do this by producing changes in our "default" patterns of neural activation, and perhaps even by altering brain circuitry—in terms of what's connected to what else and how fortified those connections are. The intriguing possibility also exists, based on preliminary research, which people practiced at meditation may be able to deliberately shift the ratio of left to right activity in their prefrontal lobes and also turn down activity in a part of the brain called the *amygdala*, which processes emotions of aggression and fear.

Certainly, outward circumstances will continue to impact those who meditate, at times inducing a sense of sadness or suffering. But the idea is that the mind could be taught to override or at least mitigate negative emotions. Neural connections could well be modified through mental exercise just as the muscles in your arms and legs can be modified by working out with weights.

Getting Ready to Meditate

Understanding that meditation can dramatically affect your fundamental capacity for happiness is, for many, a powerful incentive to consider trying it. Yet many Westerners who have not grown up with this practice as a part of their cultural heritage have an understandable reluctance to actually doing it. It's a nice idea, we think, but it's not really for us.

The truth is that anyone *can* meditate, but not everyone will. If you are sufficiently motivated, the first thing that's necessary is to look at your own objections and see if you can reconcile them. The next is to make a plan to set aside some space and time to practice on a regular basis.

Examining Your Excuses

Whenever the subject of meditation is introduced to novices, many of the same objections tend to arise. Having any of these objections—or all of them, for that matter—is only natural. Owning up to them is the first step to overcoming them.

Perhaps you say you *cannot* meditate because …

- It's not part of your religion.
- You don't have a teacher.
- You can't sit still long enough.
- It's just too hard.

As for the first objection, if you investigate you might well find that your spiritual tradition does indeed integrate some form of meditative or contemplative activity. Although we tend to think of meditation as emanating from Buddhism and Hinduism, Christianity has a long tradition incorporating chanting and centering prayer. Islam has a tradition of Sufi meditation, the goal of which is to pursue both self-knowledge and a deeper knowledge of the divine. And many Jewish people are exploring modern techniques of meditation and mysticism that were prevalent in their tradition as far back as the thirteenth century.

Moreover, it's not necessary to subscribe to *any* religious faith or spiritual path to practice and benefit from meditation. Meditation can be approached from a strictly secular standpoint—for example, as a way to relax and sharpen one's mental powers. (Although it should be noted that some people who start out this way do find themselves becoming what they would call more "spiritual" as a result.)

Having a meditation teacher is also not strictly necessary. Certainly many people do get a lot out of working with a teacher who can advise them on meditation techniques and help them through challenging periods when their commitment to the practice waivers. But it is easy enough to begin meditation on your own by consulting one of the many excellent books, audiotapes, or DVD series on the subject.

Helping Hand

Locating a meditation class or workshop can be easier than you imagine. Many are offered at local churches or community centers or through adult education programs. You might also check with your local hospitals to see if they offer instruction in MBSR (Mindfulness-Based Stress Reduction). MBSR programs, in which participants are taught to meditate for two relatively brief periods a day, have been endorsed by the medical community for many years as a means of dealing with a number of physical and emotional afflictions, and its success has been documented extensively.

As for not being able to sit still, there is no doubt that our culture does not lend itself to stillness. We are a busy, frenetic people used to multitasking. The very idea of focusing on one thing can actually seem counterproductive when we're caught up in this mindset. But when you do, you will likely find that stillness is self-reinforcing. A bit each day can make you approach the rest of your life with greater energy, balance, and contentment.

Yes, meditation is hard. The Dalai Lama himself has noted how difficult it can be, and meditation adepts have schooled him since childhood. Even very accomplished practitioners of meditation have days when they find it hard to quiet their thoughts. But what drives experienced meditators to persist is their first-hand knowledge of how great the rewards will ultimately be.

Setting Aside Space and Time

As is true with any worthwhile endeavor that you might want to incorporate into your life on a regular basis, you will find it easiest to get started with meditation if you have a plan. First, think about a place in your home where you would be able to sit undisturbed for 15 minutes or so at a stretch. If your house is a continual beehive of action, think about this creatively. Don't rule out the bathroom or a basement laundry room or an attic dormer if that's what it takes. Just make it a place where you can sit comfortably and where you will not be easily distracted by a ringing phone or pinging e-mail program.

Next, think about what time of day—and how much time—you will be able to devote to your practice. If you can find two 15-minutes blocks of time, morning and evening, that would be ideal. But if you can only find one such block of time, or two shorter periods (even 5 to 10 minutes), don't let that discourage you.

One way to find some quiet time in a busy household is to arise before the rest of your family. Early morning has another advantage in that you are less likely to be subjected to phone calls and other interruptions. Getting up 15 minutes earlier might seem like a burden, but after a few days you will adjust. And because of the beneficial way in which you are utilizing those 15 minutes, you will likely feel better rested.

Styles of Meditation

When you're ready to meditate, the next decision is how to begin. There are numerous schools of meditation, each with its own techniques, yet the basic premise is the same. The idea is to focus your attention on one thing. When the mind wanders—as it will—bring it back to the focal point.

Now you will need to find something on which to focus your attention. If you meditate with your eyes open (opening or closing the eyes is a matter of personal preference), you may choose to gaze at an object such as a candle flame, or a photograph of a peaceful place, or an object that has spiritual meaningful for you. But many beginning—and experienced—practitioners choose simply to focus on the breath.

Focusing on the Breath

Breathing is something we do all the time. Our breath is what connects us to the life-giving energy that surrounds us. Both of these characteristics make the breath an obvious choice of focus for meditative attention.

Although we are always breathing in and breathing out, we are rarely conscious of this continuous cycle. During breath meditation, the idea is to just breathe normally through the nose—no special rhythms or sound effects are required—while remaining aware of the bodily sensations that occur as you inhale and exhale.

If you like, you can "follow the breath" fully as you fill the lungs and then the diaphragm and then expel the air up and out. Or, you may find it easier to concentrate on one particular place where you experience the sensation of the breath—for example, the top of your nose, where you can feel a cool sensation as you inhale and a warm sensation when you exhale.

Another breath meditation technique is breath counting. Count your breaths starting with 1, and go up to the number 10. Then begin again. If you lose count—as you surely will at first—just begin again with the number 1.

Focusing on a Sound

Another effective way to focus attention is to concentrate on the repetition of a simple sound. You can either say a sound out loud or simply repeat it to yourself in your mind.

One mantra sound you might want to experiment with is the sound *Om*. *Om* (typically pronounced in three syllables AH-OH-UM) is said to be the sound of infinite creation. Whether you choose to believe this or not, many find there is something very soothing about repeating this sound. If you are repeating the *Om* mantra aloud, try doing it so that you feel the AH sound coming from your lower abdomen, the OH sound moving up your spine, and the UM sound vibrating in your head. The flow and vibration of the sound can be extremely calming and relatively easy to focus on.

Another common mantra is the sound SO-HUM. This is generally translated from the Sanskrit as "I am that I am." The two syllables are also said to signify the union of all energies—light and shadow, male and female, sun and moon—and so are a perfect accompaniment to inhalation and exhalation. Try repeating in your mind the syllable SO as you breathe in, and HUM as you breathe out.

If mantras from other tongues feel strange or uncomfortable to you, it's fine to stick with a word in your own language. You can choose any word you find calming. Many people simply meditate on the word "one," and some use "peace."

> **Stumbling Blocks** _____
>
> Some meditation traditions believe that each person has a special mantra upon which they should meditate, and that this should be obtained from their meditation teacher or guru. But don't let the lack of a "personalized" mantra stop you. Use a universal or self-selected mantra. Should your path take you in the direction of a teacher who wishes to counsel you on your own mantra, that's fine, too.

Focusing on Feelings of Compassion

Feelings of altruism and compassion have been shown to boost our personal happiness. And there is actually a specific technique for meditating on compassion.

The "loving-kindness" meditation (also known as the *metta* meditation in the Buddhist tradition) is said to provide a balance to other meditation practices and to help practitioners develop the mental habits and attitudes necessary for acting in a selfless manner. It is said to be effective in eliminating even very entrenched negative thought habits.

> **Helping Hand** _____
>
> There are many different levels of intensity to loving-kindness practice. What's described here is the basic technique, but you may wish to progress slowly through these stages, perhaps focusing for some length of time on loved ones before expanding your warm feelings outward. Ultimately, though, the idea is to take this form of meditating beyond a simple sitting practice and, in effect, carry it around with you so that you will direct a friendly attitude to all you encounter in your daily life. As a Buddhist teaching says, "Hatred cannot coexist with loving-kindness, and dissipates if supplanted with thoughts based on loving-kindness."

The practice of the loving-kindness meditation begins with sitting quietly and manifesting feelings of loving acceptance toward yourself. (If there is resistance to doing this fully, just make note of it and move on.) Next, think of loved ones with whom you are close and manifest warm, loving feelings toward them. Next, think of people toward whom you ordinarily feel "neutral" and expand your mental circle of compassion to include them. Finally, include those toward whom you have negative, or even hostile, feelings.

When Your Thoughts Wander

Whichever meditation method you choose, you will probably say the same thing that nearly all beginners say: "My thoughts are all over the place. I can't concentrate. I must be doing something wrong." But *when* this happens to you—not *if*—there is something very important you should know: this is what is *supposed* to happen. The trick is to recognize what is going on and why, and then to just keep going.

Our minds are continually manufacturing thoughts. And it is actually fascinating to look at what kind of thoughts these are. If you are like most people you will probably have three primary kinds of thoughts that interfere with your concentration:

◆ Thoughts about the future

◆ Thoughts about the past

◆ Judgments

Anticipatory thoughts (what might or might not happen) and retrospective thoughts (what did happen and what we wish might have happened instead) often serve as a source of stress. And thoughts of judgment—especially those involving negative judgments of others and ourselves—can keep us mired in a dissatisfied, unforgiving state. Yet we hardly notice how often we engage in such ruminations. Most of the time they are like vaguely irritating, background elevator music.

However, when we meditate we begin to realize how our minds are continually bombarding us with unhappiness-inducing thoughts. In simply noticing them, we are already changing our thought habits. Meditation is fundamentally the process of learning to notice how the mind habitually works, to gain control, and to begin to move away from unhelpful patterns.

So when you become aware of a thought crossing your mind and distracting you from the chosen object of your focus, your breath or mantra, acknowledge that thought, but try not to hold onto it or elaborate on it. Gently coax your mind back to your meditative rhythm.

Over time, you will become more adept at refocusing your mind, and at identifying less with your negative thoughts. You will recognize them as *merely* thoughts—bits of electrical impulses that pass across your mind like clouds passing across a sky. And you will understand that they are not necessarily reflective of reality.

How Long Before Rewiring Occurs?

If you're beginning to meditate with the ultimate goal of "rewiring" your brain for happiness, an obvious question you might have is: how long will that take? There is as yet no definitive answer to this question—just as no one can tell you how long it will take you to noticeably build your biceps by lifting weights.

It is a process, and the changes are subtle and gradual, but they are also cumulative. As you practice over time you should gain deeper and more lasting results. What you are likely at first to experience as isolated and fleeting moments of contentment should transform into a tendency toward better moods and, with months or years of practice, into enduring traits—traits that will themselves predispose you to a greater level of happiness.

Happy Thought

"Through attention we choose and sculpt how our ever-changing minds will work, we choose who we will be the next moment in a very real sense, and these choices are left embossed in physical form on our material selves."

—Michael Merzenich, researcher, University of California, San Francisco

The Least You Need to Know

- The practice of meditation has been cultivated in cultures around the world for thousands of years, but it was in the 1970s that most Westerners learned of this mental discipline and its physical and emotional benefits.

- Scientists who have studied meditation's impact on the brain believe the practice has the potential to raise our happiness set point by producing changes in our patterns of neural activation and perhaps even altering brain circuitry.

- Carving out some space and time for a meditation practice may require a little ingenuity and effort, but primarily it requires confronting your excuses for not meditating.

- There is a wide range of meditation methods, but what all of them share is focusing the mind on a single stimulus—this can be the breath, a sound, or even an emotion (such as a feeling of warm compassion).

- It's not known how long it takes for the mental process of meditation to exert a biological effect on the brain that, in turn, impacts happiness—but over time changes that seem fleeting can become lasting.

Chapter 21

Happiness, Hope, and Healing

In This Chapter

- ◆ Changing perspectives on health
- ◆ Learning which character traits can enhance health
- ◆ Changing poor health habits
- ◆ Learning the lessons of illness
- ◆ Aiming toward happier doctor-patient relationships

How often have you heard someone say, "If you have your health, you have everything"? It might sound cliché, but as with many clichés, it is based on a universal truth. No matter how preoccupied we are with anything else in life, no matter how fulfilled we think we are, we quickly rearrange our priorities if we become unwell.

Health *is* happiness. That much we all agree on. But positive psychology is also concerned with a corollary of that truism: can happiness help us create, maintain, and restore good health? This chapter looks at what's being learned about the links between emotional and physical wellness.

Old and New Health Views

For much of modern Western history, illness was something that "happened" to people. Until and unless it did, no one thought about the state of their health. When sickness did occur, it was treated. And although treatments became increasingly sophisticated—we went from bleeding people with leeches in the Middle Ages to treating bacterial infections with antibiotics in the twentieth century—the practice of medicine was still seen as something that was performed on passive patients. But all that is changing.

Mind and Body: Two for One

It is not uncommon today to hear physicians or psychologists talk about the mind-body system as a single entity. Virtually no one considers it a radical concept to think that our emotions and attitudes impact the state of our health. The very way we talk to one another—"Calm down, you'll give yourself a heart attack!" or "I told myself I just wasn't going to come down with a cold!"—reflects our conviction that how we behave, think, and feel can literally alter our susceptibility to illness.

Such beliefs probably seem intuitive to us. Didn't everyone always know in their gut (so to speak) that mind and body had a reciprocal relationship? In fact, some cultures did understand this principle very well. The physicians of ancient Greece, most notably Hippocrates, believed in addressing a person's psyche as part of the overall healing process. And traditional Chinese medicine has consistently viewed mind and body as inextricably bound, with the balance of vital energies being of paramount importance to health.

def•i•ni•tion

Mind-body dualism is a theory of human functioning contending that mind and body are separate entities. Sometimes called Cartesian dualism, the concept was famously espoused by French philosopher René Descartes, who maintained that the mind, which is an immaterial entity, could not affect the body, which is a material entity.

But Western medicine, for many centuries, subscribed to the philosophy of *mind-body dualism*. According to this perspective, our bodies were mechanical contraptions. Body parts, although linked in interesting and complex ways, functioned independently of mental processes.

By the 1800s, new fields of scientific inquiry—biology, neurology, and psychology among them—were upending the theory of mind-body dualism. We were now beginning to understand that mind and body were not, in fact, separate entities.

This understanding has grown significantly in recent years, particularly as we have learned more about the immune system and how that system can be impacted by psychological factors, for example by our ability (or inability) to adapt to stress. Although scientists certainly do not understand all the *hows*, it is clear that mind and body comprise a coherent, unified, and reciprocal system.

New Fields Change the Playing Field

In the past few decades, several new fields of study have arisen in the health field that are expanding our understanding of mind-body interplay.

Behavioral medicine is an interdisciplinary field that expands traditional medicine by integrating medical knowledge with the knowledge of human behavior and its impacts. Health psychology is a subfield of psychology that applies psychological research and theories to the topic of well-being, with the goal of increasing healthy habits and decreasing mortality rates. Psychoneuroimmunology (PNI) specifically investigates how psychological and neurological factors influence the operations of the immune system.

All of these fields are being watched with intense interest by positive psychology, which, in turn, is influencing the scope and the means of the disciplines' inquiry. All in all, contemporary efforts to combat illness and foster good health are broadening medicine's parameters. No doubt there are revelations and benefits in store for us all.

Proactive Wellness

When it comes to developments in the field of health, positive psychology is more than an interested bystander. Positive psychology, as we've seen, offered a new perspective on emotional life by asking, "What do successful and satisfied people do to get and stay that way?" It is now contributing to something of a paradigm shift in medicine by asking, "What do hardy people do to thrive?" To investigate such a question, we need to know what wellness means—or can mean.

> **Happy Thought**
>
> "A sound mind in a sound body is a full description of a happy state in this world."
> —John Locke

There are many definitions of health. The most basic definition is that it is the absence of disease. If we're not sick, we're healthy. Simple enough. But there are broader definitions that are not so cut-and-dry. Wellness of a somewhat more proactive sort can involve a conscious attempt to prevent illness. Someone can limit health risk factors by *not* smoking, *not* drinking too much alcohol, and *not* overeating.

But someone with a truly positive and proactive approach to wellness would be interested in more than fending off sickness. They would seek to optimize their health by doing such things as …

◆ Exercising regularly.

◆ Shopping for and preparing nutritious foods.

◆ Getting adequate sleep.

Helping Hand _____

If you are noticing that many stress-reducing strategies are the same as strategies for enhancing happiness, you are ahead of the game. A life less ravaged by stress is, *ipso facto,* a happier life. And those who are adept at managing stress will have more years to enjoy living.

Beyond this, they would find ways to manage their negative stress, the effects of which can contribute to everything from coronary heart disease to diabetes to osteoporosis to irritable bowel syndrome, and on and on. To this end, they might engage in meditation, visualization, or other attention-focusing activities, try to temper their hostilities and anxieties with humor, and take time to restore and renew their energies at regular intervals. Such a person would be taking a decisively salutary approach not only toward avoiding illness but also toward creating a state of maximum engagement in life and all it has to offer.

Wellness-Promoting Traits

Apart from redefining the parameters of wellness, positive psychology is interested in looking beyond the impact of negative emotions on health. It's long been known that negative emotions can undermine health. One well-known example involves the discovery of the correlation between heart disease and what has come to be known as "Type A" behavior.

This connection gained widespread notoriety in the 1970s, thanks to the work of two San Francisco cardiologists, Meyer Friedman and Ray Rosenman, whose nine-year study of 3,000 men showed that those who were the most verbally hostile, the most easily angered, and the most impatient were also the most at risk not only for heart attacks but also for other forms of cardiovascular problems, including stroke.

Another link between negative emotions and poor health is that negative emotions are associated with adverse health behaviors. People with high levels of anger, depression, and anxiety are apt to smoke cigarettes, consume too much alcohol, avoid physical activity, and be overweight.

But curbing negative emotions is not necessarily the same as proactively cultivating positive ones. (For example, it's one thing to be less hostile; it's another to deliberately cultivate a compassionate attitude.) Positive psychology wants to know if there are particular positive emotions that can engender optimum health. Two traits in particular are of special interest in this regard. The first is hope; the second—somewhat less predictably—is curiosity.

Happiness Trivia

A study by researchers at the Harvard School of Public Health and Harvard Medical School examined the effects of positive emotion on hypertension, diabetes mellitus, and respiratory tract infection. The results provided evidence for a protective function of positive emotion and an important association between hope, curiosity, and health.

Hope and Health

Preliminary studies show a link between hope—which is essentially a manifestation of optimism and related positive points of view—and positive health outcomes. A hopeful orientation, it is believed, can heighten immune function and create resistance to illness. It can also motivate sensible behaviors with regard to personal health. Hopeful people tend to pay increased attention to health-relevant information, and optimistic beliefs are linked to greater processing of health-risk information.

There is, however, an important caveat when it comes to health and optimism. Chapter 6 of this book mentioned that realistic optimism leads to beneficial outcomes, whereas irrational optimism does not. This principle holds true in the health realm. Individuals with an ideal level of optimism—the sort tempered by reason and logic—tend not to smoke, tend to use sunscreen, and tend to take vitamins and eat low-fat foods. Evidently, they are hopeful that both their preventative and proactive behaviors can raise the quantity and quality of their life span. On the other hand, individuals who see the future through glasses that are *too* rose-colored overestimate their life span by as much as 20 years—and then, ironically, resist doing anything to make their wildly optimistic prophecy come true. In fact they behave in ways that are actually detrimental to their health and well-being.

No one is quite sure why some people are so optimistic that they become reckless. The reason might be purely—or at least partly—neurological. Rosy thoughts are triggered on a brain region called the *rostral anterior cingulate cortex,* an olive-sized cluster of neurons that activates when we think of hopes and aspirations or when we imagine happy events in the future. We may veer into irrational exuberance if this neural hub is too active, or perhaps we overactivate this hub by willfully denying reality. Either way the result is the same: cock-eyed optimism is detrimental to your health.

Stumbling Blocks

If you feel good and want to feel even better, don't act irresponsibly. Pay attention to health facts, listen to your own body, and get regular medical checkups. In the wise words of Duke University professor and researcher Manju Pur, "Optimism is a little like red wine. In moderation, it is good for you; but no one would suggest you drink two bottles a day."

Curiosity and Self-Care

Curiosity may have killed the proverbial cat. But when it comes to humans, curiosity is another emotion that can have salutary health effects.

Scientific measures of curiosity measure the extent to which individuals in their usual environment are willing to explore novel stimuli. (For example: will a baby stop and stare at a new stuffed animal placed in its crib, or will the infant remain largely oblivious to the novel toy?) But basically, someone who is curious is someone who wants to learn, to investigate, and to incorporate new ideas and experiences. Presumably, some of the things they are likely to want to learn about and incorporate into their own lives are the latest developments in the areas of health and well-being. A curious person is far more likely than a blasé one to accumulate and draw on a rich store of health knowledge and resources.

Curiosity may also be linked to wellness because it constitutes a potential stress buffer. People who like to learn and who are able to sustain interest in engaging endeavors are the kinds of people who develop hobbies and pursue "flow" activities (see Chapter 11 for more on flow). Their periods of heightened focus and attentiveness serve to divert their minds from worry.

Changing Negative Health Habits

Positive psychology is also interested in how people can use their attitudes and strengths to alter negative health habits. One prevalent idea is that it is often easier to do away with a bad habit if a positive habit is substituted.

Even negative habits serve certain purposes that, in themselves, might not be bad. Someone might smoke to relieve feelings of stress. Someone might become a workaholic to ease a sense of loneliness. If such habits are terminated without anything to put in their place, the underlying emotions could wreak havoc. However, if the smoker substitutes deep breathing exercise for lighting up, or the workaholic finds an active social organization that will lure him out of the office, they stand a better chance of successfully disrupting their self-destructive patterns.

Researchers who study motivation and goal attainment also note that it is easier to achieve a very specific goal than it is to achieve a vague or general one. Those who wish to change a habit are better off vowing, for example, to exercise on a treadmill or bicycle for 30 minutes a day than to simply "get in shape this year."

Positive social support is also exceedingly helpful when it comes to changing a habit. Merely announcing your intentions to people who will encourage you can serve as a motivator because your commitment to change is now a "matter of record" rather than a silent wish. And should you be tempted to backslide, your supporters can remind you of your good intentions, buck up your spirits, or simply commiserate compassionately and offer you shoulders on which to cry.

Changing a habit is never easy. It involves being patient with oneself, being tolerant of frustration, being curious about what life afterward will be like, and being hopeful that things will be better. If one relies on friends and loved ones to help, then it also involves trusting them. The more one can employ their strengths in the service of change, the likelier that change is to occur.

Stumbling Blocks

How long does it take to change a habit? The expert consensus is anywhere from 21 to 30 days—never overnight! Many people give up on change too soon. On the other hand, many people feel overwhelmed by thinking of an untried habit change as something that will now last the rest of their lives. Promising yourself to change something for three weeks or a month is a reasonable trial period during which you can evaluate new behavior and start to feel familiar with its effects.

Hardiness, Resilience, and Recovery

Of course even the happiest and most optimistic people sometimes succumb to illness. The psychology of happiness is also interested in the role of positive emotions and attitudes in helping people recover from illness or, where recovery is not possible, to cope well with the effects of illness.

The idea that certain positive emotions could aid recovery from sickness took hold in the popular imagination in 1979 when Norman Cousins, a high-profile magazine editor, published a best-selling book entitled *Anatomy of an Illness*. The book recounted Cousins's recovery from a debilitating collagen disease. Cousins attributed his cure, in large part, to his decision to check out of a hospital and into a hotel, where he spent his days laughing uproariously at old Marx Brothers movies he'd rented as "therapy." Though there was some skepticism about the efficacy of his method (some said he'd have recovered anyway, and some said he owed more to getting out of a negative hospital environment than to his laugh treatment per se), Cousins's book became a potent catalyst for scientific investigations into the healing power of humor and other positive emotions.

Those sorts of investigations are ongoing. Scientists are attempting to supplement abundant anecdotal evidence with hard empirical data linking recovery from various health conditions to patient's moods, attitudes, and self-directed behaviors. And many researchers believe we are on the threshold of a new understanding of what is being called "the biology of hope."

def•i•ni•tion

Hardiness, as defined by positive psychology, is the ability to discern meaning in life and to rise to challenges in spite of taxing demands and hardships.

Still, no one would deny that there are infirmities and illnesses the effects of which are enduring. Positive psychologists are also interested in how and why certain people in the grips of chronic illnesses or permanent disabilities *still* manage to thrive. (Think about Christopher Reeves, for example, who inspired millions after his spinal cord injury.) Why do some physically challenged people still exhibit so much *hardiness?*

Although some people who are beset with illness and afflictions give in to depression and despair, others do not. The latter group …

♦ Manages to maintain a coherent view of their life, integrating all realities—even seemingly illogical and unpleasant ones.

♦ Does not dwell on the unfairness or randomness of their ailments.

♦ Is open to learning valuable lessons from the experience they've been dealt.

An individual who is determined to remain positive in the face of negative health developments does not bemoan their fate and ask the universe, "Why me?" Rather they ask, "Why *not* me? What does this challenge have to offer me?" Their attitude keeps them engaged in seeking out life's opportunities.

Positive psychology would say that such individuals refuse to participate in the *pathogenic* model of illness, which sees disease as an enemy. By focusing on what one can still accomplish and relish even in the face of illness, they are pursuing a *salutogenic* model. They look for what's right with them, rather than what's wrong with them. This does not mean they deny their illness (indeed, they will do whatever is necessary to instigate improvement) but rather that they adapt to it and manage it. The salutogenic patient refuses to feel helpless.

def•i•ni•tion

A **pathogenic** orientation on illness views sickness as an enemy invader—a purely external event. A **salutogenic** orientation views illness as an opportunity rather than an obstacle.

Researchers who focus on salutogenic individuals and their creative and adaptive strategies for dealing with ailments and afflictions often cite Beethoven as an example of a remarkable individual who lived fully and functioned with an exceptional level of creativity despite physiological limitations. The composer conveyed stirring beauty through his music despite the deafness imposed upon him. Individuals with salutogenic perspectives abound today as well—from renowned celebrities such as physicist Stephen Hawking to athletic competitors in the Paralympics's games of wheelchair tennis, archery, and rugby.

Researcher Aaron Antonovsky, a professor in the Sociology of Health department at Israel's Ben Gurion University of Negev, has noted that those who thrive despite ailments and injuries actually manifest an opposite reaction to stressful life events. Although the average person views sudden life changes and daily hassles as negative stressors, salutogenic thrivers see them as a means of becoming mentally and emotionally stronger.

Positive Doctor-Patient Relationships

Regardless of what orientation has toward illness, when one is sick, one usually consults a physician. So, another variable that affects health outcomes is doctor-patient relationships. Not surprisingly, positive interactions between physicians and their patients can have a beneficial impact.

There are many practical reasons for the positive effect a doctor can have on a patient:

♦ Patients who like their doctors are more apt to follow their instructions and more apt to make follow-up visits.

♦ Patients who are given more information may feel more in control of their condition.

♦ Patients who are listened to can provide their practitioners with valuable clues for correct diagnosis and treatment.

Beyond such pragmatic influences are more subtle—but equally powerful—ones. Doctors can provide role models for optimism. They can offer compassion that reaffirms their patients' humanity. And they can lessen fear by fostering trust.

Unfortunately, data shows many doctors today appear to be short on bedside manner. In one study, nearly 50 percent of a thousand breast cancer patients contended that their physician's explanation of their condition, diagnosis, and treatment had been difficult to understand, incomplete, or inadequate. Nearly 60 percent of these patients wished for increased communication with the medical staff.

Many doctors also appear to be short on time. The *Journal of the American Medical Association* reports that the average American patient is allotted just 23 seconds to voice their presenting complaint before their physician interrupts and redirects them. (Ironically, patients allowed to proceed until they feel they have told their story sufficiently go on no longer than two minutes.) But the mere fact that such studies are being undertaken points to a growing awareness that quality and quantity of interaction count.

Happy Thought

"Beyond the power of our most sophisticated medical equipment is a physician's humanity—the listening ear, the healing touch, the devices of healers throughout time."

—Mimi Guarneri, medical director, Scripps Center for Integrative Medicine

The good news is that the influences of health psychology, behavioral medicine, and positive psychology are acting in concert to enhance some aspects of modern medicine. Medical schools are searching for means to graduate more empathic physicians. At Columbia University and many other such institutions, programs in what is called *narrative medicine* teach literature, literary theory, and creative writing to medical students. The programs, says Dr. Rita Charon, director of the Columbia program, aim to inspire "medicine practiced with the narrative competence to recognize, absorb, interpret, and be moved by the stories of illness." Most narrative medicine programs require their students to keep personal diaries of their emotions while treating a case. A program at Harvard Medical School actually requires physicians to author an entire book about a patient and his or her disease.

Finally, in addition to calling attention to the need for increased compassion in medicine, positive psychology is creating a dynamic where physicians are being called on to take a greater role in wellness promotion. This means that doctors would make deliberate interventions to promote health, along with interventions to treat illness, and see both as a significant part of their jobs. In the long run, having doctors promote proactive heath behavior is a win-win situation. Fewer people will succumb to illness, and those who do can benefit from more of their doctors' time and positive attention.

The Least You Need to Know

- ♦ Positive psychology is interested not only in how negative emotions can cause illness but also in how positive emotions can promote well-being.

- ♦ Two traits—hope and curiosity—are of particular interest to researchers studying the psychology of optimal health.

- ♦ Drawing on personal strengths such as patience and frustration tolerance can help us change negative health habits and substitute good habits for destructive ones.

- ♦ Positive psychology is interested in examining hardiness and studying people who continue to thrive even in the face of ailment and injury.

- ♦ Modern medicine is now paying more attention to how factors such as physician empathy and compassion can benefit patients.

Chapter 22

Happiness, Aging, and Longevity

In This Chapter

♦ Having positive emotions and longevity

♦ Leveling happiness throughout the life cycle

♦ Aging with wisdom

♦ Creating a life legacy

♦ Learning the summary secrets of a happy life

Nowadays people in the developed world are, on the whole, living longer than ever before. That longevity stems, at least in part, from advances in health care as well as in sanitation and nutrition. Still, some people live longer than others. And some people age with a greater sense of contentment and engagement than others, making their elderly years rewarding.

Are life span and life attitudes connected? This chapter looks at what psychologists know about how our strengths and attitudes impact not only the length but also the quality of our lives as we grow older.

Do the Happy Live Longer?

Will we have more years if the years we do have are filled with positive emotion? If so, that certainly seems like a win-win situation. Happily, the answer appears to be yes. Research has found strong associations between positive emotional experiences and longevity.

Longevity Studies: The Proof of the Pudding

In a six-decade study analyzing autobiographies written by Catholic nuns and then following up on their mortality rates, researchers found that nuns whose writing contained less positive emotional content at age 22 were at two and a half times greater risk of premature mortality than those whose writing contained strong positive emotional content.

A study known as the Ohio Longitudinal Study has been following a group of aging peers since 1975. Its researchers have found that older people with a more positive attitude toward old age lived seven and a half years longer.

A 10-year study conducted in the Netherlands followed nearly a thousand subjects ranging in age from 65 to 85. Researchers ranked those subjects' degrees of optimism or pessimism based on answers to questions such as "I still have positive expectations concerning my future," and, "I often feel that life is full of promise." They found that subjects with the highest level of optimism were 45 percent less likely than those with the highest level of pessimism to die from all causes during the study's course.

But simply because two things—such as optimism and longevity—are correlated does not necessarily mean that one causes the other. One might look at such studies and ask if pessimists were perhaps simply sicker to begin with. But Dr. Eric Gilray, who designed the Netherlands study, carefully controlled for health risk variables such as high blood pressure, high cholesterol, smoking, and even clinical depression in his subjects and the data held up: factoring out all the other variables, the optimists still lived longer.

What could possibly explain such a link?

What's Happiness Got to Do with It?

Should additional studies continue to point to causality between long life and positive emotion, scientists will be searching in earnest for reasons *why* positive emotions lead to longevity. Some possible explanations are that positive people are more likely to …

- Promote their own health by eating well and exercising.

- Seek and benefit from the health-promoting effects of social support.

- Be married (married people, in general, live longer than single people).

- Engage in altruistic activities (do-gooders appear to be healthier for the doing).

- Use humor as a coping strategy (laughter boosts immunity).

- Deal with stress (and so avoid many of stress's illness-inducing effects).

There might even turn out to be underlying biological differences between optimists and pessimists that are themselves tied to a more robust constitution.

But whatever the explanation, if positive attitudes do indeed turn out to be a ticket to a longer life, two things are true: positive thinkers will have more time in which to be upbeat. And pessimists who obsessively worry about the future may not have as long a future to worry about.

Happiness Trivia

In 2001, researchers Donald Redelmeier and Sheldon Singh looked at the longevity of Oscar-winning actors and actresses across seven decades. Winners, on average, lived almost four years longer than nominees or actors and actresses who appeared in the same films but were not nominated. There was even a tendency for multiple Academy Award winners to outlive one-time winners. Apart from the fact that this study ought to please Sally Field, it raises a fascinating question for further study: do the psychological experiences of triumph and of receiving adulation have an impact on one's life span?

Happiness and the Life Cycle

The study of happiness and aging has led to another intriguing finding. Even those of us who are fundamentally happy, it turns out, experience varying degrees of happiness depending on what phase of life we are in. The average person will have predefined periods in their life in which they will be happier than others.

The U-Shaped Curve of Happiness

A recent study of the U.S. population showed that happiness follows what is called a "U-shaped" curve. It starts out strong, but then declines steadily between the ages of 16 and 45. Then it starts to swing upward again, and rises for 15 years. (Interestingly, the 15-year upswing in happiness that follows age 45 is stronger than the upswing that tracks doubling of income. The trend appears to be age-related rather than related to having more disposable funds or a larger nest egg.)

The U-shaped happiness pattern is not a totally new finding. However, in the past, researchers couldn't tell whether 55-year-olds were happier than 45-year-olds in a given year because the 55-year-olds had aged or because of what is known as the *cohort effect.* Maybe the older people were born to a more upbeat generation or were part of a generation that experienced less hardship throughout their lives. The recent study gets around this problem by combining data on people of different ages at different points in time over the course of a quarter-century. The authors were able to compare not only 55- and 45-year-olds today, but also people who are 55-year-olds today to people who were 55 a decade ago. Even when they accounted for *when* people were born, the U-shaped happiness pattern remained. This appears to indicate that *age itself* has a definite impact on happiness.

def•i•ni•tion

> The **cohort effect** measures effects on people's lives that arise from the characteristics of the historical periods during which they experienced stages of life such as childhood or middle age.

The Happiness Mid-Life Crisis

So why does happiness start out strong, dip in middle age, and then revive among the elderly? This is another happiness puzzle that requires further exploration.

The authors of the recent study, David Blanchflower and Andrew Oswald, are economists rather than psychologists, but they note that the pattern of happiness does *not* match the usual pattern of wealth accrual. Wealth tends to rise steadily during the life cycle, peaking around retirement age, but happiness doesn't follow the same trajectory. Once again it appears that money cannot actually buy happiness.

Blanchflower and Oswald speculate that people in mid-life experience unhappiness because they "quell the infeasible aspirations of their youth." In other words, they give up on some of their youthful dreams. But this still does not explain the upswing in happiness that occurs after one's mid-40s.

That, it turns out, could well have something to do with another quality that tends to increase as we age: wisdom.

A Wealth of Wisdom

The psychoanalyst Erik H. Erikson, well known for his theory on personality development from birth through old age, linked each stage of life with an either/or proposition. Our latter years, he said, are characterized by either a path toward despair or a path toward *ego integrity*. He also linked each stage with a virtue. The virtue of our elder years, Erikson said, was wisdom. It was wisdom that could help us avoid despair and experience a satisfying, meaningful conclusion to our lives.

However, when it came to defining, what exactly, the virtue of wisdom comprised, Erikson was less than precise. His vagueness left psychologists with open questions. As of late, more and more of them are seeking answers.

def•i•ni•tion

Ego integrity, according to the life stage theory of Erik Erikson, is the psyche's ability—accumulated during a lifetime—to view the world with a sense of order, coherence, and meaning.

Older and Wiser

The quality we call wisdom is something many people feel they simply recognize when they encounter it. And indeed our associations with it often seem to involve images of the elderly. When we imagine someone going off to see the tribal wiseman or wisewoman we picture them sitting at the feet of a thoughtful, twinkle-eyed, gray-haired sage—not consulting a lanky adolescent. When we think of one of the Waltons—the beloved TV family—needing definitive advice from a family member, we know that it was Grandma or Grandpa Walton, not John Boy, who helped them resolve their dilemma.

Wisdom, as those who are now studying it agree, is not *necessarily* a product of advanced age, but being older increases the chances of accruing the variety of life experiences and the maturity that generate the quality. Still, positive psychologists, gerontological psychologists, and even neuroscientists armed with brain-scanning equipment want to know more about how to identify and quantify wisdom. Some who are studying this virtue believe that doing so is essential to our future as individuals and as a society.

Wise Ways

Although defining wisdom presents a challenge, consistent pieces of the definition are appearing. Certain aspects of wisdom show up over and over in the growing body of literature on this topic. Elements of the evolving definition include the following:

◆ **The ability to learn from experience.** Wise people may not get things right the first time, or even the second, but at a certain point the light dawns and they change behavior that isn't serving them. Unlike those whom wisdom eludes, they don't act like mice traversing the same maze paths over and over when there's no tidbit of cheese to be found at the end.

◆ **Flexibility.** The wise are not rigidly wed to one way of doing things. They are always open to new information and new possibilities. They understand that life includes a certain amount of uncertainty, even randomness, and they are able to modify their plans accordingly.

◆ **Effective coping with adversity.** When things don't work out well, the wise don't fall apart. They are calm in the face of crisis. They adapt to misfortune in ways that can help them continue to thrive—even against the odds. After a crisis is past, they know how to rebound and move on.

◆ **Objectivity.** The wise can view situations with a certain level of healthy detachment. They try not to let personal biases determine their decisions or course of action. They lack prejudice, or at least police themselves to detect any vestiges of it.

◆ **Careful deliberation.** The wise look before they leap. They resist impulsivity and are unlikely to jump to conclusions without considering all available evidence. They ask good questions of others and of themselves.

◆ **Balance.** Wise people draw on both their logic and their well-honed emotional intelligence when making decisions. Their approach is effectively summed up in the Hebrew word for wisdom, *chochmah*, which refers to a combination of heart and mind.

◆ **A lack of self-absorption.** Wise people tend to be "other centered." They are unselfish. They exude empathy and compassion.

◆ **Humility.** Though they may be exemplary individuals, the wise are not stuck-up about it. They never assume they are infallible. As Gandhi—who often tops the list when people are asked to name a wise role model—put it, "It is unwise to be too sure of one's wisdom."

> **Happy Thought** _____
>
> "The perfection of wisdom … is to proportion our wants to our possessions and our ambitions to our capacities. We will then be a happy and a virtuous people."
> —Mark Twain
>
> "Science is organized knowledge. Wisdom is organized life."
> —Immanuel Kant

Wisdom researcher Vivian Clayton, author of numerous respected papers on the topic, believes the elements of wisdom fall under three general categories—which have since been used to develop a psychological assessment instrument known as the Three Dimensional Wisdom Scale. The *cognitive* category involves the acquisition of knowledge. The *reflective* category involves the analysis of knowledge. And the *affective* category involves filtering acquired and analyzed knowledge through the filter of the emotions.

Emotional Regulation

Within the emotional component of wisdom is what researchers consider to be an especially important ability common to people who exemplify this virtue. That quality is known as *emotional regulation*, or the ability to maintain emotional equilibrium during a wide variety of positive and negative circumstances.

There is a well-known analogy in psychology that compares humans' reaction to emotion to an image of a horse and a rider. We can either treat our emotions as a horse, with ourselves as the rider, or treat our emotions as the rider and ourselves as the horse. In other words, we can tame our emotions or let them run away with us. Wise people do the former.

Neuroscientists at the University of Wisconsin have been examining patterns of brain activity associated with emotional regulation in a group of older adults (the average age is 64). In a paper published in 2006, the team reported that the individuals in the group who regulated their emotions well (the riders) showed a distinctly different pattern of brain activity than those who did not (the horses). The former group evidently used their prefrontal cortex, the part of the brain that exerts "executive control" over certain brain functions, to moderate activity in the amygdala, the small interior brain region that processes fear, anger, and anxiety. In the latter group, activity in the amygdala was higher.

In addition, daily measurements of the stress hormone cortisol showed that it, too, was elevated in the "rider" group. The combination of high amygdala activity and high cortisol often results in poor health outcomes.

Wisconsin researcher Richard Davidson (Davidson's work on investigating meditation in the lab was mentioned in Chapter 20), noted that the subjects with lower amygdala activity were skilled at regulating negative emotion and voluntarily using their thought processes to reappraise situations. Although they registered the negative, they had somehow learned not to let it overwhelm them. Davidson added that these kinds of capabilities probably result from "something that has been at least implicitly trained over the years."

> **Helping Hand**
>
> Developing wisdom and cultivating the ability to overlook the negative is often associated with an earlier exposure to adversity or failure. Though wisdom and happiness seem to go hand in hand, it is those who weather misfortune who are most likely to end up wise. That's a silver lining worth remembering when life clouds over.

In another study, this one conducted at the University of California at Santa Cruz, neuroscientists specifically compared amygdala activity in young and old people. Neurologically speaking, it appeared that young people tend to cling to negative information, while older ones tend to shrug it off.

The bottom line: although it may not be strictly necessary to be elderly to develop and benefit from emotional regulation, practice helps. And practice takes time.

Leaving a Positive Legacy

Another element that can factor in to late-life hardiness and happiness is continuing to feel that what one does is of consequence. As it turns out, many feel that the products of their actions in their latter years are of special significance.

In a survey conducted by Dr. Tony Campolo, professor emeritus at Eastern University, 50 people older than age 95 were asked, "If you could do it all over again, what would you do differently?" Three responses came back most frequently. Nanogenarians said they would "reflect more" (reflection, as we know, is a cornerstone of wisdom). They also said they would "risk more" (courage, as we've seen, is a key character strength related to happiness). Lastly, they said they would "do things that would live beyond them." In other words, they would leave a legacy.

Leaving a legacy ties in with living a life of meaning and purpose. Not surprisingly, older individuals who have been actively engaged with leaving a positive footprint on the world and are satisfied that they will be well-remembered are likely to face their final years with a sense of satisfaction—the satisfaction that comes from a job well done.

Leaving something that lives beyond us is a goal that can be approached in many ways. Writing a will is the classic way we pass on material things. One can leave a legacy of wealth to be used for all manner of good causes—donations to charity, scholarship endowments, or sending one's own grandkids to medical school. But money is by no means the only meaningful thing we can leave behind.

Helping Hand

No matter what age you are, you can use the notion of legacy to increase your happiness. Think ahead to your life's conclusion and visualize how you want to be remembered by those closest to you. Which of your strengths do you hope they'll recall? What achievements do you want them to remember? Now spend the rest of your life, one day at a time, earning the right to a celebratory eulogy of your positive life.

We can leave the fruits of artistic endeavors—memoirs, stories, and poems we've written; artworks and crafts we've created; music we've made; photographs we've taken; sweaters we've knitted.

We can leave the fruits of our knowledge—the advice we've given, the effects of decisions we've made and helped others to make.

We can leave a business. We can leave an invention. We can leave a mathematical formula or a scientific theory, or a psychological construct.

But even if we leave none of those things, we can leave the impression we have made on those we've known. We can leave a legacy of kindness, of laughter, and of love. Even with the bulk of our life behind us, we can still keep working on our legacy. And if we believe that what survives us brings others joy, even in some small way, we can be happy about that.

Live Long and Prosper

For anyone interested in unlocking the secrets of happiness, this is an exciting time. Never before have so many fine minds and so many resources been devoted to such a life-affirming subject.

But no matter how much we as a society learn about happiness, each of us as individuals must create our recipe for a happy life. As with all good recipes, there can be many variations on a theme. But don't forget the basic ingredients:

Look on the bright side. Being optimistic is no guarantee that things will turn out as you wish. But it certainly doesn't prevent them from turning out that way, and may help you create the circumstances you seek. Much more importantly, however, optimism will enable you to weather life's storms with greater equanimity by understanding that there is often an upside to a downturn that will reveal itself in time.

Be true to yourself. Stand up for what you think is right and do what is right *for* you. Don't feel you must always conform, or you will doom yourself to an unsatisfying and endless trek on the social treadmill.

Be kind. Kindness, love, and compassion breed more of the same. In the end, your relationships with those close to you and with the world at large are a mirror of how you conduct yourself.

Be generous. Share your time and your talents with others. Giving to others not only helps them but also benefits you. The feedback loop of giving is an infinite pathway to happiness: do good, feel good. Feel good, do good.

Play with a passion. Indulge in your favorite pursuits whenever you can. Use, improve, and build on your skills in those activities. Get involved enough so that "time flies." Try to spend at least some of your work time employing your strengths and skills. The more you can do this, the more work will feel like play.

Try new things. Curiosity is curative. Always remain open to learning. Allow yourself to take some risks and stretch your comfort zone. There is nothing like the thrill of a new challenge to make you feel joyfully alive.

Look on the light side. Humor is a tonic that will perk up your energy and bolster your spirits. It will help you keep things in perspective and even rebound from crises. And there is nothing like sharing a laugh to help you bond with others.

Explore your spiritual beliefs. Even if you have no formal religious affiliation, pay attention to your soulful aspects. Notice those moments when you feel connected to something larger than yourself. Doing so can infuse your life with a profound sense of meaning.

Seek out positive people. Relationships can be great sources of happiness if the relationships you have involve reciprocal trust and respect. Seek out people whose company is enjoyable and uplifting, and who make you feel confident in yourself rather than dependent on them. Last but not least, spend time with people who are fun!

Take good care of yourself. Exercise, eat well, and make sure you get enough sleep. Try to spend some time each day in a quiet, restorative activity such as meditation. Your body needs the right fuel to maintain a long, healthy, happy life.

Express your thankfulness. Be *actively* grateful for the good things in your life. Tally them up, write them down. Express your thanks directly to people who have helped or inspired you. The more you look for things to be grateful for, the more of them you will find.

Finally, discover and fulfill your purpose. Have a reason to be excited about the future and your contribution to it. Set goals throughout the whole of your life and, as you reach them, set others—even until the end. One day your life, no matter how long, will be someone else's memory. Make it a happy memory.

The Least You Need to Know

- Numerous studies show that positive emotions correlate with increased life spans.

- Happiness tends to follow a U-shaped curve throughout our lives—it starts out strong, then dips between age 16 and 45, and then rises again.

- Wisdom—the result of accumulating knowledge and analyzing it through the filter of regulated emotions—is considered a significant source of contentment in our later years.

- Actively engaging in creating a positive legacy is another way to generate satisfaction and continue to be actively engaged in life as we age.

- When all is said and done, you can cook up a happy life with basic ingredients including optimism, love, kindness, passion, and purpose.

Glossary

appreciative inquiry (AI)   An organizational development process that focuses on what things an organization does best.

Atman   A Hindu concept that signifies the human soul in its pure form—the essence that transcends worldly existence.

autotelic experience   A self-contained activity that is done not for the sake of future reward or benefit but simply for the joy of doing it. Its opposite, an *exotelic experience*, is one in which the consequences are of primary importance.

circadian rhythm   A roughly 24-hour cycle in the physiological processes of living beings. The term "circadian," comes from the Latin *circa*, "around," and *dies*, "day." Although circadian rhythms are internally generated, they can be influenced by external cues, such as sunlight and temperature.

cohort effect   A measurement of the effects on people's lives that arise from the characteristics of the historical periods during which they experienced stages of life such as childhood or middle age.

companionate love   The basis of long-term relationships that outlast the first blush of passion. It is defined by positive psychologist Christopher Peterson as the unshakeable affection shared by two people whose lives have become intertwined.

destination addiction   A preoccupation with finding satisfaction "tomorrow," the term was coined by Dr. Robert Holden, founder of the United Kingdom's Happiness Project. He defines it succinctly as "living in the not now."

Dunbar number   According to research done in 1993 by Oxford anthropologist Robin Dunbar, this number—150—is the natural upper limit of social contacts the human brain can manage. This limit was derived by extrapolating from social groups in nonhuman primates, and then crediting people with greater capacity because of our bigger neocortex (the area of the brain used for conscious thought language).

ego integrity   According to the life stage theory of Erik Erikson, this term refers to the psyche's ability—accumulated during a lifetime—to view the world with a sense of order, coherence, and meaning.

embodied cognitive science   An interdisciplinary field of research whose aim is to explain the mechanisms underlying intelligent behavior. It evaluates psychological and biological systems in a holistic manner that considers the mind and body as a single entity.

employee engagement   The degree to which employees feel pride in their organizations, are loyal to them, and feel they are an important and respected part of them.

eudaimonia   A Greek term that literally translates as "good spirit," but that connotes the meaning "human flourishing" and "life well-lived." Noted Greek philosophers, including Socrates, Plato, and Aristotle—used the term to distinguish virtues-based happiness from pleasure-based happiness.

eustress   This term, coined by renowned stress researcher Hans Selye in 1980, refers to the modest but necessary level of stress of limited duration that we all require to feel satisfied, engaged, and capable in all areas of life.

explanatory style   The way in which we explain the causes and effects of our circumstances to ourselves; the "spin" we tend to put on events that occur during the course of our lives.

guru   From the Hindi language, this term refers to a spiritual teacher, counselor, or leader. Some think of a guru as an awakener of consciousness, or someone who can bring a pupil or follower from "darkness to light."

happiness set point   Like a set point for body weight, this is a kind of a default setting to which we tend to return over and over again. Its baseline is genetically predetermined, handed down generation to generation.

hardiness   The ability to discern meaning in life and to rise to challenges in spite of taxing demands and hardships.

hatha yoga   The aspect of yoga that focuses on physical postures, and here in the West is the typical entry point to yoga practice. *Ha* means "sun" and *tha* means "moon"—thus, the word itself incorporates the concept of natural balance.

hedonic treadmill   The phenomenon of continual dissatisfaction with the consumption of material goods. As an individual earns more money, they take their current standard of living for granted while their aspirations ratchet up. They continually aspire to the next level of consumption, which will again ultimately fail to satisfy.

helper's high   A term coined in 1988 by researcher Allen Luks, who noted that 50 percent of research subjects who helped others reported feeling "high" when doing so. Forty-three percent felt stronger and more energetic.

learned helplessness   A giving-up or quitting response. It grows out of the belief that whatever one does will have no impact.

learned optimism   The process of altering one's outlook by changing the way in which one evaluates and explains one's circumstances.

leniency   The tendency to classify a larger set of outcomes, events, and characteristics as subjectively positive. Leniency can also correspond to the adoption of relatively modest thresholds of minimum acceptability.

life-giving forces (LGFs)   This term, part of the *appreciative inquiry* process, refers to the unique structure and processes of an organization that makes its very existence possible. LGFs can be ideas, beliefs, or values.

mantra   A simple word or sound—such as *Om* or *peace* or *one*—that becomes the point of meditative focus.

Maslow's hierarchy of needs   Abraham Maslow's theory of motivation, which posits that after basic biological and social needs are met, humans will innately move toward satisfying higher needs—pursuing wisdom, aesthetics, spirituality, and personal fulfillment. Maslow's hierarchy is often pictured as a pyramid comprised of numerous levels.

meridians   One of the pillars of traditional Chinese medicine, and therefore of acupuncture and acupressure, these are the channels said to distribute vital energy throughout the body. Although meridians have no discernible physical structure, they are likened to the wiring in a house or the veins through which blood flows.

mind-body dualism   A theory of human functioning contending that mind and body are separate entities. Sometimes called Cartesian dualism, the concept was famously espoused by French philosopher René Descartes, who maintained that the mind, which is an immaterial entity, could not affect the body, which is a material entity.

modeling   Emulating what influential others say and do. Modeling is a cornerstone concept of social learning theory as put forth by psychologist Albert Bandura.

multiple intelligences   A concept, introduced by Harvard education professor Howard Gardner, which posits that intelligence can best be understood not as an all-inclusive IQ number but as a distinct group of abilities that individuals may possess in varying degrees.

neurogenesis   The birth of new brain cells.

neuroplasticity   The ability of brain systems—including visual and auditory systems, attentional systems, and language systems—to change with experience and input from the environment.

oxytocin   A hormone, secreted by the pituitary gland, that contributes to bonding behavior. It is sometimes thought of as a female hormone, because it is released during breastfeeding, but both men and women produce oxytocin.

pathogenic orientation   Viewing sickness as an enemy invader, a purely external event. *See also* salutogenic orientation.

perceived organizational support (POS)   An important determinant of employees' well-being and satisfaction in organizations, POS is a measure of how well employees feel organizations assist them in moderating the negative effect of stressors in the workplace.

power nap   A term, coined by Cornell University social psychologist James Maas, referring to a short (about 20 minutes) workday nap that leaves nappers refreshed and more productive. Power naps are associated not with slackers, but with go-getters who wish to maximize their waking time.

responsibility assumption   The belief that individuals' mental mechanisms contribute substantially to the events that occur in their lives. Whether an outcome is good or bad, someone who subscribes to responsibility assumption would concede that this is what they must have wanted.

salutogenic orientation   Viewing illness as an opportunity rather than an obstacle. *See also* pathogenic orientation.

Samadhi   A Sanskrit term for the state of consciousness induced by complete mental stillness. The word comes from *sam* (together or integrated), *a* (toward), and *dha* (to get, to hold). Taken together, the syllables connote "acquire wholeness or truth." According to the Hindu sage, Patanjali, samadhi comprises the highest accomplishment in the discipline of yoga.

self-actualization   The process of working to become one's best possible self and fulfilling one's highest potential.

self-serving bias   A cognitive distortion that occurs when people claim responsibility for successes but not for failures. It may also manifest itself as a tendency for people to evaluate ambiguous information in a way beneficial to their interests. People thinking that they perform better than average in areas important to their self-esteem is also an example of self-serving bias.

social treadmill   The dissatisfaction that occurs when we compare ourselves negatively to those whom we perceive as financially better off than we are. It is sometimes called *comparison anxiety* or *reference anxiety*.

synapse   A junction between two brain cells where fibers are close enough to transmit signals across a small gap.

tend-and-befriend response   Responding to threats by forming social alliances. The term was coined by psychologist Shelley Taylor.

yoga   From a Sanskrit word referring to the binding of opposites, yoga is comprised of eight interrelated practices: some of which have to do with purifying the body and some with purifying the mind.

Appendix B

Further Reading

Begley, Sharon. *Train Your Mind, Change Your Brain*. New York: Ballantine, 2007.

Bryant, Fred B. *Savoring: A New Model of Positive Experience*. Mahwah, New Jersey: Lawrence Erlbaum Associates, 2000.

Cloniger, C. Robert. *Feeling Good: The Science of Well-Being*. New York: Oxford University Press, 2004.

Csikszentmihalyi, Mihaly. *Flow: The Psychology of Optimal Experience*. New York: Harper & Row, 1990.

Dalai Lama and Howard C. Cutler, M.D. *The Art of Happiness: A Handbook for Living*. New York: Riverhead, 1998.

Frisch, Michael B. *Quality of Life Therapy*. Hoboken, New Jersey: Wiley, 2005.

Giacalone, Robert, Carole Jurkiewicz, and Craig Dunn (eds.). *Positive Psychology in Business Ethics and Corporate Responsibility*. Greenwich: IAP, 2005.

Gilbert, Daniel. *Stumbling on Happiness*. New York: Vintage Books, 2005.

Goleman, Daniel. *Destructive Emotions: How Can We Overcome Them?* New York: Bantam, 2003.

Holden, Robert. *Happiness Now!* London: Coronet Books, 1998.

Jameson, Kay Redfield. *Exuberance: The Passion for Life*. New York: Alfred A. Knopf, 2004.

Layard, Richard. *Happiness: Lessons from a New Science*. New York: Penguin, 2006.

Levine, Martin. *The Positive Psychology of Buddhism and Yoga: Paths to a Mature Happiness*. Mahwah, New Jersey: Lawrence Erlbaum Associates, 2000.

Linley, Alex, and Stephen Joseph (eds.). *Positive Psychology in Practice*. Hoboken, New Jersey: Wiley, 2004.

Lykken, David T. *Happiness: What Studies on Twins Show Us About Nature, Nurture, and the Happiness Set Point*. New York: Golden Books Adult, 1999.

McMahon, Darrin M. *Happiness: A History*. New York: Grove, 2006.

Post, Stephen, and Jill Neimark. *Why Good Things Happen to Good People*. New York: Broadway Books, 2007.

Provine, Robert R. *Laughter: A Scientific Investigation*. New York: Viking, 2000.

Ricard, Matthieu. *Happiness: A Guide to Developing Life's Most Important Skill*. New York: Little Brown, 2006.

Seligman, Martin, E.P. *Authentic Happiness*. New York: Free Press, 2002.

———. *Learned Optimism*. New York: Alfred A. Knopf, 1991.

———. *The Optimistic Child*. Boston: Houghton Mifflin, 1995.

Seligman, Martin, E.P., and Christopher Peterson. *Character Strengths and Virtues*. New York: Oxford University Press, 2004.

Vallant, George E. *Aging Well: Surprising Guideposts to a Happier Life from the Landmark Harvard Study of Adult Development*. New York: Little Brown, 2003.

Web Resources

Positive Psychology-Related Sites

Positive Psychology

www.positivepsychology.org

The University of Pennsylvania's positive psychology website is a good first stop for anyone interested in exploring research, training, and education in the field. There are also listings of upcoming conferences and a sample course syllabi for teachers of positive psychology.

World Database of Happiness

http://worlddatabaseofhappiness.eur.nl

This site, the World Database of Happiness, is an ongoing register of scientific research on the subjective enjoyment of life. It is useful in that it synthesizes findings that are scattered throughout many studies.

Authentic Happiness

www.authentichappiness.org

This site, associated with Dr. Martin Seligman's book, *Authentic Happiness*, promises to help you "develop insights into yourself and the world around you through scientifically tested questionnaires, surveys, and scales."

Quality of Life Research Center

http://qlrc.cgu.edu/about.htm

This nonprofit is affiliated with Claremont University's Drucker School of Management. Here you can view selected papers on topics such as creativity and optimal experience.

The Journal of Positive Psychology

www.tandf.co.uk/journals/titles/17439760.asp

Here you can view a number of free articles and even order a free online sample copy of the publication.

Values in Action Institute on Character

www.viastrengths.org

VIA is an independent nonprofit organization founded to advance the science of positive psychology. "In the pages of this site you will learn about positive psychology, the classification system and measurement tools of character strengths that serve as the backbone of this developing scientific discipline, and about the ongoing work of VIA."

Altruism-Related Sites

The Institute for Unlimited Love

www.unlimitedloveinstitute.org

The Institute, founded by Case Western Reserve University's medical school, supports scientific research and international dialogue on virtues such as generosity, compassion, and service. Many research articles and additional resources are available through the site.

Pay It Forward Foundation

www.payitforwardfoundation.org/home.html

Established in the year 2000 "to educate and inspire students to realize that they can change the world, and provide them with opportunities to do so."

The Random Acts of Kindness Foundation

www.actsofkindness.org

This site was conceived as a resource for "people committed to spreading kindness." It offers a variety of ideas for getting started spreading kindness and lending a helping hand in communities and on campuses.

The Kindness Project
www.kindnessproject.com/home.php

This is a unique website started by a group of friends from Austin, Texas, in 2005. Purchase "tokens" here to pass along to anyone who performs a simple, kind act—then encourage them to do the same. The best part: you get to track your token and read about its adventures.

Make a Wish Foundation
www.wish.org

This site is dedicated to granting the wishes of children with life-threatening medical conditions. It offers information on how to help and how to refer a child.

Big Brothers Big Sisters of America
www.bbbs.org

This renowned organization matches mentoring volunteers with youth.

Humor-Related Sites

The International Society for Humor Studies
www.hnu.edu/ishs

This site lists conferences, seminars, and workshops.

HumorRx
www.humorrx.com

The web home of an organization that researches the art and science of humor.

Laughing At & Understanding Good Humor Seminars
www.laughsrus.com

The site of L.A.U.G.H.S., a program created to help people develop their humor skills and use humor and laughter to reduce stress and promote physical well-being.

Meditation-Related Sites

The Mind & Life Institute
www.mindandlife.org

Originally started "to establish mutually respectful working collaboration and research partnerships between modern science and Buddhism." You can find on this website information about the latest research between meditation, neuroplasticity, and positive emotion.

Center for Mindfulness in Medicine, Health Care, and Society
www.umassmed.edu/cfm/mbsr

Here you can find research on mindfulness meditation and its effects on body and mind—effects that include generating increased enthusiasm for life.

Creativity and Playfulness-Related Sites

Project Zero
www.pz.harvard.edu

This is the site for a research group at the Harvard Graduate School of Education whose "mission is to understand and enhance learning, thinking, and creativity in the arts, as well as humanistic and scientific disciplines, at the individual and institutional levels."

Creativity Research Journal
www.leaonline.com/loi/crj

At this site you can read abstracts and download PDFs of full text articles.

Sociosite
www.sociosite.net/topics/leisure.php

This site offers links to studies on recreation, leisure, and sport, such as the University of Maryland's "Americans' Use of Time Project."

Work Satisfaction-Related Sites

The Testing Room
www.quintcareers.testingroom.com

At this site you can take free tests that relate to career interests and values, aimed at helping you formulate strategies to increase satisfaction in your work life.

Appreciative Inquiry Commons
http://appreciativeinquiry.case.edu

This site bills itself as "a worldwide portal devoted to the fullest sharing of academic resources and practical tools on Appreciative Inquiry and the rapidly growing discipline of positive change."

Wellness-Related Sites

National Health Survey

http://healthsurvey.org

This site provides "a free, on-the-spot analysis of your diet, physical activities, and lifestyle choices." If you choose, you can sign up to become part of an international study.

Wellness: A Positive Approach to Living

www.aug.edu/umac/aces/ace2p05.htm

This site offers free downloadable weekly planners aimed at helping visitors attain balance in their lives and make time for restorative, health-inducing practices.

Volunteer Opportunities

Volunteer Matching Services

The following Internet sites can help pair you with organizations that are seeking volunteers with your skills, talents, and interests.

VolunteerMatch
www.volunteermatch.com

This nonprofit is devoted to "helping everyone find a great place to volunteer." The organization offers a variety of online services. You can quickly find an opportunity that matches your location, interests, and skills via an easy-to-use search engine.

If you are looking for a particular organization, simply enter your location and the name of the organization on a special search form. Even if you can't get away from your desk, consider searching the Virtual Volunteer listings that let you volunteer from virtually anywhere.

The popular service welcomes millions of visitors a year and is an Internet recruiting tool for more than 50,000 nonprofit organizations. *Time* magazine has selected VolunteerMatch as one of the Top 10 Websites of 2007.

Volunteer Solutions
www.volunteersolutions.org/volunteer

At this site you can fill out an application that will match you with volunteer organizations linked to United Way. United Way, which has existed for more than a century, is "a national network of more than 1,300 locally governed organizations that work to create lasting, positive changes in communities and people's lives."

TechSoup
www.techsoup.org/learningcenter/volunteers

CompuMentor, the organization that sponsors TechSoup, is "the first full-fledged technical volunteer matching program in the U.S." Based in the San Francisco Bay Area, CompuMentor uses this site to provide matching services that link nonprofits to volunteers with technical backgrounds. If you are skilled in any aspect of information technology (computer programming, security, technical writing, and so on), this is a great place to find an organization that needs you. If you are pressed for time, you might be able to help without ever leaving your desk.

On Your Feet Project
www.oyfp.org

On Your Feet Project is a national nonprofit organization whose goal is "engaging young people in community service and activism by educating them about diverse nonprofit organizations." They also create opportunities for direct community involvement for young people in the cities of Boston, Los Angeles, New York, Philadelphia, and San Francisco.

Youth Service America
http://ysa.org

Youth Service America is "a resource center that partners with thousands of organizations committed to increasing the quality and quantity of volunteer opportunities for young people, ages 5 to 25, to serve locally, nationally, and globally." Founded in 1986, YSA's mission is to expand the impact of the youth service movement with communities, schools, corporations, and governments. YSA also has pages on MySpace and Facebook.

Organizations Seeking Volunteers

AmeriCorps
www.americorps.org

AmeriCorps is "a national network of programs that engages more than 70,000 Americans each year in intensive service to meet critical needs in communities throughout the nation." AmeriCorps offers several ways to get involved, from part-time local service programs to full-time residential programs. Members receive guidance and training so they can make a contribution that suits their talents, interests, and availability.

AmeriCorps VISTA is a national service program designed specifically to fight poverty. Founded as Volunteers in Service to America in 1965 and incorporated into the AmeriCorps network of programs in 1993, VISTA has long been on the front lines in the fight against poverty in America. VISTA members commit to serve full time for a year at a nonprofit organization or local government agency, working to fight illiteracy, improve health services, create businesses, strengthen community groups, and much more.

Senior Corps
www.seniorcorps.org

Senior Corps "connects today's over 55s with the people and organizations that need them most." If you have a lifetime of experience to share, this organization can help you become a mentor, a coach or a companion to people in need, or contribute your skills and expertise to community projects and organizations. Senior Corps was conceived during John F. Kennedy's presidency, but is enjoying a renaissance as the population ages. Today it has linked more than half a million Americans to service opportunities throughout the United States.

Senior Corps offers numerous ways to get involved. The *Foster Grandparent Program* connects volunteers age 60 and older with children and young people with exceptional needs. The *Senior Companion Program* brings together volunteers age 60 and older with adults in their community who have difficulty with the simple tasks of day-to-day living. *RSVP* connects volunteers age 55 and older with service opportunities in their communities that match their skills and availability, from building houses to immunizing children, to protecting the environment, volunteers receive guidance and training.

Citizen Schools
www.citizenschools.org

Citizen Schools operates a national network of apprenticeship programs for middle school students, connecting adult volunteers to young people in hands-on learning projects after school. At Citizen Schools, "students develop the academic and leadership skills they need to do well in school, get into college, and become leaders in their careers and in their communities." You can apply through this site to become a professional after-school educator or a Citizen teacher.

City Year
www.cityyear.org

City Year is a full-time youth service corps. Its signature program each year brings more than 1,400 young people, age 17 to 24, together for a "demanding year of full-time community service, leadership development, and civic engagement." They tutor and mentor school children, reclaim public spaces, and organize after-school programs and school vacation camps. Visit this site to learn about the application process and to watch videos that will inform and inspire you.

Experience Corps
www.experiencecorps.com

Experience Corps is an award-winning program that engages people older than 55 in 19 cities across the country (including Baltimore; Cleveland; Philadelphia; New York; Washington, D.C.; Minneapolis; Tucson; Tempe; San Francisco; St. Paul; and Portland, Oregon). Thousands of Experience Corps members tutor and mentor elementary school students struggling to learn to read. Independent research shows that "Experience Corps boosts student academic performance, helps schools and youth-serving organizations become more successful, and enhances the well-being of the older adults in the process."

Peace Corps
www.peacecorps.gov

The Peace Corps traces its roots and mission to 1960. Since that time, more than 190,000 Peace Corps Volunteers have been invited by 139 host countries to work on issues ranging from AIDS education to information technology and environmental preservation.

Today's Peace Corps Volunteers are deployed worldwide, each for a term of 27 months (including training). They work in the following areas: education, youth outreach, and community development; business development; agriculture and environment; health and HIV/AIDS; and information technology. The average age of a volunteer is 27, but 5 percent of volunteers are older than 50—and the oldest is 80.

At this site you can learn a great deal about the Corps and view testimonials from past and current volunteers.

Jesuit Volunteer Corps
www.jesuitvolunteers.org

The Jesuit Volunteer Corps is a national and international program. In all, about 250 JVs each year work in the United States and in seven countries around the world.

Hundreds of grassroots organizations across the country count on JVs to provide essential services to low-income people and those who live on the margins of our society (the homeless, the unemployed, people with AIDS, the elderly, street youth, abused women and children, the mentally ill, and the developmentally disabled).

JVC has become the largest Catholic lay volunteer program in the country. Volunteers make a commitment to serve for at least one year.

Learn and Serve America
www.learnandserve.org

Learn and Serve America supports and encourages service-learning throughout the United States, and enables more than one million K–12 students to make meaningful contributions to their community while building academic and civic skills. Service learning engages students in the educational process, using what they learn in the classroom to solve real-life problems. By engaging young people in service-learning, Learn and Serve America aims to instill an ethic of lifelong community service.

A national study of Learn and Serve America programs suggests that effective service-learning programs improve grades, increase attendance in school, and develop students' personal and social responsibility.

Teach For America
www.teachforamerica.org

Founded in 1990, Teach For America aims to connect the 13 million students in America's poorest schools (only half of whom now graduate from high school) with the country's most accomplished young college graduates.

TFA has become one of the largest recruiters of graduating college seniors in the United States. By 2010, Teach For America plans to manage 8,000 corps members, who will make up 10 to 30 percent of the new teachers in the 33 communities they serve.

Volunteers make a two-year commitment.

Landmark Volunteers
www.volunteers.com

Landmark Volunteers offers high school students 58 summer service opportunities across the country with important and dynamic nonprofit organizations. Its core philosophy is that "young people are an integral part of our society and that they have something unique and important to contribute if given the opportunity to do something real."

Most of the programs are of about a two-week duration. Keep in mind that there is a fee to participate in the programs, which includes room and board and supervision.

Big Brothers Big Sisters
www.bigbrothersbigsisters.org

Big Brothers Big Sisters matches children ages 6 through 18 with mentors in professionally supported one-to-one relationships. The organization has volunteer programs in communities across the country. Matches come together in community-based and school-based settings. Volunteers must commit one hour a week, and might spend time doing anything from tutoring to going on a hike, shooting hoops, or playing board games. If you volunteer, be prepared for an interview and background check. Matching specialists will then pair you with a youth who can benefit most from this very special relationship.

Through this site you can also link to the Malachi Program, which involves mentoring children of prisoners.

Habitat for Humanity International
www.habitat.org

Visit this site to learn about domestic and international programs for Habitat. The goal of this organization, made well-known through the work of Jimmy and Roslyn Carter, is to "eliminate poverty housing and homelessness from the world and make decent shelter a matter of conscience and action."

Here you can volunteer locally and get more information about one of Habitat's many programs, including youth programs, the Global Village Program, Women Build, Operation Home Delivery, Disaster Response, and RV Care-a-Vanes.

Meals on Wheels Association of America
www.mowaa.org

MOWAA member programs throughout the country provide nutritious meals and other nutrition services to men and women who are elderly, homebound, disabled, frail, or at-risk. These services "significantly improve the quality of life and health of the individuals they serve and postpone early institutionalization."

Visit this site to learn about volunteering in your community and to submit an application.

Boy Scouts of America
www.scouting.org

This is the website of the Boy Scouts national organization. It's a good place to get an overview of scouting programs and begin learning about the role of adult leaders in scouting. These opportunities include forming a Cub Scout or Boy Scout troop, becoming a Scoutmaster or Assistant Scoutmaster, or becoming a merit badge counselor (the latter coaches a diverse range of skills from wood carving, basketry, and archery to camping, swimming, first aid, life saving, personal fitness, communication, and environmental science).

Girl Scouts of the USA
www.girlscouts.org/for_adults

Girl Scouts of the USA is "the preeminent organization dedicated solely to girls—all girls—where, in an accepting nurturing environment, girls build leadership skills for success in the real world."

Visit this site to learn about the many opportunities available to help girls in this comprehensive program that expands horizons and builds values. The level to which you'd like to get involved can be tailored to fit your life. Here you'll find tips and tools for helping you use your creativity and great ideas to become a successful leader and advisor.

SPCA (Society for the Prevention of Cruelty to Animals) International
www.spca.com/volunteer

By registering at this site as an SPCA volunteer, you will be adding your name and contact information to the organization's list of volunteers who could be called upon to help in saving animals in times of need. This extensive database "is intended to become the largest family of animal lovers worldwide." Everybody who completes a form here will be on the SPCA's Basic Volunteer List. You can also indicate if you would like to be on the Readiness Volunteer List for disasters or the Foster Home Volunteer List for shelter animals.

If you enjoy working with animals, you should also consider contacting your local SPCA animal shelters directly. In most cases, you'll be asked to attend an initial orientation session and then be offered the opportunity to train for a position as a hands-on dog walker, cat socializer, or animal adoption counselor.

Volunteer Vacations

The following organizations offer ways to allot some of your vacation time to helping others around the world.

United Planet
www.unitedplanet.org

United Planet's Volunteer Abroad Quest program combines "volunteering abroad, language learning, cultural activities, learning excursions, and special Cultural Awareness Projects." Both skilled and unskilled volunteers of all ages and nationalities can participate from 1 to 52 weeks in 50 countries worldwide—from India to Cambodia to Costa Rica and beyond. Admission is based on "level of commitment, motivation, responsibility, flexibility, and character." Applicants represent all ages, nationalities, and backgrounds.

GlobalAware
www.globalaware.org

GlobalAware offers volunteer vacations in Peru, Costa Rica, Thailand, Cuba, Nepal, Brazil, Cambodia, Laos, Vietnam, Jamaica, Romania, Ghana, Mexico, and China. These one-week adventures in service focus on cultural awareness and sustainability, and are often compared to a "mini peace corps."

Volunteers need no special skills nor do they need to speak any foreign language to work on these meaningful community projects.

All program costs, including the cost of airfare, are tax-deductible.

ProjectsAbroad
www.projectsabroad.org

This organization sponsors volunteer programs and internships in the developing world. You can volunteer on a tremendous variety of projects in 20 destinations. Opportunities include working on environmental projects, on community development projects, and even writing for local newspapers. Two-week trips are organized for high school students during the summer.

Earthwatch Institute
www.earthwatch.org

Earthwatch Institute "engages people worldwide in scientific field research and education to promote the understanding and action necessary for a sustainable environment."

On an Earthwatch eco-tour expedition, you will be volunteering your time and energy to scientific research or a conservation project in 1 of 50 or so countries. You don't need any special skills to be a volunteer. Earthwatch volunteers range in age from 10 to 90. As a volunteer, you might choose to band penguins in South Africa or tag endangered sea turtles on Pacific beaches. You might measure snowpack density on the frontlines of climate change or map water supplies in drought-stricken northern Kenya.

Global Volunteers
www.globalvolunteers.org

Take a volunteer vacation here in the United States or abroad with this organization, which supports some 100 host communities in 19 countries year-round through short-term volunteer teams. Families, groups, or individuals can sign up for trips that last one to three weeks. No specialized skills are needed.

Cross-Cultural Solutions
www.crossculturalsolutions.org

As an international volunteer with Cross-Cultural Solutions, you will live and work with local people. The organization offers a short-term volunteer program and an Intern Abroad program for students (internships last from 2 to 12 weeks). Programs are available in Eastern Europe, Africa, Asia, and Latin America.

Meditation Resources

Meditation Instruction

The World Wide Online Meditation Center

www.meditationcenter.com

A user-friendly site that offers instruction on a wide variety of techniques—including breath meditation, mantra meditation, and light meditation.

If you are just learning to meditate, you'll find everything necessary to get started quickly and easily. If you are already practicing meditation, you may discover new methods to deepen your practice.

Shambhala

www.shambhala.org/meditationinstruction.html

This website offers a wealth of information on basic meditation techniques as well as for "post meditation practices" that enable practitioners to carry their newfound sense of happiness and well-being out of their meditation space and into their lives.

Center for Mindfulness in Medicine, Health Care, and Society

www.umassmed.edu/cfm/mbsr

Mindfulness meditation practice tapes are available here from this well-known University of Massachusetts Medical School-based MBSR center.

Insight Meditation Center

www.insightmeditationcenter.org/imc-medinstruct.html

A five-week course titled *Introduction to Mindfulness Meditation* is available to listen to or to download.

Access to Insight

www.accesstoinsight.org/lib/authors/thanissaro/breathmed.html

Basic breath meditation instruction online.

BuddhaNet Audio

www.buddhanet.net/audio-meditation.htm

This site offers a wide variety of downloadable audio files that give instruction on techniques including the "loving-kindness" compassion meditation, "cultivating peace and joy with the breath," and the "open awareness" meditation.

Spring Forest Qigong

www.springforstqiqong.com

Offers a comprehensive, easy-to-follow DVD program for meditation and healing. The program has four extensive levels, but it's simplest to begin with the "Small Universe" sitting meditation CD that eases tension and removes blockages from the body's energy pathways.

SpaSpirit

www.spaspirit.com

Click on "workshops and retreats" to find the itinerary for two amazing teachers, Michele Hebert and Dr. Mehrad Nazari, who offer instruction at various retreat centers and spas. Hebert pioneered a meditation-based Stress Management Program at the renowned Scripps Clinic in La Jolla, California, and teaches *Introduction to Meditation* at the University of California in San Diego. Nazari has been personally trained by meditation masters including Zen Master Kyozan Joshu Roshi and H. H. the Dalai Lama.

Meditation Supplies

DharmaCrafts

www.dharmacrafts.com

1-800-794-9862

High-quality meditation cushions, benches, bells, gongs, incense and incense burners, wall hangings, Japanese screens, rice paper lamps, and a beautiful collection of spiritual statuary.

Equinox Gifts

www.equinoxbooksandgifts.com
1-877-870-7369

A wide array of gongs, bells and chimes, malas (prayer beads), traveling altars and altar cards, singing bowls, and finger labyrinths.

Zen By Design

www.zenbydesign.com
1-866-903-0328

An elegant collection of meditation chairs (portable and stationary) that are said to promote spinal alignment. Select fabrics from an array of Thai silk brocades.

Samadhi Store

www.samadhicushions.com
1-800-331-7751

Cushions and benches, gongs and incense, calligraphy and flower-arranging (ikebana) supplies. A wide selection of books, audio, and video.

Four Gates

www.fourgates.com
1-888-232-7414

Meditation furniture, including "back jack" chairs for those with back problems, and a nice collection of tapestries, among other items.

Wildmind

http://secure.wildmind.org/store/customer/home.php
1-877-763-3488

A wide assortment of supplies, some quite practical, including an "invisible clock meditation timer."

3 Pound Universe

www.3pounduniverse.com
e-mail through site

The store takes its name from the weight of the brain (3 pounds)—and its concentration-enhancing supplies are geared to take that brain to a higher, calmer realm.

Well Baskets

www.wellbaskets.com

1-800-763-3488

Resources for the health and wellness of mind, body, and spirit—ideal to send to a friend or loved one you'd like to help be happier.

Ear Plug Superstore

http://store.yahoo.com/earplugstore/whitenoisecds.html

1-918-478-5500

Shop here for an array of white noise CDs and white noise machines that can help you close out distractions to your meditation practice.

Pure White Noise

www.purewhitenoise.com

e-mail through site

Choose from a broad selection of calm-inducing, meditation-enhancing sounds, including waves, wind, rain, distant thunderstorms, and the like.

An impressive array of incense and starter "sampler packs" such as "Flowers and Spice" and "Harmony and Zen."

Incense Galore

www.incensegalore.com

e-mail: webmaster@incensegalore.com

Unique, hand-dipped incense—long-lasting and fresh.

More Than Light

www.more-than-light.com

1-866-228-9132

Unique illumination and light-spreading products, such as glass oil candles, colored flame candles, and exotic tea light stands.

Illuminations

www.illuminations.com

1-800-621-2998

Every imaginable style of candle—tapers, votives, jar candles, and so on—in every color and scent. Also, a wealth of candleholders and other accessories.

Oriental Furnishings Club
www.orientalfurnishings.com
1-914-592-6320 or
1-203-853-7553

This wide collection of elegant screens in assorted sizes and materials can help you create a meditation space in a corner of any room.

Home Decorators
www.homedecorators.com
1-877-537-8539

A large assortment of room dividers that you can search by style (Oriental, Victorian, contemporary), fabric, color, or finish.

Tatami Room
www.tatamiroom.com
1-866-465-4068

Traditional and contemporary screens. Also, check out their lamp collection.

Meditation/Spiritual Retreats

Retreat Finder
www.retreatfinder.com
1-800-889-6906

For those on a quest for inner peace, this search site helps you find what you're seeking.

Zen Mountain Monastery
www.mro.org/zmm/index.php
1-845-688-2228

This upstate New York meditation training center provides Zen training for people of all ages and spiritual backgrounds. The "Introduction to Zen Training" weekend is a wonderful way to dip your toe into the well.

The Chopra Center
www.chopra.com
1-866-260-2236

Located at California's La Costa Resort and Spa, this health and wellness retreat integrates the mind-body meditation techniques as set forth by internationally acclaimed author and philosopher Dr. Deepak Chopra.

Mount Manresa

www.manresasi.org
1-718-727-3844

At this Jesuit retreat house, a professional retreat staff will help you focus your inner journey.

The Garden at Thunder Hill

www.gardenofone.com
1-518-797-3373

This retreat—describing itself as a "personal research facility"—is located on 120 acres of forest, streams, trails, and natural beauty in the Albany, New York, area. Paths through old orchards and even older forests hold the promise of serenity and simplicity.

Angel Valley Spiritual Retreat Center

www.angelvalley.org
1-800-393-6308

A nondenominational organization located on the edge of breathtaking Sedona, Arizona. The 70-acre property is surrounded by National Forest where renowned Sedona red rocks radiate their magic. The retreat offers a perfect environment for individuals and groups on retreat. If you like you can bunk in a teepee.

Seven Circles Retreat

www.sevencirclesretreat.org
1-559-337-0211

Located in foothills just outside Sequoia National Park, this retreat is situated on 24 acres of scenic hills filled with native Oak and Manzanita. Visitors can take a short hike to appreciate the sunrise over the snowcapped high Sierra. The website has an ongoing list of retreat events and programs.

Our-Lady-of-Peace Spiritual Life Center

www.our-lady-of-peace-retreat.org
1-401-783-2871

A Rhode Island retreat in the Christian tradition, the Center enables people to re-encounter their spirituality in their personal lives. It offers individual and group retreats, and a hermitage is available for private retreats.

Green Mountain at Fox Run
http://fitwoman.com/mindfulness_retreat.htm
1-800-448-8106

At this Vermont retreat, discover and practice techniques of visualization, meditation, and journaling to help yourself bring more joy and peace to your daily life.

Earth Sanctuary
www.earthsanctuary.org
1-425-637-8777

Washington State's Earth Sanctuary is an environment for personal renewal and spiritual connection, whatever your spiritual path. Accommodations are immediately adjacent to a 72-acre nature reserve, meditation parkland, and sculpture garden.

The Expanding Light Retreat
www.expandinglight.org
1-800-346-5350

Located in northern California's Sierra Nevada foothills, this retreat offers meditation workshops.

Rancho La Puerta
www.rancholapuerta.com
1-800-443-7565

A unique spa resort, Rancho La Puerta, just south of the Mexican border and about an hour from San Diego, provides an abundance of opportunities for meditation instruction and practice, including an "Inner Journey" class. Its facilities include a breathtaking meditation room overlooking Mount Kuchaama, and a tree-cloaked meditation labyrinth modeled on the one at Chartres.

Index

R

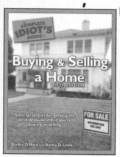

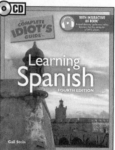

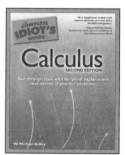

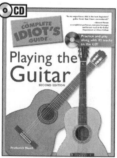